W9-CER-051

How to Adopt Internationally

A Gu   and

Mesa House Publishing
Fort Worth, Texas

Cover and text design by Jim Dodson
Cover photo © 1997 by Winn Fuqua

Library of Congress Catalog Card Number: 97-70248

Editorial correspondence and requests for permission to reprint should be
mailed to Mesa House Publishing, 1701 River Run, Ste. 702, Fort Worth,
Texas, 76107. E-mail should be addressed to mesahouse@tangram-corp.com.

This publication is intended to provide accurate information in regard to the
subject matter presented. It is sold with the understanding that the publisher is
not engaged in rendering legal, financial, or other professional services.

ISBN: 0-940352-12-5

Printed in the United States of America

Acknowledgments

We would like to thank Jo-Anne Weaver, adoptive parent of a Chinese daughter, who put us in contact with Mesa House Publishing.

Several people were kind enough to supply facts and figures. Maureen Evans of the Joint Council of International Children's Services, the staff at Adoptive Families of America, Dr. William Pierce of the National Council for Adoption, Peter Pfund, Assistant Legal Advisor for Private International Adoption Law at the U.S. Department of State, Mark Leno of the U.S. Department of Agriculture, Lorna Adams, U.S. Immigration and Naturalization Service Houston office, and Lorraine Lewis of the U.S. Department of State.

A special thank you goes to Jerri Ann Jenista, M.D., who reviewed the medical section, and to Sylvia Franzmeier, ACSW, LMSW, ACP, QCSW, who reviewed the sections on the adjustments of adoptive families.

Table of Contents

Sample Forms and Documents

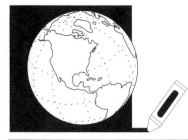

Introduction

The United States was at war in Vietnam. American political life was complicated and ugly. On the other hand, our home life was simple and beautiful. In the spring of 1972 we had a baby. Kirk was, without a doubt, the most lovable baby we had ever seen. We wanted more! Kirk's older brothers, who had already graduated high school, agreed, although they were puzzled that we would want another child. Both were absolutely flabbergasted when we told them we were flying to South America to adopt twins.

Colombian twins were not what I had in mind when I began calling adoption agencies that summer about adopting one baby girl. The media carried a lot of heart-warming stories about Korean and Vietnamese orphans being brought by the plane load for adoption by Americans. Surely there was a baby for us. I soon discovered I was wrong. We did not qualify because of our age, previous marriages, and offspring. Nor were we candidates for locally born children, for whom the wait was five years.

By fall, a breakthrough occurred via a Colombian friend, who told me she was spending the winter in her country. Her brother was an intern in a charity hospital in Bogotá. She had asked him what happened to babies abandoned there. He had given her the name of an international adoption agency, Casa de la Madre y el Niño, which she planned to visit.

Soon after her departure, a letter arrived with the referral of week-old twin girls, Rosana and Tatiana. Astonished and delighted, we began the steps to adopt them, only to discover that no one could tell us how. Up to that time, the local agency we were working with (Children's Home Society of St. Paul, Minnesota) and the Immigration and Naturalization Service (INS) had been dealing only with Korean and Vietnamese adoptions. With Heino researching new adoption procedures, the INS determined how to immigrate a Latin American orphan. Senator Hubert Humphrey had responded to Heino's plea for help by forwarding information on the difference between Eastern and Western Hemisphere orphan immigration procedures. After a two-month bureaucratic struggle and a last-minute plea for help to Senator Humphrey for immigration clearance, we jetted into the unknown. Happiness, fear, and excitement fused a four-week stay in Bogotá. The adoption of Rosana and Tatiana sparked a national trend.

In addition to our beautiful baby daughters, we returned from Colombia with pictures of eight children living at Casa de la Madre y el Niño who needed families. Children's Home Society (CHS) referred adoptive couples to us for information and insight on international adoption. We also spoke at CHS seminars for adoptive parents and gave the agency as much guidance as possible, based on our experience. We found homes for all eight children. Word spread.

People who had waited for years to adopt called us. Soon we were volunteering for three adoption agencies. On the verge of collapse, with three babies to care for, I called OURS (Organization for a United Response), now known as Adoptive Families of America. At that time, OURS acted as a support group for the aid and placement of Korean and Vietnamese orphans. OURS sent volunteers to help, but we were soon overrun by more prospective adoptive parents.

When Casa de la Madre could not keep up with all the applications, I began searching for more adoption agencies in Colombia. I came up with two more, FANA and Fundación Los Pisingos, both foundations for orphaned and abandoned children in Colombia. Within a short period of time, orphans were arriving in the Midwest from all three agencies. Over a period of eight years, our volunteer efforts led to hundreds of Colombian adoptions. In guiding prospective parents, we learned a lot about adoption agencies, and a plan began forming in our minds for an international agency of our own that would meet the needs of adoptive parents, as well as the unique needs of orphans.

Meanwhile, our little trio went to nursery school, then to elementary school. One of their teachers located us when she was ready to adopt. She never forgot Rosi and Tati. When the children were eight, we graduated with master's degrees and published *Gamines: How to Adopt from Latin America*, now out of print. A year later, we moved to Texas where no U.S.-based international adoption agencies existed and licensed Los Niños (The Children) International Adoption Center (LNI).

Following that, our family flew to Colombia. The twins were now ten years old, and we wanted them to see the nursery where they had waited for us. We were given a royal tour and shown the books in which all the pictures and letters we had sent over the years were stored. Later on, we sent a letter giving the agency the authority to show the information to the twins' birth relatives and to encourage them to write us through Casa de la Madre y el Niño. Unfortunately, the twins' birth relatives have never contacted the Casa.

During our stay, we also visited Fundación Los Pisingos. They showed us an adorable nine-year-old boy for whom they hoped we could find a home. After spending some time getting to know him, our family reached a unanimous decision to adopt him! Omar, survivor of abandonment, street life, and four orphanages, did not really believe that we would come back for him. Once back in the States, we raced along, completing the home study, formal dossier, and immigration clearance in two months. He joined our family three months later.

Until our family's trip, we had assisted in parent-initiated adoptions. Our trip to Latin America opened doors to agency-initiated adoptions. Colombian agencies in Bogotá and Medellín asked for our assistance in finding appropriate couples. Heino went on to Chile by himself to meet with adoption authorities we had discovered while researching our thesis. This pattern repeated itself over the years, as we formed agreements with child-placing entities in Bolivia, China, Colombia, Ecuador, Guatemala, Honduras, Paraguay, Peru, Romania, Russia, and Vietnam. Between 1982 and 1996, we placed more than 1,600 foreign children in loving American homes. We were able to help these countries in other ways, too, by building orphanages and buying supplies and equipment.

Many LNI placements occur in other states, where we network with licensed adoption agencies. Our files are filled with lovely pictures and glowing progress reports of LNI children. An even greater treat is seeing them at our winter parties, annual weekend celebrations, and other cultural events.

Colombia, the homeland of three of our children, has a special place in our hearts. Colombia is the prototype of good adoption practices. In 1975, its legislature passed laws to protect children from baby sellers. All placements must be approved by the national welfare department. The emergence of additional international adoption agencies, founded by Colombia's elite, have continued to shape Colombia into a pacesetter that other countries could emulate. And there are not nearly as many of the pitiful beggar children who tugged at our heartstrings twenty-four years ago.

We rejoiced in our Latin American adoption experience, which is related in the book *Butterflies in the Wind: Spanish/Indian Children with White Parents.* In elementary school, all four children worked hard at learning a language. While the first three children chose Spanish, Omar learned English out of necessity. He spoke in full sentences in less than three months and was fluent within a year. Although he had only the equivalent of a first-grade education when he arrived, he rapidly caught up to his age group by skipping a year in elementary school and attending summer sessions while in high school. An active high school student, Omar played football and had a great many friends, both Anglo and Hispanic.

In elementary school, all four children learned Latin American dances and performed at fiestas we arranged for adoptive families. As they grew older, the children participated in LNI seminars, creating colorful signs and supervising the book tables and audiovisual equipment. Since junior high, they have worked part-time in the LNI office, learning secretarial skills. They love our parent support group picnics and annual celebrations, when they get a chance to play with the babies and children. In this atmosphere, they have learned compassion and affinity with people of all races. Hundreds of LNI children view them as cousins. Many of their parents view them as role models.

One of the most meaningful experiences in the twins' lives was celebrating Casa de la Madre y el Niños' fiftieth anniversary held in Bogotá in July of 1992. Fourteen teenagers from The Netherlands, France, Italy, and the United States went back in search of their roots. The time they spent together affected them deeply. Spanish/Indian children raised by white parents, they had coped successfully with unique situations. Their meeting was like a reaffirmation.

At that time, Omar had graduated from high school. Rather than start college immediately, he joined the U.S. Army. Omar proved, as many other children have, that an older child can successfully bridge two cultures.

Twenty-four years have passed since we began our quest to adopt abroad. At that time, traveling to another country to adopt was considered only by an intrepid few. Today, television, radio, magazine, and newspaper stories on the plight of orphans abroad and their subsequent adoption are becoming commonplace. Adoptive parent support groups can be found in every major city in the United States. Licensed adoption agencies usually keep a list of these names. These groups hold informational meetings and annual conferences with workshops on every facet of adoption. They have become strong voices affecting adoption agencies.

In addition, the World Wide Web has become a source for U.S.-based international adoption agencies to present information as well as pictures of "special needs" children. On the internet, pre- and postadoptive parent newsgroups keep each other informed on the latest developments in specific countries.

Social scientists have also become very interested in the outcome of cross-cultural and transracial adoptions. LNI has been fortunate to have had the opportunity to assist in several studies examining the social and psychological adjustment of the children of such adoptions, as well as the adjustment of the entire family. The past twenty-four years of research have proven empirically what we intuited: Transracial and cross-cultural families are doing as well or better than biologically related families. A wealth of information on this topic is available through the Search Institute in Minneapolis and the Sociology Department at the University of Texas in Austin.

Our family of three biological and three adopted children may be a small sample for a study; yet, there are certain truths that apply to families such as ours. Heino and I have observed little difference in how each of our children has dealt with us as parents or with jobs, school, and our society. Each one has developed skills for successful living.

Chapter 1

Is International Adoption Right For You?

Approximately 50,000 U.S.-born children are adopted each year by unrelated adults; yet, one to two million U.S. citizens are trying to adopt. For many couples beginning to explore adoption, the process seems fraught with long waits and stringent requirements. While many older children, sibling groups, and special needs children are available for adoption, there are relatively few healthy, U.S.-born babies compared to the number of people looking to adopt. Because birth control and abortion are accessible to most U.S. citizens, fewer unplanned babies are being born. In addition, most unmarried mothers are choosing to keep their babies.

Most agencies advise couples looking to adopt a healthy Caucasian baby that the wait will be at least one year after the home study is completed, and, more typically, the wait may stretch to five or even seven years. Applicants seeking to adopt an African American or other minority child will usually have a shorter wait.

Yet, transracial adoptions are still surrounded by controversy. Although thousands of Caucasian couples have adopted minority children, most have done so through private agencies. Until recently, many states had laws and policies strongly favoring the placement of children (particularly African American and Native American children) with parents of the same race. Unfortunately, this policy resulted in continued foster care for children when same-race parents were not available. A federal law passed in 1996 forbids state public agencies from making same-race placements a priority over timely interracial placements. This law is helping children leave foster care for permanent adoptive homes. According to Adoptive Families of America, 100,000 children still wait in our foster care system, as do many newborn babies with medical complexities.

However, it can still be difficult to adopt a locally born child, whether racially matching or not. Usually, couples and singles adopting through a local social service office will be shown pictures and biographical information on children they could parent well. Applicants then select the child they are most interested in adopting. They, along with other applicants, are then considered for the same child. A social worker assigned to the child, working in cooperation with the rest of the social service staff, selects the adoptive family he or she feels is best for the child. Adoptive parents may have to apply for many different children before they are finally matched with a child. On the bright side, many individuals who might not be accepted by a private agency are accepted at county social service offices. Single men, foster parents, parents over fifty, parents with large families, and those with low incomes are eligible as adoptive parents through public social service agencies.

The procedure at private adoption agencies is quite different. When prospective adoptive parents work with a private agency, the birth mothers, under the supervision of the social workers, choose a family from their pictures and profiles. Not surprisingly, the birth mothers tend to choose people that they themselves would have wanted as parents. Young, attractive couples with an active lifestyle and an upper-middle income have the best chance of being chosen. Terms of "openness" regarding disclosure of information on the biological mother are negotiated at this time. The costs involved are similar to that of an international adoption.

To cope with the high demand for babies, private U.S. adoption agencies have established strict rules in an attempt to be fair to the adoptive parents. Childless couples take first priority. Some agencies may even require that the couple be infertile. Twenty-five- to thirty-five-year-old adopters without physical disabilities are considered to be ideal. Single parents are not accepted at many agencies. If the adoption agency is religiously affiliated, preference may be shown on the basis of religion. (As noted in Chapter 3, adoption agencies will often waive their requirements when potential clients have found a U.S.-based international agency or foreign source that will accept them as parents.)

Those who have become disillusioned with this process, who do not meet the requirements for a U.S. adoption, who believe in ZPG (zero population growth), or who simply have a strong desire to adopt a foreign child, often turn to international adoption.

In addition to shorter waits and less stringent requirements, there are many other advantages to international adoption. One main advantage is that there is no competition for a child. Once you have been approved by the adoption agency and INS and you have prepared documents for a foreign court, a child will be selected and referred to you. The U.S.-based international adoption agency's representative will locate a child based on the age, gender, ethnicity, etc. that you requested. Another compelling reason for adopting abroad is the fact that the United States has never had a case in which foreign birth parents sued for custody. Everyone in America remembers the outcome of the Baby Jessica case, and most courts now seemed inclined to rule in favor of the birth parent's rights rather than the child's rights.

Most importantly, international adoption opens a whole new dimension in your life. Suddenly, you view your child's homeland as yours, as well. You pay more attention to news of that part of the world. Your foray into another country and culture becomes a hot news item, too. Word travels fast. New acquaintances of that ethnic group and others are eager to celebrate your family's diversity. Just as suddenly, your adopted child gathers a caring flock of adults and children who become your friends, too.

Our family has extended far beyond the confines of a white middle-class community. We benefited from the companionship of children and adults of other ethnicities and nationalities we otherwise might not have met. Heino and I both feel that the time, money, and energy we expended to raise our family and to establish Los Niños International Adoption Center has been worth every minute and every penny. Sometimes our house and our office are like a joyful mini United Nations. Our lives have been enriched beyond all measure.

EVALUATING MOTIVES FOR ADOPTION

Despite all of the advantages, international adoption is not for everyone. As with a biological birth or any other adoption, the parent and child are entering a life-long relationship. Adopting a foreign child means that your family will become intercultural and perhaps interracial. You, your family, and your adoptive child will likely experience some form of racism. Furthermore, your family will remain changed for all future generations, as your child grows up, forms friendships, dates, marries (perhaps a different minority), and begins a family of his or her own.

Before even beginning the process of international adoption, potential adopters need to examine their motives and carefully consider the challenges of adopting and raising a foreign-born child.

A skilled social worker can lead prospective adopters to decide whether or not their abilities and motives are sufficient for a long-term transracial relationship. For example, one of the first questions a social worker might ask ("Why do you want to adopt a foreign child?") may bring forth a straight-forward answer, an around-the-bush answer, an angry retort, or even a shocked or baffled silence.

Some of the more common responses are:

We don't meet the age, length of marriage, religious, or other requirements of U.S. adoption agencies.

We don't want to wait three to five years for a baby.

We prefer to adopt a Third World child rather than produce a child in an already overpopulated world.

We believe in ZPG (zero population growth) philosophy: produce two children and adopt the rest.

I am still nursing my toddler; I want to adopt a tiny baby to nurse.

We want to adopt from _____ (country) because there is less prejudice toward people of that nationality than toward other nationalities in our locality.

I am single. Local adoption agencies will not place a U.S.-born baby with me.

We are an infertile couple. (About half the prospective adoptive couples we have counseled were infertile. Authorities on the subject of infertility believe that infertile parents are not able to cope well with parenthood until they learn to handle the emotional stress of infertility and to resolve their dreams of producing children.)

I have a medical problem which prevents another pregnancy.

Our family has all boys, no girls; or all girls, no boys.

We are capable of dealing with medical disabilities. We would like to adopt a handicapped child.

I have a history of stillbirths and miscarriages.

A series of artificial inseminations have failed.

Most of these responses exhibit a responsible sincerity, and few seem likely to end in failure. Whereas the responses listed below may be given in all sincerity, their potential for failure is higher.

A pregnancy may occur if we adopt first.

One of us was medically sterilized through a vasectomy or tubal ligation.

We want a child to enhance our marriage. (OK, if they don't mean to save the marriage.)

We want a child of every race. (Child collectors? Liberals out to prove their viewpoints?)

Our child died. (Counseling is needed to be certain the parents do not expect an identical replacement for the dead child.)

We want an older child because we hate the loss of sleep and the mess connected with baby care.

We want a playmate for our only child. (The children may not be able to get along with each other for a year or more.)

We want an older child, handicapped child, or sibling group unlikely to be adopted by anyone else. (Do parents expect gratitude and recognition?)

Some of the most important questions, however, cannot be answered with any degree of certainty: Will the child feel that there is something wrong with him because his mother rejected him? Will the parents and child grow to love each other? Will racial prejudice appear only after the child joins the family? Will the family stay together throughout the child's growing-up years? Adopters must learn to know themselves before they create a family in the hope of living happily ever after.

Adoptive parents must be able to acknowledge that their foreign-born children will always have a unique situation. Coping with the fact that they have another set of parents somewhere and that they are racially and/or culturally different from you can be difficult during childhood and adolescence. Counseling and/or family therapy is sometimes necessary. Adoptees end up explaining their adoptive status throughout their lives, even as adults.

Most foreign adoptions within our experience have been successful placements. However, children older than two, handicapped children, and sibling groups present a greater challenge to a harmonious family adjustment.

The most successful placements of children more than two years old occur when the parents fulfill the child's needs without expecting anything in return. These parents adopt knowing that the child may not be able to love or trust them for many years. If you are applying for a child more than two years of age, remember that he or she already has a personality, memories, habits, and probably a different language.

AN OVERVIEW OF THIS BOOK

In addition to examining individual motives, potential adopters need to have a clear understanding of the international adoption process itself and the legal requirements, expenses, and potential bureaucratic headaches that can be part of the process. This book is designed to do that by first giving an overview of the international adoption process (Chapter 3) and then providing the information for a step-by-step approach to conducting a successful international adoption (Chapters 4-15) should you decide to pursue this route. Samples of many of the documents needed for an international adoption are included at the end of the chapter in which they are discussed.

The last half of the book is a compendium of the adoption laws and other pertinent information for most countries participating in international adoption. For each country listed, the compendium includes basic information on geography, demography, language, currency, and major religions. In addition, when available, the compendium also includes information on the number of children who have immigrated to the United States from each country, a summary of the adoption laws for each country, the central authority in charge of adoption, and the address and phone number for the U.S. visa issuing post for each country.

How to Adopt Internationally also includes an Appendix and a Bibliography. The Appendix includes a collection of resources and contacts that may be helpful during the adoption process, including information on adoptive parent support groups, addresses and phone numbers for regional and district offices of the INS, INS service offices in foreign countries, and addresses and phone numbers for state departments of public welfare or social services. The Bibliography includes a list of recommended books on cross-cultural, interracial, and special needs adoption, magazines and newsletters of adoptive parent groups, information on travel and foreign languages, and other resources that may be helpful as you research and pursue an international adoption.

Finally, the book includes a glossary of common terms used in the international adoption process as well as an index to the content of the book.

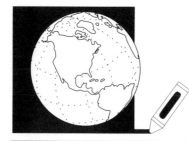

Chapter 2

A Parent's Journal

Before moving on to the more practical proceedings of international adoption, we've provided an excerpt highlighting the personal journal of one set of adoptive parents. This brief selection provides a glimpse of how foreign children and their adoptive families begin to adjust to one another and illustrates a few of the unexpected joys and bureaucratic mishaps that are common in international adoption.

Jan and Bob Ostrum, both teachers, decided to adopt rather than to produce more children in our overpopulated world. The Ostrums chose Colombia because they have a knowledge of the language and an appreciation for the culture. Jan's journal is printed here in a condensed version.

As the Ostrums' experience illustrates, there are major differences in children and how they react to an adoptive placement. Some things reported by the Ostrums appear to be related to culture. Some may be the child's temperament. Others may be related to family changes. Adoptive parents are stuck with the job of trying to separate one from the other in a child that may not have the language or emotional or developmental maturity to express his or her feelings.

Adoption is the aftermath of a tragedy. Every child who is adopted has lost a mother, a father, and other familial ties. Abandonment, relinquishment, or death are all perceived as final separations. Many social service professionals believe that even the tiniest infant feels this loss and experiences grief. These emotions affect the way that each adopted child adjusts to his or her new life in an adoptive family.

Adoption can change a child's behavior. A child's needs are intensified. He or she may be anxious and demanding and may push his new parents to prove over and over again that they will provide care and protection.

The Ostrums' Journal

April 10: Bob sends our adoption application airmail, registered special delivery, to Colombia!

April 28: Surprised by a phone call from Bogotá as I plant our first vegetable garden. So astounded when told that Bob and I have a boy, four, and a girl, two, that I forget to ask for children's names or whether they are siblings! I, of course, say yes, we will accept them. Directress wants to know when we can come down. Says the children are of medium complexion and that's it. Bob isn't home. He's pitching at a baseball game. I call and have him paged. He says, "I have to go somewhere and think about this." We are both still unbelieving.

April 30: I tell my supervisor and the staff. Everyone is so happy for us!

May 1: Receive birth certificates in the mail. Boy, Clamaco Perez, November 23, 1973. Girl, Carmen Perez, February 4, 1975. We like the name Carmen, not sure about Clamaco. We both like Maco. Take papers to the International Institute for translations. We're excited and thrilled.

June 18: Much has happened since May. Just a few days before we received notice of our approval from Immigration (INS), we got a letter from Bogotá telling us not to come down until they notified us. We called that night to find out why, but the directress told us to call the next day. Bob called. The directress said she couldn't remember; she would write us.

June 20: It was a depressing day; the day we were supposed to have left for Colombia.

We've done so much to prepare for the children. We painted their upstairs room and decorated one wall with pictures of a giraffe, a hippo, and a lion. We bought a swimming pool. Our friends gave us a party and showered us with gifts for the children. We were so busy and excited during our preparations in May. I feel lazy now but unable to enjoy my freedom and leisure before we begin our family.

July 13: Postman delivers letter from Bogotá telling us the children have *el sarampion* (the measles). The orphanage is quarantined. Our departure date is more unsure than ever.

July 24: A letter with Colombian stamps informs us that Clamaco has been reclaimed by relatives. Thankfully, they have a Felipe for us. What a beautiful name. But we haven't received Felipe's birth documents, which were mailed to us. What a mess. Now we're back to where we were in April.

July 25: Seems unbelievable, but Carmen and Felipe are no longer. Bob called Bogotá to confirm Felipe's addition, and, lo and behold, we have two different children, still a girl and a boy, two and four. Orphanage will send the birth documents special delivery.

July 30: Played tennis this morning. Just as I park in front of our house so does a U.S. Mail car. Special delivery. Birth documents for Angelita and Manuel. I spend the evening translating and typing. [Jan used the translated copy of the birth documents for the first two children assigned to them.]

July 31: I carry the documents to the [Minnesota] Department of Public Welfare office near the Capitol building in Saint Paul.

August 1: I take them to the Immigration office. Thinking of flying to Bogotá this Sunday. So scary and exciting. Two beautiful children coming home with us, changing all our lives forever.

August 4: Four-hour layover in Miami. Full of all sorts of feelings about our adventure: fear, anticipation, regret, expectations.

August 5: We arrive in Bogotá. Surprised to see many people watching us land. Must be the Sunday afternoon entertainment. (Actually, the relatives and friends waiting for the Colombian passengers.)

August 6: Arrive at the adoption agency very nervous, not knowing what to expect, realizing this is one of the most important events in our lives. Wait about fifteen minutes for our children. Bob is very, very nervous. We hear the kids coming down the hall. Angelita shyly enters and comes right to me. Manuel enters hesitantly a few seconds later and comes right to Bob. I can't voice my feelings of disappointment at that moment; both children are very fat.

Anyway, los niños are dressed really cute, blue plaid bib shorts for Manuel and skirt with suspenders for Angelita. Bob is relieved to know the children were expecting us. We are left alone, and the children sit stiffly on our laps. Angelita looks up at us shyly; Manuel looks up at us fearfully. We give Angelita a Raggedy Ann doll and Manuel a truck. We play for about an hour. The children won't speak with us except once when we ask Angelita her name. She says it so forcefully and assertively we are very surprised.

11:30 a.m.: Manuel toddles out of the room. I don't know why. I carry him back. He's screaming and crying. The maids ask him what is wrong. Manuel wants to eat–our first clue that Manuel feels very strongly about food. While the children eat, we speak with the directress. She tells us to get pictures taken of the children and to be back by 5:00 p.m. to sign the custody contract, then the kids will be ours. That doesn't sound so good. We are prepared to have the children on the evening of the second day, but not the first. We leave the orphanage to get photos taken. A surprising little one-room place. Manuel starts screaming his head off. But when our little angel smiles to have her picture taken, then what can he do?

After that we go the embassy doctor. He is also a surprise. A distinguished-looking fellow who does a cursory exam. We mention that Manual recently had surgery for a rectal obstruction. The doctor doesn't care; he allows us to write "NO" to the question on the U.S. State Department form which asks about recent operations.

We taxi back to the hotel and order food from room service. We don't order for the *gamines* thinking they weren't hungry yet. Wrong! The niños eat quite a bit. When Bob leaves the room, Manuel follows me around, demanding, "*Deme pan*" ("Give me bread!"). He is amazingly persistent. Later we leave the hotel to pick up the photos and return to the orphanage. Bob and I feel almost relieved when the directress says we do not have enough photos, and we will have to return tomorrow to acquire custody of the children. The day had seemed long and trying. The niños don't seem to mind being back home. As we talk to the directress, the children start talking and playing freely together for the first time. It's so nice they can communicate and relax together.

We feel exhausted and have a quiet evening together. There had been so much tension; not knowing how the children would respond to us, not knowing the language well, and meeting time deadlines. Bob was immediately affectionate and warm with the children. I didn't feel affection, but it was silly to think I would immediately.

August 7: Pick up the photos and go to the orphanage. Sign custody contract. Our children do not seem as scared of us. We feel more relaxed, too.

Back at the hotel and bedded down for the night, we all sleep poorly. Manuel is tossing and calling out all night; both kids seem to always be uncovered.

August 8: What a delightful day! Finally have a chance to enjoy the children and get to know them a little. It's a holiday. President Lopez's inauguration.

Big scare this morning. Manuel spit up all his eggs. The waiter says we shouldn't give him so much food.

Return to our room and read the children a story. Manuel has a temper tantrum which we ignore. Seeing him quiet down is a small triumph for us. We really feel like we're becoming parents. I feel so much closer to the children now than I did yesterday. When they wake up, we go shopping. Angelita and Manuel both get new shoes. The children are so proud when they think they look nice. Manuel has a little temper tantrum again when he can't have any candy. He's learning he can't have everything he wants; it's a nice feeling to know we're overcoming that. Angelita is just like a little angel.

We give them a bath. Manuel doesn't try it until Angelita does. We give them soap dishes, and they use them for a water fight. It's the first time they laugh so spontaneously and so much. After that, Angelita and Manuel loosen up and play freely with their toys. I'm so glad I brought matchbox cars. Then we read them a children's book. (I read; Bob does the sound effects.) We put them to bed feeling like real parents, so happy to have children.

August 9: Manuel did it again. We only ordered oatmeal and bread, but it was too much for Manuel. He spit it up while Angelita quietly polished off all of hers. It scares us. Glad we have an appointment with a pediatrician this afternoon. It takes Manuel about an hour to eat, and it's one hour of nerves for us, wondering if he'll make it. After eating we go to crowded embassy and hear good news: as soon as we get Angelita and Manuel's passports, we can fly home. Back to hotel for naps. No temper tantrum from Manuel this time, just a frown, a pout, and no kiss. Our stalwart Angelita goes right to bed.

After naps we visit pediatrician. He says Angelita and Manuel could be brother and sister. Our children are from southern Colombia (indicated by skin problems), and both have worms and malnutrition. Fat is actually bloating caused by malnutrition; with good nutrition it soon disappears. Angelita's facial scars will eventually heal and become less noticeable. She is probably $4^1/_2$ to 5 years old.

Manuel is around four, stunted from malnutrition and an intestinal problem. Testicles are undescended. Vomiting is probably due to new diet. Doctor writes prescriptions for worms.

Bedtime: Slight tantrum from Manuel when it's time to put away toys, but he comes around when it's time for the *dulce* (candy), actually worm medicine. Both jump into bed by themselves. Bob and I enjoy sharing our time with the children more each day.

August 10: Lawyer says passport will not be ready for four more days. Disappointing. Visit Plaza de Bolivar and Museo del Oro, a museum housing solid gold Chibcha Indian artworks. Always so many people on the streets. No one takes care of their vehicles. City seems always stinky and dirty.

August 11: No stomach problems for Manuel. Angelita is so good-natured, giggly, and happy. Bought souvenirs. Angelita delighted with her *ruana* (poncho). Wants to know if she can wear it *manana* (tomorrow). Manuel makes such funny faces. He has rosy gopher cheeks. Expectant eyes when about to eat; cow-eyed when wanting something. Angie tells Carlos, our waiter, that she wants Mama to help her.

August 13: Tour Zipaquira, a salt mine with a great cathedral deep inside. Los niños play all day long. We notice Angelita gives in to all Manuel's demands. Kids repeat English words: cow, sheep, tree, bath. Manuel has a speech problem; not sure if it's a lisp or an impediment. Both seem happy and secure.

Tan bueno! (So good!) is Angelita's favorite phrase. *Deme manzana* (Give me an apple) is Manuel's.

August 14: Absolutely the worst day as far as tension and worry go. Passports are to be picked up at orphanage at noon and delivered to embassy at 1:00. We don't count on two-hour lunch/siesta at orphanage. Embassy clerk says she will issue visas if we bring passports to the embassy by 3:00.

Rush to bank to get money for visas. Speed to orphanage. Kids miss their nap. Manuel has temper tantrum. We're so racked with emotion we feel like pounding him. Bob takes hopping, stamping, shrieking Manuel out to wait in the taxi while I assure directress I'll phone in our flight number if they will please give us the passports immediately. Request refused.

Rush to embassy, then to lawyer for his bill, to hotel for flight number, back to lawyer, back to embassy, back to orphanage, dash to embassy again. I notice passports have Oothoudt as last name, not ours. Then Bob reads custody contract and sees Isabel, not Angelita. Bob nearly has a nervous breakdown. *Caramba*!

Tomorrow we will repeat the race from office to office in Bogota's congestion of cars, people, trucks, burros, buses, and bicycles. It will be very nice to get home again.

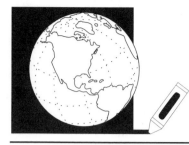

Chapter 3

Understanding International Adoption: An Overview

Should you decide to adopt internationally, it is in your best interest, and that of your future child, to learn the adoption procedures both in the United States and abroad. You will be handling much of the paperwork in cooperation with your U.S. social worker and your international agency or attorney. Your function is that of expediter. Endless delays can be avoided if you take responsibility for the paperwork shuffle; always know who has your papers, why they have them, and what happens next. While most adoption agencies, here and abroad, have years of experience in handling foreign adoptions, a few foreign adoption sources cited in the Compendium are not yet familiar with foreign adoptions; in fact, the same is true for some of the private and public agencies in the United States. And yet, some of them may be involved in processing your paperwork. The more *you* know about the process, the more likely it is that your experience will go smoothly.

STEP 1

Learn all you can about international adoption from available resources. Attend orientations and seminars hosted by adoptive parent organizations and private adoption agencies.

One of the best ways to become familiar with the adoption process itself and to understand the issues facing both the parents and children of international adoption is to attend orientations or educational seminars. These are typically sponsored by private, licensed adoption agencies to provide potential adopters with information on how a home study is conducted and to give an overview of the U.S. immigration and foreign adoption process. Adoptive parent support groups may also sponsor seminars and usually invite all of the adoption agencies to participate. (See the Appendix for a list of adoptive parent support groups.) At seminars for international adoption, postadoptive parents usually bring their children and speak about their experiences. Prospective adoptive parents find out about seminars by word of mouth, by keeping in contact with local agencies, and through public service announcements on television, radio, and newspapers. Attend as many seminars as possible before selecting an agency.

In addition, begin learning all you can about international adoption from other sources such as books, newsletters, magazines, videos, the internet, the World Wide Web, and adoptive parent groups. A list of recommended publications is found in the Bibliography. The National Adoption Information Clearinghouse also offers a series of publications on various aspects of the international adoption process. Many of these publications are free.

Write or call the National Adoption Clearinghouse at
>Box 1182
>Washington, DC 20013-1182
>703-246-9095

International adoptions occur in eight major stages:
1. Preliminary Home State Approval (Chapter 5)
2. Preliminary INS Approval (Chapter 6)
3. Application to a Foreign Adoption Source (Chapter 7)
4. Receiving Referral of the Child (Chapter 8)
5. Filing the Orphan Petition (Chapter 9)
6. Travel abroad (Chapter 10)
7. Emigration, Immigration (Chapter 12)
8. Postplacement Procedures (Chapter 14)

Twenty-three steps are dealt with, from agency registration to U.S. naturalization or citizenship (see nearby table). These steps are highlighted, beginning in this chapter and ending in Chapter 14.

It is best to follow the steps in the order they appear, whenever possible. Based on our experience and that of the many adoptive parents we have guided, prospective U.S. adopters who try to alter this approach will encounter serious difficulties along the way.

TABLE 3-1 STEPS IN THE INTERNATIONAL ADOPTION PROCESS

Step 1   Learn all you can about international adoption from available resources. Attend orientations and seminars hosted by adoptive parent organizations and private adoption agencies.

Step 2   Collect agency information.

Step 3   Choose an international adoption agency.

Step 4   Choose the agency that will conduct your home study (if different from your international adoption agency).

Step 5   Initiate home study by registering with appropriate agency.

Step 6   Obtain documents required for home study.

Step 7   Prepare documentation required for I-600A (Application for Advance Processing).

Step 8   File I-600A (Application for Advance Processing) and the FD-258 (Fingerprint Charts).

Step 9   Apply for a passport.

Step 10   Select an adoption program in a foreign country.

Step 11   Obtain documents required for your foreign dossier.

Step 12   Obtain translations for documents in your foreign dossier.

Step 13   Obtain notarization, verification (or apostille), and authentication of documents in your dossier.

Step 14   Prepare for the referral of your child.

Step 15   Obtain visa or tourist card (if necessary) for travel to your child's country.

Step 16   File the I-600 (Orphan Petition) if this is to be filed in the United States. (This is usually filed abroad if the adoption is finalized in the child's country and both parents travel to meet the child.)

Step 17   Prepare for your adoption trip.

Step 18   Meet your child.

Step 19   Obtain the guardianship or final adoption decree.

Step 20   Apply for the orphan visa and file the I-600 (Orphan Petition) if this was not filed earlier.

Step 21   Participate in postplacement supervision.

Step 22   Readopt your child in your county of residence.

Step 23   File for U.S. citizenship for your child.

REQUIREMENTS FOR ADOPTIVE PARENTS

In reviewing the Compendium at the back of this book, most prospective adoptive parents are pleased to see that the adoption requirements of many foreign adoption agencies are less stringent than those of local adoption agencies in the United States. At most U.S.-based international agencies, single persons and couples married one year or more, between the ages of twenty-five and fifty, with or without children, of all races and religious affiliations, as well as persons who were previously divorced, can find adoption programs in countries to accept their applications. Prospective adoptive parents must be in the middle to upper income bracket, able to expedite documents, and able to travel abroad if required.

However, prospective adoptive parents must also meet the requirements of the Immigration and Naturalization Services (INS). The INS requires that at least one spouse be a citizen of the United States. The INS will not approve welfare recipients, unmarried couples, or persons who have a history of felonies, drug or alcohol abuse, mental illness, or who are carriers of the virus that causes AIDS.

AGENCY-INITIATED AND PARENT-INITIATED ADOPTIONS

There are two major types of legal foreign adoptions: agency-initiated adoptions and parent-initiated adoptions (also known as direct or independent adoptions).

In an agency-initiated foreign adoption, prospective parents work with a U.S.-based international adoption agency, which handles paperwork and communications, and assigns a child to a client through a child-placing agreement or contract with a foreign source. This is the most common type of international adoption. Upon the assignment of a child, the foreign child-placing entity sends the U.S.-based agency copies of the mother's release or the decree of abandonment and the child's birth certificate. The U.S. agency, in turn, presents these documents to the adoptive parents. In addition, the foreign source will send medical and biographical information, and a picture and/or video of the child for the U.S. agency to share with you. Once the adoptive parents have accepted the referral, the U.S. agency coordinates their adoption trip. The agency and its bilingual representatives take responsibility for assisting you with the child, your lodging, and obtaining the final adoption decree and the child's passport and exit visas. They will also provide the documents required for the orphan visa by the American Consulate. (A more detailed description of the different types of agency-initiated adoptions is given in Chapter 7.)

Parents do not have to travel to some countries. For example, Korea arranges proxy adoptions and allows for escorts to bring the child to you. The U.S. adoption agency is the guardian of the child until you adopt about six months later. Guatemala also permits adoption by proxy; when the final decree is issued, the child can be brought to you.

This type of escort service has a down side. The most obvious problem is that the child becomes a part of your family sight unseen. Parents usually have very little idea about the behavior of these children until they are in their new home. The other problem with escorting is that it takes longer to arrange than it would if you traveled there yourself, and it is not substantially cheaper.

In a parent-initiated adoption (also known as an independent or direct adoption), prospective parents obtain a home study from a licensed adoption agency or social worker. After this point, they are on their own as far as filing with the INS and preparing a dossier of documents for the court abroad. The adoptive parents are solely responsible for selecting and securing a foreign lawyer or agency who will, in turn, refer a child to them.

The foreign agency or lawyer tells the adoptive parents when to take their adoption trip. After that, the parents are again on their own. They must take full responsibility for the child as well as obtaining the proper documentation for the child's adoption, passport, and orphan visa.

While independent international adoptions are certainly possible, the risks are much higher than in agency adoptions, which are regulated by the state. In addition, many foreign countries do not allow independent adoptions. According to the National Adoption Information Clearinghouse, the risks of an independent adoption include involvement in the black market; loss of confidentiality; infringements upon the child's privacy; inadequate medical information; the possibility of outright fraud; and the lack of proper documentation of the child's status as an orphan.

The safest way to adopt a foreign child is to involve a licensed adoption agency or social worker (if individually licensed) in your state of residence and adopt the child through an international adoption agency or public welfare department abroad.

Over the years, we have heard of many sad cases in which a missionary or foreign lawyer, rather than an international agency abroad, assigned a couple a child but was unable to obtain the birth documents needed for a legal international adoption. The prospective adoptive parents send money overseas for years in the hope that the child can be legally freed for adoption. We usually meet them when they have given up hope and want to start over with an agency-initiated adoption.

TYPES OF U.S. ADOPTION AGENCIES

Licensed U.S. adoption agencies fall into three general categories: public adoption agencies, private local adoption agencies, and U.S.-based international adoption agencies. (All U.S.-based international agencies are private.) In addition, some states also license individual social workers to conduct home studies and supervise adoptive placements. Understanding the functions of and differences between these types of agencies will help in your understanding of the adoption process.

Although there are no special standards set forth for international adoption agencies, *all* adoption agencies in the United States are mandated and licensed by the state. Lawyers, facilitators, or other professionals involved in an independent adoption, but not working with an adoption agency, are not regulated by the state.

Public Adoption Agencies

Public adoption agencies are funded by your tax dollars. They are set up to provide social services to children in their counties. Public adoption agencies maintain the cases of children in foster care who have been removed from their parental home due to abuse or neglect. If the parents terminate their parental rights, the children are placed in adoptive homes. There is very little cost to prospective parents adopting children through a public adoption agency. However, because of their ever-growing case loads, these agencies seldom have time to conduct home studies for international adoptions.

Private Adoption Agencies

Private adoption agencies are funded in many different ways. If they specialize in placing children from the public adoption agencies, they are usually funded by the state. If they specialize in handicapped children or locally born infants, they usually rely on client fees. However, many of them receive funding through a church or synagogue affiliation, the United Way, Independent Charities of America, Children's Charities of America, and so on.

Most local, private adoption agencies will usually perform casework and a home study for foreign adoptions, even though they will not be able to refer a child for adoption. Such agencies, which include nonprofit, licensed private, church-funded, or community organization-funded placement agencies, charge fees or need donations of anywhere from $2,000.00 to $4,000.00 for pre- and postadoptive services. Each agency has its own set of requirements for applicants. If the agency is church-funded, it may require church membership in that denomination. (Many private agencies may waive their own requirements if the adopter has found an international agency or foreign source that will accept him or her as an adoptive parent.)

U.S.-Based International Adoption Agencies

U.S.-based international adoption agencies have child-placing contracts with foreign government child welfare departments, adoption agencies, liaisons, or attorneys in foreign countries. U.S.-based international agencies handle the foreign application, coordinate the referral of the adoptive child, and coordinate state, foreign, and emigration/immigration procedures. In addition, such agencies do the casework and perform the home study and postplacement supervision for residents of the state where the agency is licensed. (If an applicant lives in another state, a locally licensed private agency or licensed, certified social worker must conduct the home study and postplacement supervision.)

When traveling for an adoption, a liaison of the international agency will meet you at the airport and assist you throughout the process in the child's country of origin. In foreign countries where adoption sources permit proxy adoptions or guardianships, international agencies may arrange to escort the assigned child to the United States if laws permit this. International agencies usually charge fees or need donations.

Social Workers and Certified Adoption Investigators

Social workers are the largest professional group providing mental and social health services. Every state has different standards for social workers, but the minimum is usually a bachelor's or master's degree in social work (BSW or MSW, respectively) and certification with the state board. State certification includes credentials such as a Certified Social Worker (CSW) or an individual with a master's degree, an Advanced Clinical Practitioner (ACP). To keep their licenses current, social workers are required to continue their education and must submit proof of this on an annual basis.

Some states license individual social workers to conduct home studies and supervise adoptive placements. Prospective adoptive parents will need to get in touch with their district INS office to see if it will accept a study written by a social worker independent of an agency.

The advantage to using an independent certified social worker over an agency might be that they are less expensive and possibly speedier. If the social worker is networking with an international adoption agency, there should not be any problems. Otherwise, adoptive parents may discover that their home study is not accepted by the INS or government abroad. U.S.-based international adoption agencies have a full-time or part-time social worker with a master's degree who reviews the home study to be certain that it is in compliance with the requirements of the state, the INS, and the foreign country prior to signing it. Another disadvantage to using an independent social worker is that most don't have access to the current international adoption situation or the cross-cultural educational and parenting resources of a large adoption agency.

U.S. SAFEGUARDS
FOR FOREIGN ADOPTED CHILDREN

Any adoption can be a legally complicated affair, but in international adoptions the typical issues are compounded by U.S. immigration requirements, the legal requirements of the country from which the child is originating, and the requirements of the state in which the child will ultimately live.

Immigration and Naturalization Services (INS) laws are strict. Adopters must have documents to prove their identities, whom they are married to, whom they are no longer married to, and how much money they have to support a family. INS will not approve advance applications for the orphan petition until the adopters get FBI clearances to prove they have no criminal records. U.S. immigration laws are designed to prevent criminal activities by foreign and U.S. citizens who are involved in the adoption process. Without a doubt, unscrupulous persons with criminal intent would import large numbers of children if they could.

A number of legal and procedural safeguards have been enacted by the federal and state governments to ensure the success of foreign adoptions by U.S. citizens.

On the federal level these actions include:

A home study performed by a licensed agency or a licensed social worker in the adopter's home state.

INS orphan immigration petition requirements.

FBI check of every preadoptive parent.

Good practice, intercountry adoption guidelines established by the U.S. Departments of Health, Education, and Welfare.

U.S. citizenship for every legally immigrated orphan.

Those actions on the state level are as follows:

Postplacement visits by a licensed social worker.

Social worker's recommendation for readoption.

Issuance of a new birth certificate (in most states).

ICPC

Also, be aware that if an agency, parent group, or individual in one state causes a foreign child's placement in another state, the Interstate Compact on the Placement of Children (ICPC) regulates these placements. The ICPC applies when a child is escorted, or when only one parent (of an adopting couple) has observed the child prior to adoption. An exception to the ICPC usually occurs when both spouses or a single parent travel abroad to observe the child prior to the adoption. ICPC filings and approvals are handled by the adoption agency.

The ICPC was never intended for use in intercountry adoptions, only for child placements between U.S. states. In many ways, the ICPC illustrates the almost *ad hoc* evolution of laws and regulations governing international adoption in the United States.

In his article, "Transnational Adoption of Children,"[1] Richard R. Carlson describes the international adoption process as it has evolved, identifies deficiencies in the existing process, and proposes legislative reform.

---

[1] Richard Carlson, "Transnational Adoption of Children," *The University of Tulsa Law Journal,* Volume 23, No. 3, 1988.

Here, he describes some of the difficulties and frustrations in foreign adoptions:

Transnational adoption is an increasingly important facet of immigration and adoption in the United States. However, transnational adoption has received surprisingly little attention from lawmakers and legal scholars. Congress has enacted legislation facilitating the immigration of prospective adoptive children, but has not endeavored any substantial regulation of the adoption process. A few states have enacted special legislation dealing with transnational adoptions, but the great majority continue to rely on the same legislation that was enacted primarily for adoption of locally-born children.

The adoption of a foreign-born child, however, can raise difficult legal problems that are rare or unknown in the adoption of American-born children. These problems arise partly from the difficulty of reconciling foreign and domestic law, and partly from the failure of American lawmakers to develop a rational allocation of authority among foreign, federal, and state officials.

Despite the early views of Congress that large-scale transnational adoption was a temporary phenomenon, transnational adoption has not only grown over the past forty years, but is likely to continue for the foreseeable future. Transnational adoption is both an important solution to the shortage of adoptable children in the United States and the shortage of adoptive parents in many developing nations. Greater attention must now be focused on the unique problems of transnational adoption in order that the process will not be jeopardized by poorly formed rules and standards at the immigration phase, and overly-restrictive rules at the state adoption [or readoption] phase.

THE HAGUE CONVENTION

An international law affecting intercountry adoptions was put forth by the Hague Conference on Private International Law. The final text of the law (known as the Convention on Protection of Children and Cooperation in Respect of Intercountry Adoption) was passed at the conclusion of the organization's seventeenth session in May of 1993. The law applies to all adoptions between countries that have accepted and ratified the intercountry adoption law.

The intent of the law is to regulate intercountry adoptions by setting forth minimum standards and procedures designed to protect the interests of the children being adopted as well as those of the birth parents and the adoptive parents. However, the law does not prohibit countries party to the Convention from setting additional requirements and standards governing international adoption.

So far, more than twenty countries have signed the Convention. The United States signed the Convention in May of 1994; however, this act was mainly symbolic, showing an intent to ratify, rather than an immediate commitment.

Disunity in the U.S. adoption community has led to delays in its implementation leading to ratification. Ratifying the Hague Convention would require the establishment of a central authority for U.S. international adoptions, and only recently have the larger social service groups and adoption groups come to an agreement on what they believe should be included in such an authority. Currently, the United States has no national adoption law; each state has its own laws regulating adoption.

No one knows whether ratifying the Hague Convention will help or hinder U.S. citizens adopting abroad. However, without ratifying the Convention, the United States, as the largest recipient of intercountry adoptions, certainly lacks some clout in the international adoption community.

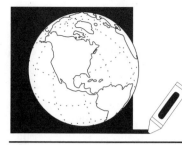

Chapter 4

Choosing the Right Agency

In the years following World War II, when U.S. citizens were first trying to adopt abroad, it was difficult to find a local agency to conduct pre- and postadoption services. The first U.S.-based international agency was Holt International Adoption Services of Eugene, Oregon, which was founded in the 1950s. That agency made arrangements with private agencies in various states to provide services to Korean orphans being placed through Holt. However, prospective adoptive parents who did not fit the requirements for Holt because of their age, length of marriage, or religious beliefs had a difficult time finding alternatives.

International adoption nowadays is a completely different story. So many agencies exist and so much information is available that potential parents are overwhelmed.

STEP 2

Collect agency information.

Most potential adoptive parents find an international adoption agency by word-of-mouth, through recommendation by their local adoption agency or parent group, or by researching all available books on the subject. Adoption information and referral services have popped up in many states to help adoptive parents find the most suitable agency for their needs. Annual adoption conferences are held in many states. This gives preadoptive parents the chance to talk to all the agencies, both local and out of state, and to take home their literature. Most local agencies hold their own seminars or orientations to present an overview of their services. Another method for finding information is to surf the World Wide Web. Not every agency has a home page, but this is a convenient method to collect needed information from those who have.

Several excellent directories of agencies are also available. Two sources for this kind of information are the *Report on Foreign Adoption* and *The Adoption Directory,* which list the names, addresses, and telephone numbers of U.S.-based international agencies that process guardianships and adoptions in other countries. Information on both of these publications is found in the Bibliography.

Other resources include your state department of public welfare or social services, Adoptive Families of America, National Council for Adoption, and the Joint Council on International Children's Services. The Appendix includes phone numbers and addresses for each of these organizations, as well as a list of state departments of public welfare. In addition, many adoption agencies have web sites on the Internet.

Los Niños International Adoption Center (LNI) provides adoption services to residents in Texas and to residents of states where LNI networks with other licensed adoption agencies. Many other U.S.-based international adoption agencies also network with private adoption agencies in other states.

CHOOSING AN INTERNATIONAL ADOPTION AGENCY

Once you have gathered information on the agency or agencies you are interested in contacting, you may wish to prepare a list of questions for each one. That done, you can ask the questions not covered in the litera-ture by phone, e-mail, or in person. Since some agencies work with several different countries, the answers to questions regarding requirements, waits, and fees may differ according to country. In addition, each agency should be able to provide you with names and telephone numbers of postadoptive parents who enjoy discussing their adoption experiences. What follows is a sample of some helpful questions for evaluating an international adop-tion agency.

International Agency Administration

Q: Is your agency licensed and nonprofit? Which government body licenses you?

Q: Who directs the agency, human service professionals, business administrators, or lawyers?

Q: How many years have you been placing children?

Q: May I have a copy of your policies and the contracts for adoptive parents?

Q: Who helps me prepare a dossier of documents for the child-placing authorities?

Q: What types of education and support services do you provide before, during, and after the placement of a child?

Q: Are you licensed or approved by the foreign governments in countries where you have programs?

Q: Do you have bilingual staff abroad to obtain the referral of a child and to assist the adoptive parents while they are there?

Q: May I have names of people who have recently adopted from _____ (country)?

Q: Are you planning to obtain national accreditation when Congress ratifies The Hague Convention?

Placement Procedures
Q: How many children did you place last year?

Q: What are the ages and nationalities of the children you place?

Q: What is their behavior like?

Q: What is their general state of health?

Requirements for Adoptive Parents
Q: What are your requirements for adoptive parents, relating to age, income, religion, marital status, living arrangements, length of marriage, divorce, state of health, or records of a legal misdemeanor?

Q: What is your policy regarding single applicants?

Q: Which countries do you think might accept my application?

The Referral of a Child
Q: After my dossier is completed, how long is the wait for a girl/boy of ___ years of age from _____ (country)?

Q: When I am referred a child, what kind of information will I receive?

Q: What happens if I don't feel I can accept this referral?

Q: Once I accept the referral, how long will it be until I can travel to _____ (country) to immigrate the child? Will that be one trip or two?

Q: How long will I need to stay abroad? If I choose a country where the child will be escorted, how long does it take for the child to be brought to me?

Q: What happens if the child becomes too ill to be adopted before or during my stay? What happens if I decide I don't wish to adopt that particular child?

Q: What happens if we can't adjust to this new child?

Expenses
Q: What is the total cost for an adoption from _____ (country)?

ESTIMATING THE COSTS OF AN INTERNATIONAL ADOPTION

The costs of an international adoption vary greatly depending on the agency you use, the range of services provided, the country from which you adopt your child, the cost of travel, present exchange rates for the U.S. dollar, and a host of other factors. The average cost for an international adoption in 1996 was between $12,000 and $20,000.

TABLE 4-1   ESTIMATING ADOPTION EXPENSES

The fees listed below are estimates only and will vary according to the agency you work with, the country you adopt from, and your individual situation. We've made these estimates based on the fees charged by adoption agencies with which we are familiar. To determine your approximate cost, select only the expenses that apply to your individual case or choice of country. Most countries have a widely varying rate of inflation generally much higher than in the United States, as well as fluctuating exchange rates vis-à-vis the U.S. dollar.

PREADOPTION U.S. AGENCY FEE
Registration with agency ....$50 to $600

Home study fee..$600 to $2,500
(Assumes international agency also conducts home study)

Agency fee for services ....$3,000 to $6,000
(Some agencies do not list this fee separately, but combine
it with the program fee.)

Preplacement checklist update ....$150 to $300

OTHER ADOPTION-RELATED EXPENSES INCURRED IN THE UNITED STATES
INS filing fee for Orphan Applications...$155
(There is no filing fee for the Orphan Petition if done in the
same year as the application.)

Certified copies of birth, marriage, and divorce certificates ....$10 to $60
(Fees range from $5-$10 per document)

Notarization and verification fees ....$200 (average)
     (Varies according to state and number of documents.
      Most states charge $10 per document.)

Translations of documents ....$350 (average)
     (Averages $300-$400 when done in the United States.
      If done overseas, costs vary and are often included in the program fees.)

Authentication of documents by the foreign consulate ....$375 (average)
     (Ranges from free to $500.00)

Program fee for child...$3,000 to $30,000
     (If agency fee for services is separate)

TRAVEL-RELATED COSTS

One round-trip ticket per person traveling ....$600 to $2,000
     (Varies tremendously depending on country traveling to,
      time of year you are traveling, and type of ticket you buy)

One-way ticket for child to United States..$100 to $900
     (Tickets range from $100 to $120 for infants and children
      up to age two. Tickets for children age three and older generally cost
      about sixty percent of the adult fare.)

Food and lodging...$30 to $100 (per day)
     (Varies depending on whether stay is in a major city,
      an average hotel, or with a family)

U.S. consular service Orphan Visa fee $200

Orphan's photos for passport and visa..$25 to $35

Orphan's passport ....$25 to $100

POSTPLACEMENT EXPENSES

Postplacement supervision...$800 to 2,500
     (Varies according to agency and whether international agency
     or network local agency conducts supervision. Also varies
     according to the number of supervision contacts required.)

Legal fees for readoption...Fees vary
     (Legal fees may vary tremendously. Call a lawyer in your state for an
     estimate. If you are conducting a *pro se* adoption, you will only be responsible for court fees.)

U.S. Citizenship filing fee $90.00

*POSSIBILITIES FOR ADDITIONAL COSTS:

Other less common costs that may come into consideration, depending on the country and the type of program you choose, include the costs of foster care for the child, escort fee for bringing the child to the United States if you do not travel overseas, fees for transferring INS paperwork if you change foreign programs, fees for professional handling of documentation, fees for obtaining visas (required for China, Russia, Vietnam, Bolivia), etc.

The only way to get a firm handle on what an adoption will cost is to keep track with a sheet of estimated expenses (see nearby table). Whatever the figure you arrive at, the amount will be trifling in comparison to the costs of actually raising the child. The U.S. Department of Agriculture estimated that a moderate-income family will spend $145,320.00 to raise a child born in 1995 until he or she is 17 years old.

Although an international adoption agency should be able to provide exact figures for costs such as the agency's international processing fee and the foreign program fee, other costs such as document preparation and travel may vary considerably according to the adoptive parents' individual situation and the country from which they are adopting. For example, a single or a couple in Pennsylvania who adopts through a U.S. based international agency in Texas will know ahead of time what the pre- and postadoption fees will be for their adoption agency in Pennsylvania. However, the costs of obtaining their certified documents and getting them translated, notarized, and verified will differ, since a typical single will have fewer documents than a couple who have both been divorced.

One of the most expensive parts of many adoptions is travel. The costs of air travel, hotels, food, and transportation within the country will vary according to the part of the world you are traveling to and the exchange rate at the time of your trip. Miscellaneous expenses such as fees for photos and the medical examination required for the orphan visa will also vary. A good, up-to-date travel guide book will help you estimate most of your travel expenses. The travel book will also provide information about tipping and whether or not small gifts are expected by officials.

One of the easiest ways to calculate travel expenses is to talk to several adoptive parents who have recently returned from their adoption trip.

However, since we all have different spending and saving habits, you may find a difference of several thousand dollars. Some folks spend hundreds of dollars to phone home every day, or even include the cost of expensive souvenirs in their accounts of travel and adoption expenses.

While international adoption is costly, the fees can be paid over a series of months. Payments are due in increments as you move through the process. Be sure you know what all of the fees will be (excluding travel) before you begin the process. Some people finance their international adoption by applying and qualifying for an unsecured loan.

EVALUATING YOUR OPTIONS

Choosing an adoption agency is an act of faith. The agency assumes a lot of responsibility toward coordinating an adoption. Trust is the key word. And a lot of paperwork.

Warning signs that may make you decide against using a certain agency boil down to communication, administration, and finances. Was your initial phone call, fax, or e-mail requesting information during business hours responded to within five working days? If not, the agency may be understaffed or overextended. Are the administrators experienced enough in international adoption to be able to solve all the complex problems that arise? Does the agency work in more than one country? If a foreign country changes its adoption requirements and you no longer qualify, will they help you to apply in a different country? Does the agency have sufficient financial reserves to cover losses due to major changes in a foreign adoption program and the resultant loss of income?

Other factors to consider are expenses and the extent of service provided. Not surprisingly, the more work an agency does for the adoptive parent, the higher the agency fee is likely to be. For example, some agencies assist the adoptive parents in filing with the INS as well as preparing the dossier of original documents for the foreign court, while other agencies show the adoptive parents how to do it themselves. Either the international agency or its networking agency must be licensed in the state where you reside in order to handle the documentation for you. Generally there is a separate fee for this service that can range from $3,000 to $4,000.

Your choice of an international agency will also be driven by the country or countries you are most interested in adopting from, as well as whether you qualify in terms of age, length of marriage, and so on. No agency has adoption agreements with every country in which it is possible to adopt.

It's best to have more than one country in mind when selecting an agency. Choose an agency with several foreign programs that interest you. For example, a lot of potential parents decide to adopt from a particular country because they have met an adoptive family or seen a television show on adopting in that country. This has been particularly true of Romania, Russia, and

STEP 3

Choose an international adoption agency.

TABLE 4-2   INTERCOUNTRY ADOPTIONS 1990-1995

	1990	1991	1992	1993	1994	1995
ALL COUNTRIES	7093	9008	6536	7248	8195	9679
EUROPE	262	2761	874	1521	2406	2711
Romania	121	2552	145	88	199	275
Russian Federation	-	-	-	-	1530	1196
Other Former USSR	-	*12	*432	*1107	268	341
Other Europe	141	197	297	326	409	199
ASIA	3779	3194	3032	3163	3641	5040
China, total	95	157	263	388	856	2193
China-Mainland	29	62	201	330	787	2130
China-Taiwan	66	55	35	31	35	23

	1990	1991	1992	1993	1994	1995
Hong Kong	-	40	27	27	34	40
India	348	448	348	342	406	371
Japan	57	83	71	59	49	63
Korea	2620	1817	1787	1765	1795	1666
Lebanon	16	17	16	24	16	20
Pakistan	14	9	15	12	17	6
Philippines	421	417	353	358	314	298
Thailand	100	127	90	65	47	53
Vietnam	-	-	23	105	88	318
Other Asia	108	119	66	45	53	52
AFRICA	52	41	63	59	91	101
OCEANIA	10	16	13	1	7	8
NORTH AMERICA	959	1047	1136	1133	846	771
Canada	8	12	6	7	1	3
Mexico	112	106	104	97	85	83
Carribean	156	159	134	150	132	124
Dominican Rep.	58	50	41	39	17	15
Haiti	64	52	49	49	61	49
Jamaica	28	39	29	48	35	45
Other Carribean	6	18	15	14	19	15
CENTRAL AMERICA	683	770	892	878	628	561
Belize	10	4	8	5	3	1
Costa Rica	105	55	65	48	29	19
El Salvador	103	122	115	97	38	30
Guatemala	257	324	428	512	436	449
Honduras	197	244	253	183	77	28
Nicaragua	7	11	8	9	18	10
Panama	4	10	15	24	27	24
OTHER N. AMERICA	0	0	0	1	0	0
SOUTH AMERICA	1995	1949	1418	1471	1204	1048
Bolivia	30	51	74	123	37	21
Brazil	228	178	139	178	149	146
Chile	302	263	176	61	79	90
Colombia	631	527	403	416	351	350
Ecuador	59	11	36	48	48	67
Paraguay	282	177	244	405	483	351
Peru	440	772	324	230	37	15
OTHER S. AMERICA	23	20	22	10	20	8

National Adoption Reports, January/February 1996

China, where the media has given the orphans a lot of coverage. The couple's next step is to contact an agency with a program in that country. However, if that agency only has one viable program, and that country changes its requirements or puts a moratorium on adoptions, the couple may be left without other options.

The determination of some couples to adopt from a particular country can sometimes get in the way of good sense if they do not fit the age restrictions, length of marriage, and so on. If the prospective parents are unusually persistent, they will call every agency in America until they find one that will take them as clients, not fully realizing that they could be turned down at the end of the process by a judge who reviews that country's national adoption law before granting a final adoption decree.

WORKING WITH THE INTERNATIONAL AGENCY

While prospective parents expect to be guided and kept informed, agencies have certain expectations, as well. They expect the potential parents to read their contracts, handbooks, and program packets of directions before calling for help. They also trust that the documents required from the prospective parents will be sent to the agency in a timely fashion. They also expect that prospective parents will be prepared to take an adoption trip abroad on short notice. More importantly, the agencies abroad have the expectation that the adoptive parent has applied to only one foreign child-placing entity.

You may be required to sign a contract that specifies the services performed by the international agency. It should cover the illness or death of a child awaiting adoption, as well as relatives reclaiming the child and adoption disruptions. Waiting pool policies and a postplacement supervisory agreement are usually outlined, as is the addition of a child to the adopting family during the waiting period by pregnancy or adoption through another agency. A reimbursement schedule for international processing and foreign program fees should be included, usually with a disclaimer such as one posted in ICCC's Report on Foreign Adoption:

> *Due to circumstances beyond the control of any agency, the possibility exists that the adoption process could be discontinued by foreign nations, governmental action, or judicial decrees beyond the control of the agency. You must further understand that it is necessary to advance funds to accomplish agency objectives and that the portion of those funds already utilized very possibly cannot be recovered in the event of such discontinuance. You need also to understand that in spite of information to the contrary, the child, when received, might have some undiagnosed physical or mental problem or might develop such a problem at a later date. You need to know, finally, that*

*despite agency effort to work with competent and honest lawyers,
their actions are beyond agency control. This is by no means meant
to scare you, but to tell you simple facts about intercountry adoptions.*

Chapter 5

Obtaining State Approval: The First Steps

O nce you have learned as much as you can about the international adoption experience, attended as many educational seminars as possible, talked to prospective parents and visited with adoptive parents and their children, and thoroughly evaluated the agencies you are interested in working with, you are ready for the next formal step in the adoption process: registering with the licensed agency or certified registered social worker that will conduct your home study and any postplacement supervision required.

If the U.S.-based international agency you plan to use to adopt your child is located and licensed in your state, it will be the one to conduct your home study. When the potential adoptive parents live in a state where the international agency is not licensed, they will need to find another agency or a certified social worker to conduct the home study. Thus, in some cases, you will actually need to formally register with two agencies: a local agency that is close enough to your residence to do your home study and an international agency that will connect you with a child overseas. Fortunately, because most international adoption agencies use a network of local agencies across the United States, finding a local agency to do your home study is usually not difficult.

The agency conducting your home study must have a countywide or statewide license, but it does not necessarily need to have an office in your city. Many agencies utilize social workers in other cities and counties on a contract basis in order to provide services for a wider area.

> **STEP 4**
>
> Choose the agency that will conduct your home study (if different from your international adoption agency).

THE HOME STUDY

The INS mandates that all states require a home study by a licensed social worker or adoption agency in the adopter's home state before a child is adopted abroad or is brought into the United States for adoption. The home study must follow the requirements of the state licensing department for child-placing agencies. INS requirements must also be included. You will need an adoption agency or social worker to conduct a home study even if you plan to enter into an independent or parent-initiated adoption.

A home study usually consists of an orientation meeting, registration, a private interview, a home visit, and group discussions led by a social worker. Data gathered at the study meetings is summarized by the social worker in a document that becomes the official home study. The home study may take anywhere from six weeks to six months depending on individual circumstances.

Home studies deal with the dynamics of the individual adopter, the marriage, the challenges of transracial and cross-cultural adoptions, and the subsequent adjustments of parent and child. Social workers are professionally trained to help prospective adopters explore the many facets of adoption and to help them make the best possible decisions for the family they are planning. This study process ends when a mutually agreed upon decision is reached either to proceed toward adoption or to withdraw the application.

REGISTERING WITH YOUR LOCAL AGENCY

STEP 5

Initiate home study by registering with appropriate agency.

Every adoption agency has a registration form or application that must be filled out before the home study begins. If you have a history of mental illness, alcohol or drug abuse, or a criminal record, discuss your problem with the director of the agency before registering. You may be requested to provide a letter of recommendation from a psychiatrist, counselor, or probation officer before you register. Many agencies also request that you fill out a form indicating your level of acceptance of certain medical conditions in the child you wish to adopt. (See sample list of handicapping conditions of waiting children at the end of this chapter). This list ranges from conditions as minor as a lisp or small scar to much more serious health issues. Adopting parents who want a completely healthy child may answer "no" to all listed conditions or may decline to fill out the form.

You may also be required to sign a home study contract, which outlines the agency's responsibilities and your own. If, for some reason, your agency or social worker does not offer a home study contract, you might request one. The home study sessions and the conditions necessary for approval are set forth in the contract. Most contracts or agreements will state the conditions under which some or all of the fees you pay will be refunded.

Before you commit to any agency, you should know exactly what services this agency will perform and what its fees will be. Call or write to request literature explaining the agency's requirements for adoptive parents, fees, policies, and length of licensure.

Two separate entities are involved in licensing adoption agencies and social workers. Social workers are licensed in their state by the State Board of Social Worker Examiners. The board issues a directory of social workers each year. Adoption agencies are licensed by the licensing division of their state adoption unit. There is a unit in each county. State adoption units go by different names. In Texas, it is the Department of Protective and Regulatory Services. To ensure that you are registering with a qualified adoption agency or social worker, check with the appropriate licensing agency. (Note: In most states, a home study conducted by an agency is required; however, in some states, such as New York, Iowa, Florida, Louisiana, and Texas, a licensed social worker may conduct the study instead.)

In addition, before you commit to having an agency conduct your home study, you should know the answers to the following questions:

What does your home study consist of?
Who will conduct it?
How soon will the social worker contact me after I apply?
How long will it take for approval?
Why would someone not be approved?
What happens after the home study?

OBTAINING DOCUMENTS FOR THE HOME STUDY

Once you have registered with an agency to conduct your home study, you should begin to collect the documents needed to meet your home study requirements and the requirements of other federal and foreign agencies that will be involved in your adoption. Many of the documents assembled for your home study will also later be used to prepare a dossier (or collection of documents) for the foreign court or central authority.

STEP 6

Obtain documents required for home study.

You will be collecting a combination of certified and original documents. A certified document is an official document issued by the state or county, as opposed to a document issued by a hospital for a birth or a document issued by a church for a marriage. Original documents are individually generated. Job letters, health certificates, police clearances, letters of reference, and your home study are all considered original documents.

Each prospective adoptive parent must obtain the following documents before the home study can be approved. (You can initiate the home study before you have all of the documents.)

Required Documents

1. Certified birth certificates for each member of the family. Order three for each spouse (one for the foreign dossier, one for the passport, and one for the INS) and one for each child.

Certified birth certificates can be ordered from the Bureau of Vital Statistics in the state where you were born. If you need help finding this office, contact directory assistance in the capital city of the state where you were born. Obtaining certified birth certificates takes about four weeks by mail or two hours in person, unless you use express mail services.

If you are a naturalized citizen, use your naturalization certificate for evidence at the INS Office and Passport Office. Use a certified copy of your birth certificate for the formal adoption dossier. This can be accomplished through the consul of your native country, who will authenticate a photocopy of your original. If you are from a country which does not have a consul here (i.e., Cuba), you may request the consul of the country from which you are adopting to handle this step. If you do not have a birth certificate, ask INS for form G-342. With this, they can certify your name, birth date, and birthplace.

2. Certified marriage license. Order two (one for the foreign dossier and one for INS).

Certified marriage licenses are available from the County Clerk in the county where you were married. These usually cost between $3.00 and $10.00. This takes one week by mail or two days if you call ahead and pick it up. Tell them the month, day, and year of the marriage, the names of both parties, and your return address.

3. Certified death certificate, if applicable, of former spouses. Order two of each (one for the foreign dossier and one for INS). Certifed death certificates are available from the Bureau of Vital Statistics in the state where the death occurred.

4. Divorce decree, if applicable. Order two of each (one for the foreign dossier and one for INS). If both you and your spouse are divorced, you will each need two copies of both divorce decrees. Divorce decrees are available from the Clerk of Court in the county in which the divorce occurred.

5. Job letter from your employer stating your length of employment and annual salary. (You need one letter for each applicant.) If you are self-employed a public accountant may prepare the statement.

6. A statement of net worth written by you or your accountant. (See sample net worth statement at the end of this chapter.)

7. Copies of your insurance policies. You need only the page showing the company name, beneficiary, and amount. A photocopy will usually suffice. (Note: Not all states require this.)

8. Medical examination forms for all household members signed by the family physician. (See medical history form at the end of this chapter.) The date of the exam must be included on the form. The medical examination form is good for one year from the date of the exam.

9. A photocopy of last year's federal income tax return (first and second page only).

10. For all household members over age eighteen, a letter from your local police department stating that the individual has no criminal record. (See sample police clearance form at the end of this chapter.) You will usually need a separate letter for each applicant. Try to get the signature of the Chief of Police notarized at the same time. Ask at the police station for information on doing this.

11. Letters of reference from at least three people who are acquainted with you and your family. These letters should come from professionals or community leaders if at all possible. (See sample format for letters of reference at the end of this chapter.) Try to obtain letters of reference from people in your locality. Then, the same notary public, Secretary of State, and foreign consul can be used to sign, stamp, verify, and authenticate all or at least most of your documents.

12. Pictures of applicants in front of their home and individual close-ups (or passport pictures). You should also include photos of existing children. You need at least three sets of photos. Pose in business attire. Jeans, shorts, swimsuits, and bare feet will not make a favorable impression, since your dossier should be presented with as much dignity as possible. (See sample photos at the end of this chapter.)

Submit photocopies of your documents to the agency conducting your home study. You must retain the originals for your foreign dossier. Documents not usually required abroad are birth certificates and medical forms on children already in your family and insurance policies.

Documents for the foreign dossier may need notarization or apostilles, verification, and authentication, depending on the country you adopt from. (Some adoptive parents notarize each of the original documents as they are gathered.) Chapter 7 explains the process for ensuring that your documents are appropriately endorsed. Try to get all of your original documents generated in the same state. This way, you may need only one notary public to sign all of your documents. This also makes them easier to verify.

SAMPLE GUIDELINES
FOR A TYPICAL HOME STUDY

Most U.S.-based international agencies have a specific guide for social workers conducting the home study as well as the postplacement supervisory reports. Your international agency will inform you if your local agency or social worker needs to follow a specific format.

Since many foreign adoption agencies will ask to see a translated copy of the home study, adopters should ask their social worker to make the home study as brief as possible. In most cases, eight to ten pages is adequate.

What follows is an example of a set of home study interview guidelines used by the administering agency or social worker. This particular home study guide incorporates Texas Minimum Standards, the INS regulations cited in form I-600A, and those of Los Niños International Adoption Center. Although the home study guidelines of other agencies may vary somewhat, you can expect that all of these topics will be brought up at some point in the home study process.

In addition, the social worker will also conduct an environmental evaluation of your house to be sure the home would be safe for a newborn or child. (See sample environmental health checklist at the end of this chapter.)

THIS GUIDE IS FOR THE EXCLUSIVE USE OF NETWORKING AGENCIES

Revised from the Federal Register/Vol. 59, No. 146
Re: INS regulations 9/30/94
Texas Minimum Standards 5/10/94

PREPARING THE HOME STUDY & DOCUMENTS
A Guide for Social Workers
Copyright 1995 Jean Nelson-Erichsen

If this guide is not followed, we must request a rewrite or an addendum. The home study report should be eight to ten pages. Use agency letterhead.

(Name of State) CHILD-PLACING LICENSE

THIS STUDY IS APPROVED FOR THE SOLE USE OF LNI FOREIGN ADOPTION PROGRAMS.
Name of prospective adoptive parents.
Address (Street, City, State, and Zip).
Home and work telephone numbers.
(Name) have met all the preadoption requirements for the State of _____.

HOME STUDY APPROVED: _____ (date). A complete set of supporting documents was presented to this agency prior to approval.

INS and LNI standards require these separate interviews and their dates:

First consultation or orientation _____ (date).

An individual interview with each applicant _____ (date).

Interviews with school-age children or other persons living with family _____ (date).

At least one visit to home with all present _____ (date).

At least one interview with adult children living at home who are over 18: _____ (date).

Interview either by phone or in person with each adult child no longer residing in the home: _____ (date).

The applicants answered "No" to the questions "Have you ever had a negative home study or been rejected by another child-placing agency?"

TOPICS REQUIRED

Child Desired: Prospective adoptive parents must accept a child of either sex. However, they may state a preference along with a solid reason for their choice.

State the minimum and maximum ages, sex, ethnicity (Asian, Asian/Caucasian, Asian/Hispanic, Asian/Black, Hispanic, Hispanic/Caucasian, Hispanic/Black, Caucasian, Gypsy), a newborn with low birth weight or correctable/noncorrectable handicaps, or a sibling group, or twins they wish to adopt.

Note whether one or both parents will travel abroad for the legal proceedings and to bring their child home. Do not specify country, since the international adoption situation changes often. The description of the child desired must match one(s) in your recommendations on the last page.

Adoptive Mother: State the adoptive mother's birth date and birthplace and describe her family constellation and work and play activities. What were the expectations of the parents for their daughter? Their methods of discipline? Was she emotionally abused? Physically abused? Sexually abused? How does the adoptive mother feel about her parents and childhood? What are her feelings about herself now?

Adoptive Father: Same as for the adoptive mother.

Children (this includes adults over 18): State the age, sex, personality, and physical description of any school-age children. What are their attitudes toward this adoption? For children over 18, include an evaluation of the relationship they plan to have with the child.

Roomers and Boarders: Do the applicants have nonrelated persons in their home? If so, please describe the physical characteristics, age, and sex of this individual. In addition, what is the attitude of the roomer toward the adoption? What is the relationship of the applicant(s) with the roomer? What will the roomer's relationship with the child be?

Marital Relationship: How do the individuals view each other and their partnership? Include their feelings about their inability to produce children biologically, if applicable. Are they trying to conceive a child now? Could the wife possibly be pregnant or become pregnant during the adoption process? If so, will they agree to put the adoption plan on hold until the biological child is six months old? Are they trying to adopt a child through another source? If they do receive a child, their present adoption plans must be put on hold for six months. In both cases, an update must be written for the home study.

Have they ever been separated or threatened divorce? Do they believe that a new child will stabilize their relationship? Have they ever received marriage counseling? If so, when and for how long? What was accomplished? Were there any previous marriages? Did they end by death or divorce? Were any children produced? What are the custody and child support arrangements?

Lifestyle: What is their philosophy toward society? What activities do they enjoy together and separately? What is their religion(s) and the extent of their involvement in church activities?

Occupation, Educational Level, and Aspirations: Write a statement on each of these topics for the adoptive father and adoptive mother.

Personality and Physical Description: Write a statement on each of these topics for the adoptive father and adoptive mother.

Physical Health of the Adoptive Parents: Write a statement for the adoptive father and adoptive mother on their general health as well as chronic health problems, if they exist, and how they are being controlled. If applicable, include a statement covering the diagnosis of their infertility. Is their age such that they can meet the needs of the child? Is their state of health verified by the medical examination forms provided? (Studies will not be approved until medical forms are on file.)

Have they ever been treated for mental illness? What was the treatment? Duration? Have they ever received counseling for emotional problems? Treatment? Duration? Name and address of doctor or therapist who will recommend this patient for adoptive parenthood must be obtained. He or she will be sent a psychological/psychiatric report to fill out and return. Out-of-state clients must also obtain a letter of recommendation from their networking adoption agency.

Mental Health: A typical statement is, "_____ (names) appear to have healthy, well-rounded, functioning personalities. There is no evidence of any type of psychopathology. Further, they have a good maturity level and a good ability to handle stress. They are both independent thinkers and demonstrate good overall judgment and logical thinking."

Economic Situation: Sufficient income and management ability must be substantiated in order to provide for the child's needs. Include each adoptive parent's income and any investments, etc. Mention the insurance coverage for health and life. Do their employers provide some benefits which pay part or all of their adoption expenses?

Housing: Are the physical environment, the home, and the outdoor surroundings appropriate for the care of a child? What are the housekeeping standards? Include the approximate size of the child's room, a description of the play room, and the play area outdoors. Is it clean? Is the yard fenced? If the prospective parents plan to move or if they live abroad but plan to raise the child in the United States, include a description of the house where they will reside, if this is known. Will the space meet state requirements?

Safety, Water, Firearms, Fire, and Home Health: Discuss water hazards near the property and how to protect the child. Does an existing pool have an alarm? How does the family handle fire practices? Do they have fire alarms? How many?

If they own guns or firearms, where do they keep them? Have they or will they babyproof their house? Do they practice safety by keeping children away from dangerous liquids, tools, and machines?

Child Raising: Will one of them provide care and guidance or will they handle this as a couple? In the case of older child placements, have they thought about traumas the child suffered, loss of biological parents, institutional care? Are they ready to write and then manage a daily routine for a child over two?

Parenting Skills: Is the motive for adoption shared equally by husband and wife? Why does he or she wish to adopt? How does their extended family and community view adoption? What are their expectations for the child? Are they adopting to fulfill the need to love and nurture? Are they adopting to help humanity? Do they think that adoption is different from biological parenting?

How will they help the child understand adoption? Will they explain that the child was born to another set of parents, but is theirs now, both in love and in law? What do they think about the biological parents of the child? Was the birth mother poor? Unwed? Did she ask an adoption agency for help? Were there no relatives able to help? Should a young child know this? What will they tell the child about his or her birth parents? What are the reasons a child may be abandoned? Do they think the child's birth mother remembers them on birthdays and holidays? How can they help a child prepare an answer for other children when they ask, "Why are you adopted?" or worse, "Didn't your mother want you?" Do they plan to adopt more than once?

Discipline Policy: Are they ready to write, and continually revise as the child matures, a set of household rules? Do they fully understand the need for structure in a formerly institutionalized child? Can they limit the sensory bombardment of television and toys until the child has settled into the family?

What discipline methods will they use? Will they abide by the agency's discipline policy? Will they seek family counseling or therapy if necessary for a child or teenager if he/she encounters difficulties in school or socially? How long before seeking counseling should adoptive mothers absorb a child's misplaced anger because he or she is angry with the birth mother over his or her perceived rejection? How and when will they discuss the issue of illegitimacy with their child? How will they guide their child in accepting his or her sexuality and taking responsibility for himself or herself?

Adopting Siblings: Will the adopters feel threatened by the closeness of the siblings who will probably speak another language for a while? How will the adopters be able to win the trust of the oldest child, so that he or she will let go of the parental role?

Transracial, Cross-Cultural Adoption: Many people find it difficult to love another person's child as their own. Some find it easy to love a child of their own race and culture, but find it difficult to love a child whose race or culture is vastly different. It takes special people with extra sensitivity and understanding to parent a child of a different race in our society.

How can they become more sensitive to racial differences? Do they live in an integrated neighborhood? Is this a plus or a minus? Will the child attend an integrated school? Are they willing to move if necessary to a more supportive environment?

The family will be interracial for future generations. Adoption of a child of another race is not just a question of a cute little baby or a child, but a commitment to a lifetime of growing. How do they feel about interracial marriages? How will they feel when people assume they are married to a person of their child's race? How will they feel when their child invites minorities to their home? Do they have friends or intend to cultivate friends of their child's race or national origin? How do they feel about lots of public attention, stares, etc.? How will they raise a foreign child in an American family? Have they considered adopting more than one child of similar ethnicity so that the child has someone with whom to share the experience? Will adopting a second or third time help children see that their parents feel very positive about adoption?

Culture: How can they help their child understand his or her culture and feel comfortable answering peers' questions of "What are you?" How much do they know about differences in child raising in the culture from which they wish to adopt? Are they interested in learning about them? Should they keep the child's name or part of it, or select an African, Oriental, or Latin name if the child was not named? (Research indicates the wisdom of keeping the name the child is called. Many seriously disturbed adoptees had their names changed at placement.)

Do they believe there is a need to stimulate a sense of pride about the child's family of origin, by participating in cultural activities (attending parades, visiting museums, eating ethnic foods, obtaining books, listening to music, watching ethnic programs of

various kinds, i.e., television, movies, live shows)? Will they help in celebrating culturally associated holidays such Cinco de Mayo, Chinese New Year, etc.? Will they prepare
a life story book with emphasis on family background, ethnicity, and culture? How do
they feel about teenagers who decide they want to visit their place of birth? What are the
risks? How would they feel if their teenager wanted to search for his or her birth parents? Do they feel that contact with the birth mother is beneficial to the child?

How will the child benefit from this adoption? Describe as much as possible
the kind of life potential parents envision for their child.

Does the prospective adoptive parent agree with agency policies regarding
cross-cultural and foreign placements (quote this paragraph):

"_____ (names) do not expect their child to resemble
them physically, and do not have any rigid expectations for him or her. They plan
to learn about the child's cultural background and to incorporate some of that
knowledge into their own family's lifestyle and tradition. They realize they may
have little or no medical information on the child or the biological parents and
they have considered the fact that their child may have physical or psychological
problems at the time of placement. Also, they are aware of the possibility of their
child developing a previously undiagnosed health problem. They are accepting of
this and willing to take that risk. _____ (names) will assume full responsibility for the medical and financial needs of their child after placement."

"_____ (names) are willing to know and to understand the laws of
_____ (name of state) pertaining to international adoption, the requirements of the Immigration and Naturalization Service, the delays caused by
Interstate Compact Placement (ICPC)* procedures, and the adoption process in
general. _____ (names) understand that copies of the supporting documents must be presented to this agency before the home study can be approved.
_____ (names) are also aware of the INS requirement that this home study
must be filed within six months of the approval date. _____ (names) are
informed that the I-600A Advance Processing form is valid for 18 months."

*ICPC applies to out-of-state home studies, if no final decree is issued in the
country of origin.*

READINESS TO ADOPT (QUOTE IN HOME STUDY)

"Prior to and during the home study, _____ (names) were counseled
regarding the processing, expenses, medical risks, difficulties, and delays associated with international adoptions. After their initial consultation, or orientation,
_____ (names) proceeded with their home study interviews and with a
social worker. During this time, they followed a systematic approach to international adoptions and became knowledgeable about cross-cultural, transracial
parenting by reading texts and following their agency handbook."

Work: Are the adoptive parents changing their priorities concerning their jobs and other activities to allow ample time to spend with the child? Will one or both parents take maternity or paternity leave?

References (paraphrase in home study): Three letters of reference from professionals, clergy, neighbors, and/or community leaders provided by the applicant(s) testify to the stability, maturity, financial responsibility, and sensitivity of the individuals as these qualities relate to adoptive parenting. References from attending physicians and therapists cannot be accepted.

Police clearance for all household members 18 and over (including children away at school) must be completed (quote in home study):

" _____ (name) answered Yes/No to the question, 'Were you ever arrested?' on the application form. A letter from the local police verifies that _____ (name) has no criminal record. Also must specifically address topics of domestic violence and substance abuse."

If a potential adoptive parent was arrested for a misdemeanor, such as one DWI (Driving While Intoxicated) or smoking marijuana at a party five years or more ago, state the nature of the incident and whether the client has successfully changed his or her behavior. If a potential adoptive parent has been arrested for any reason, this must be discussed before completing the study. (The agency may decide to tell the client to get counseling and to shelve the study temporarily or permanently.)

Ask the prospective parent if the record of his or her arrest can be expunged. They may need to consult an attorney for this. If the offense cannot be expunged, the agency may not complete the study or approve them for adoption.

Child abuse clearance for all household members 18 and over (including children away at school) must be completed (quote in home study):

" _____ (name) answered yes/no to the question 'Have you ever been accused or charged with child abuse or neglect?' The state of _____ does/does not provide child abuse clearances for prospective adoptive parents registered with private licensed nonprofit adoption agencies. The child abuse registry in the state of _____ has verified that _____ (name) does not have a criminal record of child abuse."

PREPLACEMENT PROCEDURES (QUOTE IN HOME STUDY)

" _____ (names) realize that they must prepare a dossier of original documents for a foreign court, with the assistance of the agency, in order to adopt or to secure a guardianship abroad.

_____ (names) are also aware that upon presenting this formal dossier that they will begin a weekly series of adoptive parent training classes through the agency correspondence course."

INS Regulations: They realize that a child must be adopted in the United States if the single adopter or both spouses have not seen the child prior to being granted the final adoption decree. They also realize that they must adopt if they were granted a guardianship.

POSTPLACEMENT COUNSELING (QUOTE IN HOME STUDY)

" _____ (name) agrees to at least six months of postplacement supervision, required by the State of Texas, or longer if required by the foreign child-placing entity involved."

Texas Preplacement Checklist Update: Upon the assignment of a child, a social worker must conduct a face-to-face in-the-home interview using the agency checklist. This is applied if a child was referred six months or more after the home study was approved. Quote this paragraph in home study:

" _____ (name) is aware that if this study has not been submitted to INS within six months, an update must be written, or for significant changes such as a change of residence, marital status, criminal history, financial resources, and/or the addition of one or more dependents prior to the orphan's immigration. _____ (name) will take responsibility for arranging for a preplacement checklist update at the time a referral is made, a minimum of 30 days prior to the placement of a child in the home or prior to the expiration of the home study with INS."

Social Worker's Impressions and Recommendations: List impressions and recommendations as well as your signature and credentials on the last page.

AFTER THE HOME STUDY

Immediately upon the approval of your home study by the supervisor of social work, copies of the home study, supporting documents, and the I-600A application (including fingerprint charts) should be filed at INS. Do not forward these documents to the INS until you have formally registered with a U.S.-based international agency. Chapter 6 explains the process for filing the I-600A.

Updating the Home Study

A home study is valid 6-12 months depending on state law. A home study update must be written if the home study has expired, or if you have moved or experienced some other major life change. If you move out of state, you must register with an agency there to update your study according to their state requirements. INS fingerprint charts and petitions must also be updated and/or transferred to your new local INS office.

Each home study topic must be covered in the update. If a topic remains the same, "No changes" may be written below the topic heading. Dates on preceding documents 5 through 11 expire after six months to one year. These items must be updated during the time the home study update is in progress.

Handicapping Conditions of Waiting Children

Indicate your level of acceptance of a child who has the following problems:

		Indicate		
NEWBORNS		YES	NO	MAYBE
A.	Low Apgar score, prognosis uncertain	☐	☐	☐
B.	Birth mother on drugs or alcohol, prognosis uncertain	☐	☐	☐

CHILDREN

1.
  A. Slight limp ☐ ☐ ☐
  B. Leg braces ☐ ☐ ☐
  C. Missing limb ☐ ☐ ☐
  D. Is in a wheel chair. ☐ ☐ ☐
  E. Is paraplegic ☐ ☐ ☐
  F. Is quadriplegic ☐ ☐ ☐
  G. Cerebral Palsy ☐ ☐ ☐
  H. Cystic Fibrosis ☐ ☐ ☐

2.
  A. Seizure disorder that is controlled by medication ☐ ☐ ☐
  B. Seizure disorder not controlled but child has infrequent seizures ☐ ☐ ☐
  C. Seizure disorder not controlled and has frequent seizures ☐ ☐ ☐

3.
  A. A blood disorder that requires blood transfusions every 3 months ☐ ☐ ☐
  B. Blood disorder that requires hospitalization once a month ☐ ☐ ☐
  C. Blood disorder resulting in a limited lifespan ☐ ☐ ☐

4.
  A. Heart murmur, activity not curtailed ☐ ☐ ☐
  B. Heart murmur, vigorous activity curtailed ☐ ☐ ☐
  C. May require open heart surgery at a later date but at placement needs only to be watched ☐ ☐ ☐
  D. Definitely will require open heart surgery ☐ ☐ ☐
  E. Will require more than one open heart surgery ☐ ☐ ☐

5.
  A. Sight in both eyes but vision is limited and special glasses needed ☐ ☐ ☐
  B. Sight in one eye only ☐ ☐ ☐
  C. Blind but surgery may give partial sight ☐ ☐ ☐
  D. Blind and will never have sight ☐ ☐ ☐

6.
  A. Hearing problem with only partial hearing and surgery may help. ☐ ☐ ☐
  B. Hearing problem with partial hearing but surgery will not help ☐ ☐ ☐
  C. Hearing in only one ear ☐ ☐ ☐
  D. No hearing, deaf and does not speak. ☐ ☐ ☐

7.
  A. Deformed hand ☐ ☐ ☐
  B. Deformed arm ☐ ☐ ☐
  C. Deformed leg ☐ ☐ ☐
  D. Deformed face ☐ ☐ ☐
  E. Two deformed arms ☐ ☐ ☐
  F. Two deformed legs ☐ ☐ ☐

Handicapping Conditions of Waiting Children

				YES	NO	MAYBE
8.	A.	In special education		☐	☐	☐
	B.	In EMR		☐	☐	☐
	C.	In TMR		☐	☐	☐
	D.	Retarded and will always need supervision, such as sheltered home		☐	☐	☐
	E.	Downs syndrome		☐	☐	☐
9.	A.	Hyperactive		☐	☐	☐
	B.	Hyperactive, requires medication but functions relatively normal		☐	☐	☐
	C.	Hyperactive, requires medication and some kind of special classroom setting		☐	☐	☐
10.	A.	Emotionally damaged, very withdrawn and will require therapy for an extensive period of time		☐	☐	☐
	B.	So emotionally damaged he/she is very abusive toward other people; a child who is abusive to animals		☐	☐	☐
	C.	Emotionally damaged; he/she is very abusive toward his/her person, such as pulling out hair, pinching himself/herself		☐	☐	☐
11.	A.	Stutters		☐	☐	☐
	B.	Lisp		☐	☐	☐
	C.	Speech at age 6 is very hard to understand		☐	☐	☐
	D.	Will always have trouble speaking and being understood		☐	☐	☐
12.	A.	Hare lip		☐	☐	☐
	B.	Cleft palate		☐	☐	☐
	C.	Both hare lip and cleft palate		☐	☐	☐
13.	A.	Had one parent who is schizophrenic		☐	☐	☐
	B.	Had two parents who are schizophrenic		☐	☐	☐
	C.	Schizophrenic, but medication helps		☐	☐	☐
14.	A.	Sickle Cell carrier		☐	☐	☐
	B.	Sickle Cell Anemia but relatively controlled		☐	☐	☐
	C.	Sickle Cell Anemia with frequent episodes		☐	☐	☐
15.	A.	Burn scars		☐	☐	☐
	B.	Slight		☐	☐	☐
	C.	Extensive, needing surgery		☐	☐	☐
16.	A.	Birth marks		☐	☐	☐
	B.	Small		☐	☐	☐
	C.	Large or extensive		☐	☐	☐

Statement of Net Worth

NAME(S): _____

ADDRESS: _____

_____

Home Telephone Number: (   )   —

ASSETS

Cash on hand & in banks $ _____
Investments   _____
Savings accounts   _____
Cash surrender value
  of life insurance   _____
Other Stocks & Bonds   _____
Real Estate: _____
1. _____   _____
2. _____   _____
Automobile   _____
Trucks, boats, planes   _____
Personal property   _____

TOTAL ASSETS $ _____

LIABILITIES & NET WORTH

Mortgages & real estate notes $ _____
Notes payable   _____
Credit card (balances):   _____
            _____ _____
            _____ _____
            _____ _____
Loans (balances): _____   _____
            _____ _____
            _____ _____
            _____ _____
            _____ _____

TOTAL LIABILITIES $ _____

NET WORTH* $ _____
(*Net Worth is the difference between Assets & Liabilities)

Date _____ Signature _____

Date _____   Signature _____

SUBSCRIBED AND SWORN to before me on the _____

day of 199__ . To which witness my hand and seal of office. _____

Notary Public in and Or the State of _____ , county of _____

My commission expires:. _____ .

Medical History

Last Name	First Name	Age

Address: _____

Relationship to Adoptive Parent(s): _____

PRESENT CONDITION:

Weight: _____ Height: _____ Blood Pressure: _____ Heart Rate: _____

Maintenance medication : _____

General physical condition: _____

How long has this patient been known to you? _____

MEDICAL HISTORY: YES   N O

		YES	NO
A	Is the applicant in good mental and physical health?	—	—
B	Does applicant have a personal or family history of any significant disease or chronic disabling condition?	—	—
C	Does applicant suffer from any contagious disease?	——	—
D	Has applicant ever been hospitalized?	——	——
E	Has applicant ever been treated for emotional problems or mental illness?	——	——
F	Has applicant ever had major surgery?	——	——
G	Has applicant ever been treated for chemical dependency?	——	——
H	(Prospective parents only) Has applicant undergone infertility tests and/or treatment?	——	——
I	(Prospective parents only) is the applicant infertile?	——	——

If the answers to any of the questions A to H are "yes," what implications might this have for the applicant's functioning as an adoptive parent?

_____

_____

Physician's Signature   Date of Exam

AUTHORIZATION FOR RELEASE OF MEDICAL INFORMATION: I authorize my physician or clinic to release any medical information pertinent to the application for adoption to _____ (agency name).

_____

Signature of Prospective Adoptive Parent to be notarized   Date

SUBSCRIBED AND SWORN to before me this _____ day of _____ , 199 __. to which witness my hand and seal of office.

_____

Notary Public in and for the State of _____ , County of _____

Police Clearance

NOTE: This form is not accepted in all states. If so, request a letter on their letterhead. If at all possible, get fingerprinted at your local police or sheriff's office. Before making an appointment, obtain the packet of forms for an orphan visa from your local INS office. Take the FD-258 fingerprint chart with you. You will file the chart with INS for FBI clearance.

Dear Sir/Madam:

Our adoption agency requires that all applicants have a record check. Please check this information through the NCIC and, (for Texas residents) the TCIC. In some localities, neither police nor sheriff offices can produce fingerprint charts. In this event please return the chart to our clients.

MALE APPLICANT: _____ Date of Birth: _____

Social Security No.: _____ Place of Birth: _____

Present Address: _____

Father's Full Name: _____

Mother's Full Name: _____

FEMALE APPLICANT: _____ Date of Birth: _____

Social Security No.: _____ Place of Birth: _____

Present Address: _____

Father's Full Name: _____

Mother's Full Name: _____

RELEASE OF INFORMATION PERMISSION: I willingly give my permission for the above information to be
checked and released in full to _____ (agency name) at _____
_____ (agency address).

MALE APPLICANT: _____ Date: _____

FEMALE APPLICANT: _____ Date: _____

TO BE FILLED OUT BY LAW OFFICER

TO WHOM IT MAY CONCERN: The subject has been checked by our department. Records were also checked through TCIC/NCIC and were found to be clear.

The record of this male subject is: _____
_____

The record of this female subject is: _____
_____

Signature of law officer: _____

SUBSCRIBED AND SWORN to before me this _____ day of _____ , 199 ___ .

_____

Notary Public in and for the State of _____ , County of _____

My commission expires: _____ .

Letter of Reference

Try to obtain letters of reference from people in your locality. Then the same notary public, Secretary of State (verification), and foreign consul (authentication) can be used to stamp and sign all or at least most of your documents.

Photocopy three copies of this form for the persons you have selected to write your letters. Ask them to give you the letter for your formal adoption dossier.

TO: _____

FROM: _____

DATE: _____

RE: Letter of Reference: A letter must be typed and signed before a notary.

We have applied to _____ (agency) for assistance with our adoption plans. We hope that you will be able to write a letter of reference for us, and return it to us by _____ (date). Following are seven categories which the agency wishes you to consider and to include in a letter of reference.

1   How long have you known us and in what capacity?

2   Have you observed us around children? Under what circumstances?

3   Do you believe we can easily handle the problems that could arise when an adopted and/ or foreign child enters our home?

4   Have we discussed our adoption plans with you? How do you feel about our plans?

5   How do you think an adopted and/or foreign child will be accepted in our community?

6   Do you believe we manage our money responsibly?

7   How would you rate our homemaking and property upkeep?
    We will appreciate any additional comments and/or information you would like to include.

Sample Photos for Home Study

Environmental Health Checklist

		YES	NO	N/A
1.	Home is clean and maintained in good repair	☐	☐	☐
2.	Furnishings and equipment used by an ill child are cleaned with soap and water	☐	☐	☐
3.	Sheets and pillowcases are washed before use by another child	☐	☐	☐
4.	Yard is free of hazards to children	☐	☐	☐
5.	Rooms are adequately ventilated and without objectionable odors	☐	☐	☐
6.	Windows and doors used for ventilation are screened	☐	☐	☐
7.	Plumbing appears in good repair. Home is free of water stains or other indications of water leaks	☐	☐	☐
8.	Home has hot and cold water available	☐	☐	☐
9.	Glasses are used by only one child between washings	☐	☐	☐
10.	Outside area is free of indication of sewage overflow or related problems	☐	☐	☐
11.	Home uses a public water supply. NOTE: Where a private well is used, the Texas Department of Health Resources or the local health department may be requested to provide assistance in regard to standards and sampling	☐	☐	☐
12.	Home uses a public sewage disposal system. NOTE: If problems are observed with private sewage disposal systems, assistance may be requested to provide assistance in regard to standards and sampling	☐	☐	☐
13.	Adequate number of garbage containers available	☐	☐	☐
14.	Garbage containers have tight fitting lids	☐	☐	☐
15.	Garbage containers designed for reuse are kept clean	☐	☐	☐
16.	Garbage is collected from the premises at least once a week	☐	☐	☐
17.	Garbage is disposed of in a sanitary manner if collection is not available	☐	☐	☐
18.	Yard is well drained and there is no standing water	☐	☐	☐
19.	Premises are free of garbage and rubbish	☐	☐	☐
20.	Steps have been taken to keep the premises free of insects (flies, mosquitoes, cockroaches) and rodents.	☐	☐	☐
21.	Label instructions on rat and pest poisons are followed	☐	☐	☐
22.	Pesticides and other poisons are kept in areas not accessible to children	☐	☐	☐
23.	Food is prepared, stored, refrigerated, and served under safe and sanitary conditions	☐	☐	☐
24.	Food is obtained from approved sources in labeled containers	☐	☐	☐
25.	Eating and cooking utensils are properly washed	☐	☐	☐
26.	Food preparation area is cleaned after each use	☐	☐	☐
27.	Eating and cooking utensils are stored on clean surfaces	☐	☐	☐
28.	Medication is stored separately from food	☐	☐	☐
29.	Animals are vaccinated for rabies and other diseases as recommended	☐	☐	☐
30.	Bathrooms are located inside home	☐	☐	☐
31.	A minimum of one toilet, lavatory, bathtub, or shower is available	☐	☐	☐
32.	Each child is provided with own clean towel or single use towels are available	☐	☐	☐
33.	Adequate soap and toilet paper are available	☐	☐	☐
34.	Bathroom floors, walls cabinets and work surfaces are clean and easily cleanable	☐	☐	☐
35.	Plumbing facilities are in good working condition	☐	☐	☐

Comments:

_____   _____   _____
Signature   Title   Date

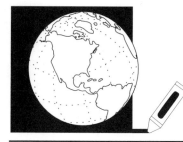

Chapter 6

Preliminary INS Approval

Although adoption or readoption procedures are defined by the laws of the county of the state in which you reside, the federal government has an interest in the fact that your child is entering the United States legally. You will be dealing with two different departments of the U.S. government: the Department of Justice, Immigration and Naturalization Services (INS), which processes orphan visa petitions and applications for citizenship, and the Department of State (U.S. Consular Service office abroad), which issues the orphan's U.S. visa.

Once you are sure you are going to adopt internationally, you should begin advance placement for INS by filing the I-600A (Application for Advance Processing) and supporting documents. With advance filing, INS processes paperwork on the adoptive parents first, so that later it is only necessary to process the child's paperwork. This helps to keep the approval procedures moving as fast as possible.

This chapter will cover advance filing of the I-600A. More detailed information on working with the INS and finalizing the immigration of your adoptive child will be covered in Chapters 9 and 12.

A United States citizen who plans to adopt a foreign orphan but does not yet have a specific child in mind can have the immigration paperwork done much faster by advance processing. Even though you may not yet know what child you will adopt or even what country you will adopt from, advance filing will help expedite INS clearance when you are ready to bring your child home.

Advance processing can also be applied in the following case: the child is known, the prospective adoptive parents are traveling to a country where there is no INS office, and the petitioners wish to file an orphan petition at a U.S. consulate or embassy in the country where the child resides.

Until you obtain citizenship for your child–an event which occurs more than six months after your child enters the United States–he or she is classified as a permanent resident but is legally an alien. If you try to have your child enter the United States under a nonimmigrant student or visitor visa, changing his or her status from a nonimmigrant to a permanent resident and finally to a naturalized U.S. citizen can be difficult, time-consuming, and expensive.

PREPARING THE NECESSARY DOCUMENTATION FOR FILING

STEP 7

Prepare documentation required for I-600A (Application for Advance Processing).

U.S. Immigration and Naturalization Service (INS) forms may be ordered ahead of time by calling your District INS office and requesting the packet of forms to immigrate an orphan as an immediate relative. This package should include Forms I-600A (Application for Advance Processing); I-600 (Petition to Classify Orphan as an Immediate Relative); FD-258 (Fingerprinting Chart), and I-134 (Affidavit of Support). Keep the I-600 (Orphan Petition) and I-134 (Affidavit of Support) in your files. You will need these forms after a child has been assigned to you. (Filing the I-600 petition is covered in Chapter 9.) Consult the Appendix to find the INS office nearest you.

Required Documents

To utilize advance processing, only three items are needed initially: the I-600A Advance Processing form, the FD-258 Fingerprint Charts, and the filing fee. The rest of the items listed below can be filed when the home study is approved.

INS does not require notarization of documents.

1. Form I-600A. Both spouses must sign the form. (See sample form at the end of this chapter.)

2. Home study, which covers criteria set forth in form I-600A. (If your home study is not yet complete, include a statement in your cover letter noting that you will forward the completed home study as soon as final approval is obtained.)

3. Birth certificate, or other proof of birth and citizenship (such as a baptismal certificate), or an original naturalization certificate, or an up-to-date U.S. passport. You need one birth certificate for each applicant, as well as for any other adult or child residing in the home.

4. Form I-134, Affidavit of Support. Copies of your federal tax returns for the past three years must accompany the affidavit. Whether or not to file this form depends on the American Consulate requirements in each country.

5. Marriage certificate, if applicable.

6. Divorce decree, if applicable.

7. Evidence that your state's preadoption requirements have been met, such as a statement to that effect in the home study, or a Consent and Approval form, if required by your state. (See sample Consent and Approval form at the end of this chapter.) U.S. Consular service offices abroad are usually not aware of the adoption laws in each of the fifty U.S. states. They may require proof that you have met the preadoption requirements of your state and that your home study is valid there. (See first page of home study guidelines.) Information on how to establish that these requirements have been met may be obtained from public and private adoption agencies.

8. Forms FD-258, Fingerprint Charts. (See sample charts at the end of this chapter.) You will need two fingerprint charts for every household member over the age of 18. There is no additional charge for filing these.

The fingerprint charts must be completely filled out with the special orphan address included. The INS will only accept fingerprint charts from Designated Fingerprint Service (DFS) sites. Your district INS office should be able to provide a list of DFS locations. (For a list of district INS offices, see the Appendix). Take care not to smudge the charts. INS sends your charts to the FBI to check for a criminal record. This search can take 30 to 60 days.

Fingerprint charts are valid for 18 months. If the orphan has not immigrated before then, you must repeat this step.

FILING FORM I-600A

As soon as you initiate your home study, you should file the completed form I-600A. If you don't know all the details about the proposed adoption, write "unknown at this time" in the appropriate blank. Include a cover letter with your name, day phone number, and address. Most INS offices will let you file the Fingerprint Charts (Form FD-258) with the Advance Processing Application (I-600A) and fee before the home study is approved, in order to save time. The rest of the documents may be forwarded when the home study is complete.

You may file the previously mentioned forms and fee in person or send them by mail. Some INS offices will let you send copies. Others will accept copies after they see the originals. Do not leave the original home study with the INS unless you have more than one copy. You will need the original home study for your foreign dossier. The current fee of $155.00 is best paid by money order. Cash and personal checks are not always accepted.

STEP 8

File I-600A (Application for Advance Processing) and the FD-258 (Fingerprint Charts).

When you file form I-600A, ask for the name of the "adoption officer," so you will be able to call about your clearance later on. The INS will start a file on your case that they will maintain throughout the child's U.S. orphan visa application and U.S. citizenship.

Be certain to photocopy one full set of documents, including form I-600A, to hand-carry abroad. In the event that your child is ready to immigrate before the U.S. Consulate receives your file of the above documents sent by diplomatic pouch, you may be able to obtain the visa with your set of copies, in addition to a copy of the I-171H (Notice of Favorable Determination), which is described below.

APPROVAL OF FORM I-600A

INS must decide from the facts listed in the home study whether the prospective adoptive parent is able to take care of one or more orphans properly, depending on the number of children being adopted. Form I-171H (Notice of Favorable Determination Concerning Application for Advance Processing of Orphan Petition) is sent to you if you appear to qualify for further processing. This notice will also state the date of the determination and the location of the filing of the petition. (A sample of the I-171H is included at the end of this chapter.)

You must send a copy of I-171H to your U.S.-based international agency immediately upon receipt.

INS does not permit convicted felons to adopt. A misdemeanor that appears on your records must be discussed with the adoption agency if you failed to mention it on your application. Depending upon the nature of the misdemeanor, the agency may request documentation from you and proceed, or they may close your case.

A Notice of Favorable Determination does not guarantee that the Orphan Petition (I-600) will be approved. An Orphan Petition may still be denied because the child does not qualify as an orphan or for other proper cause.

Filing to approval of I-600A takes about 30-60 days, and sometimes even longer.

Unfavorable Determination

When there is unfavorable information about the prospective adoptive parent(s) and INS concludes that proper care could not be given to a child or children in that case, INS makes an unfavorable determination. You are advised of the reasons for the unfavorable determination and of the right to appeal the decision.

Updating the I-600A

The I-600A is valid for eighteen months. If an orphan has not immigrated before then, a new application, updated home study and documents, and new fingerprint charts must be filed again, and another $155.00 fee must be paid.

OBTAINING YOUR PASSPORT

Once your dossier is complete and your child is assigned, you will need to be ready to go abroad on short notice. Since it can take three to four weeks to receive your passport in the mail and you will need your passport to apply for a visa or tourist card (which may take a number of weeks depending on the country), you should apply for your passport early in the adoption process. In addition, in some countries, a photocopy of your passport is required for the dossier of documents.

STEP 9

Apply for passport.

Passport numbers are often demanded in foreign courts as another means of identification; each spouse should apply for a passport, even if only one plans to travel.

The passport application form can be picked up at your local post office. To acquire a passport, you will need this form, two 2" x 2" color photos, and a certified copy of your birth certificate. You can get one-day service on passport photos at many places, such as the American Automobile Association (AAA). Passports are valid for ten years.

One-day service for passports can also be found in most major cities. You will need to present proof that you have a ticket or a travel itinerary. Call ahead for information about this service and office hours.

I-600A (Application for Advance Processing)

OMB No. 1115-0049

U.S. Department of Justice
Immigration and Naturalization Service

Application for Advance Processing
of Orphan Petition [8CFR 204.1(b)(3)]

Please do not write in this block.

It has been determined that the
☐ Married   ☐ Unmarried
prospective petitioner will furnish proper care to a beneficiary orphan if admitted to the United Sates.

There
☐ are   ☐ are not
preadoptive requirements in the state of the child's proposed residence.

The following is a description of the preadoption requirements, if any, of the state of the child's proposed residence:

The preadoption requirements, if any,
☐ have been met.   ☐ have not been met.

Fee Stamp

DATE OF FAVORABLE DETERMINATION

DD

DISTRICT

File number of petitioner, if applicable

Please type or print legibly in ink.

Application is made by the named prospective petitioner for advance processing of an orphan petition.

BLOCK I - Information About Prospective Petitioner

1. My name is: (Last)   (First)   (Middle)

2. Other names used (including maiden name if appropriate):

3. I reside in the U.S. at: (C/O if appropriate)   (Apt. No.)

(Number and street)   (Town or city)   (State)   (ZIP Code)

4. Address abroad (if any): (Number and street)   (Apt. No.)

(Town or city)   (Prcvince)   (Country)

5. I was born on: (Month)   (Day)   (Year)

In: (Town or City)   (State or Province)   (Country)

6. My phone number is: (Include Area Code)

7. My marital status is:
☐ Married
☐ Widowed
☐ Divorced
☐ Single
     ☐ I have never been married.
     ☐ I have been previously married _____ time(s).

8. If you are now married, give the following information:

Date and place of present marriage

Name of present spouse (include maiden name of wife)

Date of birth of spouse   Place of birth of spouse

Number of prior marriages of spouse

My spouse resides ☐ With me   ☐ Apart from me
                    (provide address below)

(Apt. No.)   (No. and street)   (City)   (State)   (Country)

9. I am a citizen of the United States through:
☐ Birth   ☐ Parents   ☐ Naturalization   ☐ Marriage
If acquired through naturalization, give name under which naturalized, number of naturalization certificate, and date and place of naturalization:

If not, submit evidence of citizenship. See Instruction 2.a(2).
If acquired through parentage or marriage, have you obtained a certificate in your own name based on that acquisition?
☐ No   ☐ Yes
Have you or any person through whom you claimed citizenship ever lost United States citizenship?
☐ No   ☐ Yes (If yes, attach detailed explanation.)

Continue on reverse.

Received	Trans. In	Ret'd Trans. Out	Completed

Form I-600A (Rev. 8/25/89) Y

I-600A (Application for Advance Processing)

BLOCK II - General Information

10. Name and address of organization or individual assisting you in locating or identifying an orphan

    (Name)

    (Address)

11. Do you plan to travel abroad to locate or adopt a child?

    ☐ Yes   ☐ No

12. Does your spouse, if any, plan to travel abroad to locate or adopt a child?

    ☐ Yes   ☐ No

13. If the answer to question 11 or 12 is "yes", give the following information:

    a.   Your date of intended departure _____

    b.   Your spouse's date of intended departure _____

    c.   City, province _____

14. Will the child come to the United States for adoption after compliance with the preadoption requirements, if any, of the state of proposed residence?

    ☐ Yes   ☐ No

15. If the answer to question 14 is "no", will the child be adopted abroad after having been personally seen and observed by you and your spouse, if married?

    ☐ Yes   ☐ No

16. Where do you wish to file your orphan petition?

    The service office located at

    The American Consulate or Embassy at

17. Do you plan to adopt more than one child?

    ☐ Yes   ☐ No

    If "Yes", how many children do you plan to adopt?

Certification of Prospective Petitioner

I certify under penalty of perjury under the laws of the United States of America that the foregoing is true and correct and that I will care for an orphan/orphans properly if admitted to the United States.

(Signature of Prospective Petitioner)

Executed on (Date)

Certification of Married Prospective Petitioner's Spouse

I certify under penalty of perjury under the laws of the United States of America that the foregoing is true and correct and that my spouse and I will care for an orphan/orphans properly if admitted to the United States.

(Signature of Prospective Petitioner)

Executed on (Date)

Signature of Person Preparing Form if Other Than Petitioner

I declare that this document was prepared by me at the request of the prospective petitioner and is based on all information of which I have any knowledge.

(Signature)

Address

Executed on (Date)

Consent and Approval

This letter verifies that prospective adoptive parent(s)_____

of this address: _____

has/have met the preadoption requirements of their state of residence.

   A home study, conducted by a certified social worker, which meets the standards of their state of residence, has been completed and approved. Supporting documents provided by the prospective adoptive parents validate the data therein.

   I hereby grant consent and approval of an adoptive placement for the aforementioned person(s).

_____   _____
Date   Supervisor of Adoptions (agency name)

SUBSCRIBED AND SWORN to before me on the _____ day of _____ , 199__,
to which witness my hand and seal of office.

FD-258 (Fingerprint Chart)

APPLICANT	LEAVE BLANK	TYPE OR PRINT ALL INFORMATION IN BLACK LAST NAME **NAME** FIRST NAME MIDDLE NAME	FBI	LEAVE BLANK

SIGNATURE OF PERSON FINGERPRINTED

RESIDENCE OF PERSON FINGERPRINTED

ALIASES AKA

O R I

NBINSORPZ
USINS
LINCOLN, NB

DATE OF BIRTH DOB
Month   Day   Year

CITIZENSHIP CTZ

SEX	RACE	HGT.	WGT.	EYES	HAIR	PLACE OF BIRTH POB

DATE   SIGNATURE OF OFFICIAL TAKING FINGERPRINTS

YOUR NO. OCA

EMPLOYER AND ADDRESS

FBI NO. FBI

LEAVE BLANK

ARMED FORCES NO. MNU

CLASS _____

REASON FINGERPRINTED

SOCIAL SECURITY NO. SOC

REF. _____

MISCELLANEOUS NO. MNU

1. R. THUMB	2. R. INDEX	3. R. MIDDLE	4. R. RING	5. R. LITTLE

6. L. THUMB	7. L. INDEX	8. L. MIDDLE	9. L. RING	10. L. LITTLE

LEFT FOUR FINGERS TAKEN SIMULTANEOUSLY	L. THUMB	R. THUMB	RIGHT FOUR FINGERS TAKEN SIMULTANEOUSLY

I-171H (Notice of Approval)

United States Department of Justice

Immigration and Naturalization Service

509 NORTH SAM HOUSTON PARKWAY EAST
HOUSTON, TEXAS   77060

Name and Address of Prospective Petitioner

•   •

Name of prospective petitioner	
Name of spouse, if married	
Date application filed	Date of completion of Advance processing

•   •

NOTICE OF FAVORABLE DETERMINATION CONCERNING APPLICATION
FOR ADVANCE PROCESSING OF ORPHAN PETITION

IT HAS BEEN DETERMINED THAT YOU ARE ABLE TO FURNISH PROPER CARE TO AN ORPHAN OR ORPHANS AS DEFINED BY SECTION 101(b) (1) (F) OF THE IMMIGRATION AND NATIONALITY ACT. A SEPARATE ORPHAN PETITION, FORM I-600, MUST BE FILED IN BEHALF OF EACH CHILD WITH DOCUMENTARY EVIDENCE AS DESCRIBED IN INSTRUCTIONS 2c, 2d, 2e, 2f, 2g, AND 2h OF THAT FORM. A FORM OR FORMS FOR YOUR USE ARE ENCLOSED. NO FEE WILL BE REQUIRED WITH FORM I-600 IF YOU FILE ONLY ONE FORM I-600 WITHIN ONE YEAR FROM THE DATE OF COMPLETION OF ALL ADVANCE PROCESSING. IF YOU DO NOT FILE FORM I-600 WITHIN ONE YEAR FROM THE DATE OF COMPLETION OF YOUR ADVANCE PROCESSING APPLICATION, YOUR APPLICATION WILL BE CONSIDERED ABANDONED. ANY FURTHER PROCEEDINGS WILL REQUIRE THE FILING OF A NEW ADVANCE PROCESSING APPLICATION OR AN ORPHAN PETITION.

Form I-600 should be filed at the Service office or American consulate or embassy where your advance processing application is being retained or has been forwarded as indicated by an "X" mark below:

1. ☐ YOUR ADVANCE PROCESSING APPLICATION IS BEING RETAINED AT THIS OFFICE.

2. ☐ YOUR ADVANCE PROCESSING APPLICATION HAS BEEN FORWARDED TO OUR SERVICE OFFICE
   AT _____ .

3. ☐ YOUR ADVANCE PROCESSING APPLICATION HAS BEEN FORWARDED TO THE AMERICAN CONSULATE OR
   EMBASSY AT _____ .

In addition, please note the following:

☐ Any original documents submitted in support of your application are returned to you.

☐ Your home study is returned to you.

THIS DETERMINATION DOES NOT GUARANTEE THAT THE ORPHAN PETITION(S) WHICH YOU FILE WILL BE APPROVED. AN ORPHAN PETITION MAY BE DENIED BECAUSE THE CHILD DOES NOT QUALIFY FOR CLASSIFICATION AS AN ORPHAN OR FOR OTHER PROPER CAUSE. DENIAL OF AN ORPHAN PETITION, HOWEVER, MAY BE APPEALED.

Form I-171H
(12-15-82)

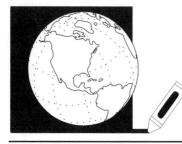

Chapter 7

Application to
a Foreign Source

I f you have not already done so, now is the time to make a decision on the country from which you would like to adopt. After your home study is approved and you have completed your preliminary INS paperwork, assess the current international adoption situation with your international adoption agency. Requirements for adoptive parents, the age and ethnicity of the children available, the length of wait until the assignment of a child, the number of trips required, the length of your stay abroad, program fees, and numbers of children being assigned monthly by each adoption program are all factors you should consider. If you are having difficulty making a decision, consult the agency staff or director, or seek further information from an adoptive parent support group.

STEP 10

Select an adoption program in a foreign country.

METHODS OF ADOPTION REQUIRED BY FOREIGN COUNTRIES

A final important factor to consider before choosing a country program is the legal means by which an adoption is facilitated. This is determined by the child's country of origin. One of six different methods may be used to meet the various legal requirements of foreign countries. (See the adoption law summary for each country listed in the Compendium.)

For example, a power of attorney form is used in most countries to initiate adoption procedures prior to the arrival of the adoptive parents. An attorney acts on behalf of the prospective parents. This saves the adopters from spending time abroad at all the appointments with government officials and court hearings and waiting there for legal custody. Power of attorney forms are also used in some countries for a guardianship or a final adoption by proxy. They are also utilized in certain countries for authorized escorts to immigrate children to their new parents. (A sample of a power of attorney form can be found at the end of this chapter.)

Advantages and disadvantages are inherent in each of the six methods. Adoptive parents may choose one country over another simply because they prefer the power of attorney method to avoid making one long stay or two short trips abroad. Other couples might decide that they prefer to adopt in a country where they can go to see the child immediately after the referral and to be involved in all the adoption proceedings. Adoption by proxy carries more risk for the adoptive parents, since they have not observed the child prior to his or her final adoption and/or immigration. There are more cases of disrupted adoptions in this method, since the families are not always pleased with the child that is delivered to them. The child does not meet their expectations, and they cannot overcome their disappointment.

Method 1: U.S. parents plan to assign a power of attorney to a foreign adoption agency or attorney who initiates the adoption. The parents present themselves later in the foreign country to complete the remaining adoption procedures. This is the most common method used and is found in both agency-initiated and parent-initiated adoptions.

If you are conducting a parent-initiated adoption and the country you are adopting from uses a power of attorney, request the power of attorney form and custody contract as soon as the adoption source has agreed to place a child with you. Power of attorney procedures can be quite time consuming. From the time you receive the forms, it takes from two to eight weeks for them to be signed, authenticated, and returned unless air courier services are used instead of air mail.

Method 2: Proxy adoptions or proxy permanent guardianships are also initiated by a foreign adoption agency or attorney who has been given power of attorney by preadoptive parents. The assigned child is escorted to his or her adoptive family by a person designated by the foreign child-placing entity. INS requires that the adoptive parents must readopt in their state of residence.

This method is mainly used in agency-initiated adoptions, especially by countries such as India. The country, in turn, has child-placing agreements with U.S. adoption agencies. In this case, the child remains under the managing conservatorship of the U.S. adoption agency until the child is legally adopted in the child's new country of residence. Guatemala is one of the few countries that grants a final adoption decree by proxy. The children in these cases are immigrated and escorted by an individual authorized by the U.S. adoption agency or the adoptive parents.

Method 3: The orphan emigrates the foreign country under a permanent guardianship agreement, usually with the adoptive parents or an authorized escort. Some countries consummate the adoption six to twelve months later.

The prospective adoptive parents must promise to adopt the child in their state of residence in order to comply with INS regulations.

Method 4: Formal final adoption decree preceded by a permanent guardianship agreement may be necessary in some countries when the adopters are not old enough or have not been married long enough to meet the adoption requirements.

This method is used in both agency- and parent-initiated adoptions in Chile and in Argentina. The adoptive parents immigrate the child under a permanent guardianship.

Method 5: Custody transfer, usually with escort service, is used by some international adoption agencies with child-placing agreements abroad. It transfers custody of the child from the foreign institution to a U.S. international agency until the child is adopted in his/her state of residence. This method can only by used by international agencies.

Method 6: A final formal adoption decree, issued at the end of the adoption process.

PREPARING YOUR FOREIGN DOSSIER

Once you have made a decision, your agency or its foreign counterpart will provide you with a packet of materials and instructions for preparing your dossier for the foreign country. Completing the dossier is a big task, but you will have already done much of the work in preparation for your home study.

Cover Letter

Your completed dossier will need to be accompanied by a cover letter. If you are working with an international agency, you typically won't need to write the letter yourself, unless it is specifically requested by the child-placing country. The letter should be translated, but notarization is not usually required.

The cover letter should describe your motive for adoption. In the length of two or three pages, your cover letter must clearly explain why you plan to adopt.

Formally request the child you wish to adopt with a description: State your preference for a boy or girl. Specify the age of the child. Explain your preference, if any, for the child's ethnic background. Indicate the name(s) you have chosen for the child, or if you will consider keeping all or part of the child's original name. (Research indicates that children whose names are retained have an easier adjustment.) Your wait will usually be shorter if you will accept a boy or a girl and if you will accept a child within the age range of one to three years. If you are considering a child with a chronic illness or handicap, state the medical conditions you are willing to accept.

Through the activity of formulating your ideas and communicating your knowledge of international adoption, you will create a letter which should lay to rest some of the fears we have heard foreign nationals express concerning international adoptions. (Occasional rumors assert that Americans are adopting children to use as servants, or for organ transplants. Nothing of the sort has ever happened.)

Required Documents

STEP 11

Obtain documents required for your foreign dossier.

Most likely you will have already assembled many of these documents to support the facts you gave the social worker during the home study process. Now is the time to check to make certain you have all of the necessary documents and to move them into a complete dossier for the foreign country. See Chapter 5 for specific details on requesting this information.

Foreign countries change their documentation requirements occasionally; however, they will inform you or your agency of their current procedures. They will also state which documents need notarization, verification, authentication, and translation. (A section at the end of this chapter describes this process.)

It's best to keep this information in a protective folder or binder, just be sure not to punch holes in the documents.

Required documents for your dossier will include:

1. Application form of the child-placing entity. Government authorities in charge of adoption in many countries have their own application forms. These forms are also used by their adoption committees for preapproval in some countries.

2. Certified birth certificates for each member of the family.

3. Certified marriage license, if applicable.

4. Certified divorce decrees, if applicable.

5. Certified death certificates of former spouses, if applicable.

6. Job letter (one for each applicant) from your employer, stating your length of employment and annual salary. If you are self-employed, a public accountant can provide this.

7. A statement of net worth written by you or your accountant.

8. The first two pages of last year's federal income tax return.

9. Current medical examination forms for all household members. (Good for one year from the date of the exam.)

10. Letters of reference from at least three people who are acquainted with the family unit. These letters should come from professionals or community leaders, if at all possible.

11. Letter(s) from your local police, stating that you have no criminal record.

12. Pictures of you in front of your home and individual close-ups (or passport pictures), three of each. Pose in business attire for all photos.

13. Specific forms particular to the foreign child-placing entity.

14. International processing contract. This document explains the agency's responsibilities and yours in locating a child for you and arranging your legal custody.

15. Copies of the first two pages of your passports.

TRANSLATING SERVICES

Your international agency or foreign liaison will advise which documents need translating and at what point this should take place. Most translations of dossiers are accomplished abroad by official translators. If translations must be accomplished in the United States, most U.S.-based international agencies can recommend a skilled translator who can produce legal documents for review by a foreign court. In addition, skilled translators can be found through International Institutes. About forty International Institutes are located around the nation in the larger cities. Consult the telephone book to find the institute nearest you. Before submitting your letter to a translator, agree on a price. Seventeen dollars or more per typewritten page is typical.

STEP 12

Obtain translations for documents in your foreign dossier.

A cover letter certifying the translator's competency must be attached to the translated document. One letter will suffice for all documents translated by the same person. Notarize and verify this letter. Some countries also require authentication of this letter. (A sample for the translator's statement of competency appears at the end of this chapter.) On the other hand, some countries require that translations be accomplished in their Department of Foreign Ministry. In this case, your U.S.-based international agency will courier your documents there. Whether you work with an independent translator or a Department of Foreign Ministry, you should supply the translator with a photocopy rather than the original document in order to keep the originals pristine.

NOTARIZATION, VERIFICATION OR APOSTILLE, AND AUTHENTICATION

STEP 13

Obtain notarization, verification (or apostille), and authentication of documents in your dossier.

All documents must go through the process of notarization and verification before they can be authenticated by the consul of the country from which you are adopting. To make sure that the information you provide is reliable, the consulates require that the papers sent to them for authentication be notarized by a notary public and verified by your county clerk or secretary of state.

Check with your international agency or foreign source to find out exactly what documents need to be notarized, verified, and authenticated. Any supporting documents that you choose to submit, such as a cover letter or tax return, probably need not be notarized.

Obtaining Notarization

A notary public verifies that the signatures on your documents are valid by affixing his or her seal.

You can find a notary public in the phone book. Fees may range from free to $5.00 per document. Legally, the persons who provide the documents or letters of reference–your doctor, banker, employer, friends, and so on–must sign their name in the presence of the notary public. If a doctor, police chief, or so on, cannot leave the office to sign before a notary, the alternative is for you to also sign the form as a release of information and have your signature notarized. Ask your notary to use a jurat form similar to the one at the end of this chapter.

Sending for Verification or Apostille

Verification or an apostille is the process by which the state or county verifies the validity of the notary's signature. (Mexico and some Eastern European countries request apostilles rather than verifications. All former Soviet Union republics do.) Verification and apostille sheets are available from the county clerk or secretary of state who verifies that the notary's signature and seal are valid. Fees for verification or apostille vary from state to state. Do not verify or apostille documents until you have chosen an adoption source. Not every country requires this step. (Samples of verification and apostille forms for the state of Texas can be found at the end of this chapter.)

Send a typewritten sheet with the name, county, and expiration date of your notary's commission, along with the fee for each signature, to obtain apostille or verification sheets with state seals to the secretary of the state in which the document was issued. Check with the appropriate office before sending in your fees and sheets. In some other states, you send a photocopy of each original document. Check before sending. Remember that even if one notary signs six documents, you will need six verifications, not just one.

Birth and marriage certificates are certified documents; they should not require additional verification before they are accepted by the consul.

A county clerk can legally verify the seals of only those notary publics who reside in his or her county and register with his or her office. *All* notaries, however, must register with the secretary of state.

All documents must be verified in the states where they originated; for this reason, it is advisable that all of your documents be prepared by persons living in your present state of residence. Out-of-state documents will require verification out of state, which just creates one more hassle.

Obtaining Authentication

After notarization and verification, most countries require that certain documents be authenticated by a consul representing the country from which you wish to adopt who has jurisdiction in your locality. Consuls attest to the authenticity of the document or the signer of it by their seal, stamp, and signature. U.S.-based international agencies will provide a list of documents requiring authentication by the country from which you plan to adopt. Check with your international agency or foreign liaison to ensure that you follow the correct steps, especially if you are adopting from a country not mentioned here.

To locate the nearest consul, look in the phone book under U.S. Government Offices, Federal Information Center. These centers have consulate addresses and phone numbers. The INS also has the addresses and phone numbers of various consulate offices.

The process with foreign consulates is as follows: send your notarized and verified documents, with translations if required, to the foreign consulate for authentication. Enclose a check or money order for the total amount and a stamped, self-addressed envelope when you send your documents. Obviously, you will have to call the consulate first to inquire about the fees per document. Fees for authentication range from a free service by Chile to $40.00 per document by Costa Rica.

If the consulate is located in your city, you may be able to handle this much more quickly in person. Be certain to dress in business attire since the cooperation of the consul is essential. Treat the consul with the dignity to which he or she is accustomed. However, if the consul is not cooperative, call the embassy of the country from which you are adopting for help. All of the foreign embassies are located in Washington, D.C. Ask your telephone operator for the number.

Some states near the Washington, D.C. area and some foreign countries without consulates outside of Washington, D.C. require that the U.S. Department of State certify the notarized and verified documents before they will authenticate them. This is always required if you deal with a consulate attached to a foreign embassy. For instance, Russia has only two consulates in the United States, one attached to their embassy. Romania has no consulates outside the D.C. area, nor does Vietnam. At present there is a $4.00 charge per document for this service. Call them before sending your money order or certified cashier's check. The address and telephone number are as follows:

Supervisor, Authentication Office
   U.S. Department of State
   2400 M Street, N.W., Room 101
   Washington, D.C. 20520
   Telephone: (202) 647-5002

A WORD OF CAUTION: DOCUMENTS AND FEES

Safeguard your documents. After your documents have been notarized, verified, and authenticated, make one photocopy of each before they are sent abroad. This is your proof in case of loss in the mail or elsewhere. Hand-carry these copies with you on your adoption trip abroad.

Do not give your dossier of original documents to anyone in the United States except a licensed adoption agency or licensed social worker. Be suspicious of unlicensed individuals who for any reason keep their sources secret, insist upon handling your dossier, or expect payments, whether these payments are to be made in advance or at a later date.

INTERNATIONAL COMMUNICATION

If you are working with a U.S.-based international agency, your agency will send your dossier to their representative abroad and handle the communications for you. If you are not using an agency, you should send this information to your lawyer or foreign representative. Several methods of international communication are available.

1. Telegrams. Many foreign businesses and institutions have short, registered cable addresses, usually acronyms. A return voucher is sent along with the message if a reply is expected.

2. Faxes. Faxes are becoming quite common around the world.

3. Telephone. Long-distance phone calls range from $4.00 to $12.00 per minute, person-to-person.

4. Courier Service. International courier services guarantee service from pickup in a foreign country to personal delivery here. The cost varies. U.S. Postal EMS (Express Mail Service) is the least expensive and now goes to most foreign capital cities.

5. E-mail. Check to see if your foreign child-placing entity has this service.

Power of Attorney

TO WHOM IT MAY CONCERN:

This is to certify that we, the undersigned _____

presently living at _____

are herewith granting full power of attorney to _____

presently living at _____

to carry through and complete on our behalf any and all formalities required for the process of

the adoption of a _____ born child.

This is also to confirm that we herewith grant full power of attorney to _____

to carry through and complete on our behalf any and all formalities required by the American

Consulate in _____ in this matter.

Name _____ Date _____

Name _____ Date _____

Subscribed and sworn to before me on the _____ day of _____ 199__ to which

_____

Notary Public

My commission expires: _____

Statement of Competency

I, _____ , hereby certify that I am competent to translate from the _____

language to the _____ language and that the above translation is accurate.

Date: _____   _____ (name printed or typed)

                     _____ (address)

                     _____

Jurat

Subscribed and sworn to before me on the _____ day of _____ , 199 ____
to which witness my hand and seal of office.

_____

Notary Public in and for the State of _____ , County of _____

My Commission Expires _____.

Verification

The State of Texas
Secretary of State

I, _____ , Secretary of State of the State of Texas, DO HEREBY CERTIFY that according to the records of this office,

(name of notary)

qualified as a Notary Public for the State of Texas on July 27, 1995, for a term ending on July 27, 1999.

Date Issued: November 13, 1996

_____

Secretary of State　　sai

Apostille

STATE OF TEXAS

APOSTILLE
(Convention de La Haye du 5 Octobre 1961)

1.   **Country:**   **United States of America**
This Public document

2.   **has been signed by**   (name of notary)

3.   **acting in the capacity of Notary Public, State of Texas**

4.   **bears the seal/stamp of**   **, Notary Public,**
State of Texas, Commission Expires:
07-27-99

CERTIFIED

5.   **at Austin, Texas**   6.   **on December 3, 1996**

7.   **by the Deputy Assistant Secretary of State of Texas**

8.   **Certificate No. N-118607**

9.   **Seal**   10.   **Signature:**

Deputy Assistant Secretary of State
LSW/NO/ sai

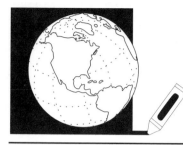

Chapter 8

The Referral

O nce your completed and authenticated dossier has been sent, you are ready for a referral for your child. Waiting for a child to be assigned is the most difficult part of the process. Make good use of the time by volunteering to babysit for friends, taking child care classes (see the section below), finding a good pediatrician or family doctor (consider looking for a foreign-born pediatrician or one who specializes in health conditions in developing countries), attending adoptive parent support group functions, subscribing to their newsletters (see Bibliography), and researching the culture and customs of your child's native land. Buy a book on child care that explains the signs and symptoms of childhood illnesses. Study the language. Assemble what you will need to pack, using our tips in Chapter 10.

STEP 14

Prepare for the referral of your child.

PREADOPTIVE RESOURCES

The American Red Cross, local hospitals, and some adoption agencies offer courses on infant care. While these courses are essential for every inexperienced new mother, the courses do not cover problems typical of Third World orphans and malnourished babies with infectious diarrhea. (See Chapter 13 for more information on health issues of Third World babies and children.)

Other excellent resources are the La Leche League's publications, counselors, and members. Their focus is on good mothering, understanding and satisfying the needs of babies with the loving help and support of fathers whether a mother chooses to nurse or not.

Local groups may be listed in the telephone directories in most cities. Or, for further information on mothering and adoptive nursing, write:

La Leche League International
9616 Minneapolis Avenue
Franklin Park, Illinois 60131

For information on nursing an adopted baby with the Avery Lact-Aid Nursing Supplementer, contact:

J.J. Avery, Inc.
P.O. Box 6459
Denver, Colorado 80306

Also contact adoptive parent groups and child development centers for information. Also, see Chapter 15 for more information on parenting adopted children and refer to the Bibliography for additional resources.

THE REFERRAL CALL

When the call comes with the referral of your child, panic may render you nearly witless and speechless. So, somewhere near your phone, tape a list of questions you have about the child such as the name, age, and clothing size. Ask if the child has any health problems, and, if a baby, whether the child needs a special formula. Have names ready in case the child does not have a name.

In the event that you are assigned an abandoned child without a name, your foreign lawyer will draw up a birth certificate with the name you have chosen. You can find books of names for children in the public library that list endless derivations of names along with their foreign origins.

Don't hang up without asking for the name and the phone number of the person who is calling you. Write it down. You will need to contact that person again. Then collapse on the couch.

Usually, you are given several days to make a decision. In the meantime, depending upon the policies of the child-sending country, you will be sent a photograph or possibly a video, health, educational, social, and genetic information, possibly a power of attorney form, and a custody contract. After telephoning your acceptance of the child to your adoption agency, follow this up formally by mail or fax. The child-placing entity will send copies or fax the child's documents to your agency or you if required by INS, the Department of Public Welfare in your state, or ICPC. The originals are retained for their court.

Most people are quite happy with the babies they are assigned, unless they object to the color or there is a health problem they are worried about. In Russia, for example, infants are overdiagnosed to make certain that the child will qualify for medical services provided by the state. While the medical record can be alarming, the video may show a normal, healthy child. Medical information and tests are not always accurate; record keeping is poor.

You can take the translated information, photos, and videos to discuss with a pediatrician. In addition, you might contact an international adoption clinic (see Chapter 13 for names and contacts) and send them the information for an opinion. Developmental delays in orphanage children are common. Your child may lag far behind infants and children of the same age level in your neighborhood. Generally, the children overcome developmental delays fairly quickly.

The same is even more true for older children. The social worker at the orphanage will include her observations about the child's personality and behavior. However, the behavior may be different for a while when the child is interacting in a family. The other scenario is that the parents and established siblings may have more trouble adjusting to the child than the child does to the family. The main reason adoptive parents reject children after adoption is not health, but behavior.

However, if the child's medical information indicates problems you cannot or do not wish to handle, or if the child does not fit the guidelines you originally specified, then by all means, turn down the referral. You will be given another. If you are in a foreign country when you make a decision not to adopt a particular child, it is extremely important that you cooperate with the authorities abroad and also with your child-placing agency in the United States if you wish to try again.

The referral of a child is a nerve-wracking time for everyone. The new parents start worrying about who is taking care of the child, his or her state of health, and possible legal hitches. The agency starts worrying about getting the adoptive parent's approval in order to begin coordinating the travel itinerary with the adoption hearing. An aggravating problem at this point can be the rescheduling of the adoption hearing. That means changing travel plans and days off at the workplace.

You can help prepare a child over two for adoption. Mail the following items to the authorities in charge of your child: pictures of yourselves, your home, your parents, and, if applicable, the child's future siblings. Also include pictures of the local playground, pets, and/or a fabulous toy like a tricycle. And, include translations of short letters from new family members which can be read to him or her.

OBTAINING A VISA OR TOURIST CARD

American citizens do not usually need visas except in formerly or presently communist countries. If you are adopting from Africa, China, Vietnam, or Russia, your international agency or the consulate of that country will advise you regarding the type of visa needed. They will also tell you how to use special expediting services in order to get the visa in a day or two.

Once the authorities abroad know that you have accepted the referral of a child, they will send you an invitation to travel to their country. When you

STEP 15

Obtain visa or tourist card (if neccessary) for travel to your child's country.

have this letter and your travel itinerary, you will fill out their visa application forms. If you are adopting from an international agency, they will furnish these forms. Otherwise, they can be obtained at the consulate of that country. The length of stay will depend on the length of the adoption process; about one or two weeks in the afore-mentioned countries should be sufficient. The question regarding the object of the journey should be answered. "To conclude business and carry out humanitarian aid." Be certain to sign and date the form.

Send copies of the letter and itinerary along with the visa application to the consulate. Obtaining a visa can take a week or two unless you use special expediting services.

Most tourist cards or visas are issued in duplicate. The original is surrendered upon entry. The copy is turned in at the time of departure. The other documents required to enter a country are needed again to leave it.

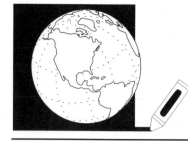

Filing the Orphan Petition

ELIGIBILITY TO FILE FOR AN ORPHAN PETITION

In order to be able to file a petition, parents must meet INS eligibility requirements.

A petition to classify an alien as an orphan for issuance of a visa may be filed by a married or unmarried United States citizen. (If married, they must adopt jointly; if unmarried, the citizen must be at least twenty-five years of age.) The spouse need not be a United States citizen. It must be established that both the married petitioner and spouse, or the unmarried petitioner, will care for the orphan properly if the orphan is admitted to the United States. If the orphan was adopted abroad, it must be established that both the married petitioner and spouse, or the unmarried petitioner, personally saw and observed the child prior to, or during the adoption proceedings. If both the petitioner and spouse, or unmarried petitioner, did not personally see and observe the child during the adoption proceedings abroad, they must establish that the child will be adopted in the United States and that any preadoption requirements of the state of the orphan's proposed residence have been met; and the petitioner must submit, if requested, a statement by an appropriate official in the state in which the child will reside that a regular adoption can be accomplished in that state. If the orphan has not been adopted abroad, the petitioner and spouse, or the unmarried petitioner, must establish that the child will be adopted in the United States by the petitioner and spouse jointly, or by the unmarried petitioner, and that the preadoption requirements, if any, of the state of the orphan's proposed residence have been met.

DOCUMENTATION OF ORPHANS

In addition, in order for approval of the I-600, it is crucial that the child you are adopting meets the INS definition of an orphan and that proper supporting documentation of the child's status be available.

In the first paragraph of the application and the petition, the INS definition of an orphan is provided:

> *"The term orphan under the immigration laws means a foreign child who is under the age of 16 years at the time the visa petition in his behalf is filed and who is an orphan because both parents have died or disappeared, or abandoned or deserted the orphan, or the orphan has become separated or lost from both parents."*

> *"If the orphan has only one parent, that parent must be incapable of providing for the orphan's care and must have in writing irrevocably released the orphan for emigration and adoption. An illegitimate child whose father acknowledges paternity and signs a relinquishment along with the mother is also considered an orphan. In addition, the orphan either must have been adopted abroad or must be coming to the United States for adoption by a United States citizen and spouse jointly or by an unmarried United States citizen at least 25 years of age." [Section 101] (b)(i)(F) of the Immigration and Nationality Act.*

A child who is abandoned to a government institution by both parents may qualify for classification as an orphan under immigration law, but immigration law does not define the term abandonment, and the subject is only discussed once in INS regulations.

According to the regulations, a child who has been unconditionally abandoned to an orphanage is considered to have no parents. A child is not considered to be abandoned, however, when he or she has been placed temporarily in an orphanage, if the parent or parents are contributing or trying to contribute to the child's support, or the parent or parents otherwise show that they have not ended their parental obligations to the child.

DIFFICULT ISSUES IN ORPHAN CASES

Under U.S. immigration law, the child of a sole or surviving parent may be considered an orphan if that parent is unable to care for the child properly and has forever or irrevocably released him or her for emigration and adoption. The child of an unwed mother normally may be considered to be an orphan as long as the mother does not marry. The child of a surviving parent may also be considered to be an orphan if it is proven that one of the child's parents died, and the surviving parent has not since married. However, marriage results in the child's having a stepfather or stepmother under immigration law.

Legitimate versus Illegitimate Designations

Most countries have legal procedures for the acknowledgment of children by their natural fathers. Therefore, adoptive and prospective adoptive parents of children who were born out of wedlock in any country should find out whether the children have been legitimized. Legitimized children from any country have two legal parents and cannot qualify as orphans (until the passing of the proposed amendments).

Some countries have passed laws which eliminate all legal distinctions between legitimate and illegitimate children. In those countries, all children are considered to be legitimate or legitimized children of their natural fathers as of the effective date of the laws in question. Of course, paternity must be established. A child born out of wedlock and living in a country that has such a law and whose paternity has been legally established has two parents even though the parents never married and may not be living together.

Adoptive and prospective adoptive parents of children who were born out of wedlock should become familiar with the legitimacy laws in the countries where the children are born and reside. If a child born out of wedlock is from a country that has eliminated all legal distinctions between legitimate and illegitimate children, the child could still qualify for classification as an orphan under immigration law.

FILING THE I-600 ORPHAN PETITION

Normally, an Orphan Petition is filed at the same INS office where the Advance Processing Application was filed. In fact, when an Advance Processing Application is still pending, the Orphan Petition *must* be filed at the same office.

Otherwise, where you file the I-600 Orphan Petition depends upon the kind of adoption you are planning, such as an agency-initiated adoption requiring one or both spouses to travel abroad; an agency-initiated adoption with escort for the child to the United States; or a parent-initiated adoption. Your U.S.-based international adoption agency or INS will advise you whether to file the Orphan Petition with your INS district office, the appropriate INS service abroad, or the U.S. Embassy or Consulate in the child's native country. If the petition is filed in the United States, information on its approval will be forwarded to the appropriate U.S. visa-issuing post abroad. The orphan visa will then be issued abroad.

STEP 16

File the I-600 (Orphan Petition) if this is to be filed in the United States. (This is usually filed abroad if the adoption is finalized in the child's country and both parents travel to meet the child.)

Filing in Absence of the I-600A

If no Advance Processing (I-600A) application has been filed because you located a child who meets INS criteria before you knew and understood their requirements, file the I-600A and the I-600, then register with an adoption agency and follow the remaining steps, beginning in Chapter 3.

Required Documents

1. Form I-600. (See sample form at the end of this chapter.) Both spouses must sign the form. The $155.00 fee is payable by money order or a cashier's check drawn on a U.S. bank, unless the adoptive parent resides and files abroad. When more than one petition is submitted by a prospective adoptive parent on behalf of orphaned siblings, only one fee is required.

2. Birth certificate of orphan. If it cannot be obtained, the prospective adoptive parent should submit an explanation together with the best available evidence of birth.

3. Death certificate(s) of the orphan's parent(s), if applicable.

4. Form of relinquishment, if applicable, which shows evidence that the orphan's sole or surviving parent cannot provide for the orphan's care and has in writing forever or irrevocably released the orphan for emigration and adoption. If the orphan has two unmarried parents, both must sign relinquishments. However, a child with two parents must be relinquished to a government agency.

5. Certificate of abandonment, if the orphan is institutionalized, which shows evidence that the orphan has been unconditionally abandoned to an orphanage.

6. A final decree of adoption or permanent guardianship.

7. Evidence that the preadoption requirements, if any, of the state of the orphan's proposed residence have been met, if the child is to be adopted in the United States. If, under the laws of the state of the child's proposed residence, it is not possible to submit this evidence when the petition is first filed, it may be submitted later. The petition, however, will not be approved without it.

8. The home study and supporting documents previously listed in the I-600A (Application for Advance Processing), unless this evidence was submitted with a pending I-600A or it is within one year of a favorable determination in a completed advance processing case.

Documents 2-6 are obtained by the foreign lawyer or foreign child-placing entity, who also arranges for the translation of these documents. Two sets of certified copies are needed to complete the legal immigration and readoption in your home state. The adoptive parent, or international agency in the case of an escort, is responsible for submitting a complete set of these translated originals to the American consulate abroad. If you are traveling to meet your child, be sure to take the originals on your adoption trip.

Exceptions to the Process

If documentary evidence relating to the child or the home study is not yet available, the I-600 Orphan Petition and fee may be filed without that evidence. The FD-258 Fingerprint Chart and all other evidence must be submitted with the petition.

If the necessary evidence relating to the child or the home study is not submitted within one year from the date of submission of the petition, the petition is considered abandoned and the fee is not refunded. If the petitioner later decides that he or she wants to petition for the same child or a different child, it will be necessary to file a new Advance Processing Application or Orphan Petition and pay a new fee.

U.S. CITIZENS RESIDING ABROAD

Transferred business employees of international companies, military personnel and U.S. government employees, missionaries, students, Peace Corps volunteers, and other U.S. citizens who are not expatriates (residing abroad voluntarily without a contract or military orders) and who will be residing abroad should follow these procedures for the following situations:

U.S. citizen departing for a foreign post. Filing the I-600A

Advance application will be easier if your move is still in the planning stages. Ask an adoption agency to give you top priority if you are planning to leave the United States in the near future. You must get advance processing before you leave if you wish to avoid future delays.

U.S. citizens residing abroad who have been living with an adopted orphan for less than two years.

At least three to six months before you plan to return home, you must process an I-600 petition for the orphan. Consult the nearest U.S. Consulate to find out which foreign INS office has authority to act on your petition. Allow enough time before your departure to obtain a home study that meets the legal requirements of your state of residence. The department of public welfare in your home state may agree to let you fill out your own home study forms.

U.S. citizens who have adopted abroad or had legal custody and have been living abroad for two years with the foreign orphan.

You may file form I-130, Petition to Classify an Alien as an Immediate Relative. I-130 is for aliens of any age who can be classified as immediate relatives. The U.S. Embassy located in the country where you reside will provide you with the I-130 form and with the list of supporting documents that you will need in order to file for the child's IR2 visa. If you can prove that the child has lived with you for two years, you do not need a home study or an FBI clearance.

Updating the I-600 Orphan Petition

As with the I-600A, the I-600 is valid for eighteen months. If an orphan has not immigrated before then, a new application, updated home study and documents, and new fingerprint charts must be filed again.

OVERSEAS ORPHAN INVESTIGATION

When an I-600 Orphan Petition is sent to an American Consulate or Embassy for possible issuance of a visa to the child or when an Orphan Petition is filed there, a Consular officer conducts an overseas orphan investigation as part of the normal processing. This is usually done quickly, and the adopting parent need not do anything to initiate, expedite, or finalize this process. The purpose of the investigation is to make certain that the child is an orphan as defined in immigration law, and the child does not have a significant illness or disability not described in the Orphan Petition. A sample of Form I-604 (Request for and Report on Overseas Orphan Investigation) can be found at the end of this chapter.

If a child is not eligible for classification as an orphan under immigration law, INS notifies the petitioner and spouse, if married, and gives them the choice of withdrawing the petition or having the question considered in revocation proceedings. When there are revocation proceedings, the petitioner is given a chance to submit evidence to overrule the stated grounds for revoking the approval of the petition.

I-600 (Orphan Petition)

U.S. Department of Justice		
Immigration and Naturalization Service		

OMB No. 1115-0049

Petition to Classify Orphan as an Immidiate Relative [Section 101 (b)(1)(F) of the Immigration and Nationality Act, as amended.]

Please do not write in this block.

TO THE SECRETARY OF STATE:

The petition was filed by:
☐ Married petitioner   ☐ Unmarried petitioner

The petition is approved for orphan:
☐ Adopted abroad   ☐ Coming to U.S. for adoption.
Preadoption requirements have been met.

Remarks:

Fee Stamp

File number

DATE OF ACTION

DD

DISTRICT

Please type or print legibly in ink. Use a separate petition for each child.

Petition is being made to classify the named orphan as an immediate relative.

BLOCK I - Information About Prospective Petitioner

1. My name is: (Last)   (First)   (Middle) (name of notary)

2. Other names used (including maiden name if appropriate):

3. I reside in the U.S. at: (C/O if appropriate)   (Apt. No.)

(Number and street)   (Town or city)   (State)   (ZIP Code)

4. Address abroad (if any): (Number and street)   (Apt. No.)

(Town or city)   (Province)   (Country)

5. I was born on: (Month)   (Day)   (Year)

In: (Town or City)   (State or Province)   (Country)

6. My phone number is: (Include Area Code)

7. My marital status is:
☐ Married
☐ Widowed
☐ Divorced
☐ Single
   ☐ I have never been married.
   ☐ I have been previously married _____ time(s).

8. If you are now married, give the following information:
Date and place of present marriage

Name of present spouse (include maiden name of wife)

Date of birth of spouse   Place of birth of spouse

Number of prior marriages of spouse

My spouse resides ☐ With me   ☐ Apart from me
(provide address below)

(Apt. No.)   (No. and street)   (City)   (State)   (Country)

9. I am a citizen of the United States through:
☐ Birth   ☐ Parents   ☐ Naturalization   ☐ Marriage
If acquired through naturalization, give name under which naturalized, number of naturalization certificate, and date and place of naturalization:

If not, submit evidence of citizenship. See Instruction 2.a(2).
If acquired through parentage or marriage, have you obtained a certificate in your own name based on that acquisition?
☐ No   ☐ Yes
Have you or any person through whom you claimed citizenship ever lost United States citizenship?
☐ No   ☐ Yes (If yes, attach detailed explanation.)

Continue on reverse.

Received	Trans. In	Ret'd Trans. Out	Completed

Form I-600 (Rev. 8/25/89) Y

I-600 (Orphan Petition)

BLOCK II - Information About Orphan Beneficiary

10. Name at birth (First) (Middle) (Last)	20. To petitioner's knowledge, does the orphan have any physical or mental affliction? ☐ Yes ☐ No If "Yes", name the affliction.
11. Name at present (First) (Middle) (Last)	
12. Any other names by which orphan is or was known.	21. Who has legal custody of the child?
13. Sex ☐ Male ☐ Female 14. Date of birth (Month/Day/Year)	22. Name of child welfare agency, if any, assisting in this case:
15. Place of birth (City) (State or Province) (Country)	23. Name of attorney abroad, if any, representing petitioner in this case.

16. The beneficiary is an orphan because (check one):
   ☐ He/she has no parents
   ☐ He/she has only one parent who is the sole or surviving parent.

Address of above.

17. If the orphan has only one parent, answer the following:
   a. State what has become of the other parent:

24. Address in the United States where orphan will reside.

   b. Is the remaining parent capable of providing for the orphan's support? ☐ Yes ☐ No

25. Present address of orphan.

   c. Has the remaining parent, in writing, irrevocably released the orphan for emigration and adoption? ☐ Yes ☐ No

25. If orphan is residing in an institution, give full name of institution.

18. Has the orphan been adopted abroad by the petitioner and spouse jointly or the unmarried petitioner? ☐ Yes ☐ No
   If yes, did the petitioner and spouse or unmarried petitioner personally see and observe the child prior to or during the adoption proceedings? ☐ Yes ☐ No
   Date of adoption

   Place of adoption

26. If orphan is not residing in an institution, give full name of person with whom orphan is residing.

27. Give any additional information necessary to locate orphan such as name of district, section, zone or locality in which orphan resides.

19. If either answer in question 18 is "No", answer the following:
   a. Do petitioner and spouse jointly or does the unmarried petitioner intend to adopt the orphan in the United States? ☐ Yes ☐ No
   b. Have the preadoption requirements, if any, of the orphan's proposed state of residence been met? ☐ Yes ☐ No
   c. If b. is answered "No", will they be met later? ☐ Yes ☐ No

28. Location of American Consulate where application for visa will be made. (City in Foreign Country) (Foreign Country)

Certification of Prospective Petitioner

I certify under penalty of perjury under the laws of the United States of America that the foregoing is true and correct and that I will care for an orphan/orphans properly if admitted to the United States.

(Signature of Prospective Petitioner)

Executed on (Date)

Certification of Married Prospective Petitioner's Spouse

I certify under penalty of perjury under the laws of the United States of America that the foregoing is true and correct and that my spouse and I will care for an orphan/orphans properly if admitted to the United States.

(Signature of Prospective Petitioner)

Executed on (Date)

Signature of Person Preparing Form if Other Than Petitioner

I declare that this document was prepared by me at the request of the prospective petitioner and is based on all information of which I have any knowledge.

(Signature)

Address

Executed on (Date)

I-604 (Overseas Orphan Investigation)

U.S. Department of Justice
Immigration and Naturalization Service

Request for and Report on Overseas Orphan Investigation

TO:　　U.S. CONSUL, _____ 　　　　　　　　　　　　　(City and country)	File
FROM:　DISTRICT DIRECTOR, _____	Date

☐ 1. Attached is an approved visa petition in behalf of an orphan. Please complete this form concerning the orphan. If you develop information which indicates that the child is not an orphan as defined in section 101(b)(1)(F) of the Immigration and Nationality Act or that the child has an affliction or disability not set forth in the petition, suspend action on the visa application and return this form with the attached petition to the INS office of origin. If no adverse information is developed, attach this form and the petition to the visa application.

☐ 2. Attached is an application for advance processing of an orphan petition with a favorable determination concerning the prospective petitioner's ability to furnish proper care to a beneficiary orphan. When the prospective petitioner files an orphan petition at your post, please complete this form concerning the child. If you develop information which indicates that the child is not an orphan as defined in section 101(b)(1)(F) of the Immigration and Nationality Act, forward the petition with this form, Form I-600A and all attachments to the Service office having jurisdiction over the beneficiary's place of residence. If you determine that the child has an affliction or disability not set forth in the petition, furnish all details to the petitioner, and spouse, if married. Should the petitioner and spouse, if married, elect to proceed with the petition, the information concerning the affliction or disability should be incorporated at the bottom of page 1 of Form I-600 and initialed by the petitioner and spouse, if married. If the petitioner and spouse, if married, choose not to proceed with the petition, Form I-600A should be returned to the INS office of origin with Form I-600, this form, and all attachments.

Orphan's present name

Date and place of orphan's birth

(name of notary)

Ethnic origin of orphan	Does orphan live in an orphanage?	If not, where does orphan live?

If orphan lives with relatives, what are their relationships to the orphan?

If orphan lives with non-relatives, explain.

How many years of formal education has orphan received?	As a student, orphan is ☐ Average　　☐ Above average　　☐ Below average

Is child's mental level the same as that of other children the same age?	Does child get along well with other children the same age?

Does child participate in games or athletic activities with other children the same age? If not, explain.

Has the orphan had serious difficulties with any adult authority, including the persons having charge of the orphan? If so, explain.

Form I-604 (Rev. 12-15-82) N

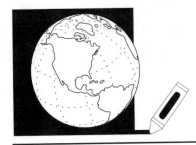

Chapter 10

The Adoption Trip

Your adoption trip will be planned down to the last detail if you are adopting through an international agency. They will make certain that you are in the right place at the right time for all of your appointments. If this is a parent-initiated adoption, you will plan the trip yourself.

Depending upon the country you have chosen, you might leave in just a few weeks to initiate the adoption. If you have chosen a country where power of attorney is used, you may not leave for one to three months.

Your adoption experience in a foreign country is uniquely your own. If you have never spent much time in a foreign country before, the food, customs, and language can give you a first-rate case of culture shock. The average stay for adopters is two weeks, just long enough to reach a peak in exasperation, frustration, anger, and shock. No one has ever died of it, but recovery requires several months. After a year back home, almost everyone has fully recovered and wants to make the trip again–either to adopt more children or to visit.

INTERNATIONAL TRAVEL

Adopters traveling to foreign countries become unofficial ambassadors for the United States, especially for the U.S. adopters who come after them. Adopters who wish to make and leave a favorable impression do their homework first—a study of the host country's language, culture, and etiquette. While orphans are usually from the lower classes, social workers, directors, lawyers, and liaisons are from the privileged classes. Proper social form and behavior are important to them. Most North Americans are in a hurry to return home. This is understandable. What is not understandable is rude and pushy behavior, which, incidentally, does not get the family home any faster.

Several excellent travel books explain how we should behave in foreign countries as well as 1,001 things every traveler should know. New editions are published each year. The language barrier appears to present the greatest obstacle to bridging the gap between the two cultures. Books, tapes, records, and hand-held computers are available to assist or teach you in most of the major languages. In most cases, a representative associated with your U.S. agency will meet you abroad and stay with your group, but the more you know, the more independent you will be when you arrive at your destination. Consult your library for more information.

As you prepare for your adoption trip, learn the travel requirements and procedures in the foreign country, too. After sending your dossier, gather your travel documents together; then you will be ready to travel when your referral comes. While the average adoption stay is two weeks, your stay could last up to eight weeks, depending upon your foreign source and other variables.

Following the Entry and Exit Requirements

Foreign immigration authorities only permit travelers with proper documents to enter their countries. Be aware that many foreign governments change their entry and exit requirements frequently. For up-to-date information on entry and exit regulations, contact your airline or the consulate of the foreign country you wish to visit.

If you are working with an international agency, they will advise you about your travel documents. Otherwise, you will need to consult a travel agent.

Generally the following documents are required:

1. A passport. Married couples should obtain separate passports since one spouse may need to return home ahead of the other spouse.

2. A tourist card or visa (if required).

3. A round-trip ticket. Nonpenalty tickets are more expensive, yet they are the best way to purchase airline tickets for an adoption. That way, if the hearings are rescheduled or other problems occur overseas, you won't lose any money. You can exchange the tickets.

4. Identifying photos. A passport photo will be sufficient.

If for some reason you were not able to get your passport earlier, keep in mind that one-day service for passports can be found in most major cities. You may need to present evidence that you must leave the country within forty-eight hours. Call ahead about this as well as their office hours.

Most tourist cards or visas are issued in duplicate. The original is surrendered upon entry. The copy is turned in at the time of departure. The other documents required to enter a country are needed again to leave it.

Making Travel Arrangements

Arrange your trip by phone. U.S.-based international agencies as well as some travel agencies are aware of adopters' needs and will advise you about fares and nonpenalty tickets. Please do not make reservations until INS sends a cable of clearance, and/or ICPC has granted approval (if your international agency is out of state), and the court hearing is scheduled. Remember to arrive at the airport three to four hours before any international flight and two hours before a domestic flight.

Since different excursion rates are offered from time to time by various airlines and since airfares are subject to sudden changes, you should check the fares of several airlines before your adoption trip is scheduled. You will also need to purchase a one-way ticket back to the United States for your child. Because adoption hearings are sometimes rescheduled or the process takes longer than planned, you should look for nonpenalty tickets that can be exchanged without additional costs.

In most circumstances, your international agency will arrange for your lodgings. If you are traveling by yourself to adopt, the agency staff will help you find lodgings according to your taste and budget. If you are traveling in a group, your lodgings will be arranged ahead of departure.

HEALTH PRECAUTIONS FOR TRAVELERS

Your adoption trip will be one of the peak experiences in your life. It's definitely not the time to get sick. Taking some simple precautions listed below should minimize your risk of becoming ill while overseas.

Travelers to Third World countries must be extremely careful about what they eat and drink if they want to avoid spending three or four miserable days in the bathroom. Rule number one is to eat only in first-class restaurants or to dine in the homes of the upper-class nationals. However, this is not always possible.

Even then, do not eat raw salads. And, don't eat raw vegetables or fruits unless you disinfect them with iodine before peeling them yourself. Do not eat raw meat or fish. Don't eat or drink milk products unless you know they are pasteurized. And avoid foods, including condiments, that have been sitting around at room temperature for long periods of time.

So what do you do if you are far from a AAA-rated restaurant and hungry? Find a bakery and buy some just-out-of-the-oven rolls or the equivalent staff of life for that country. Clean your hands before you eat with the packaged pre-moistened towelettes you brought from home. Or, stash some U.S. breakfast bars or other high protein bars in your pockets.

What should you drink? Bottled mineral water, with or without carbonation, or other carbonated beverages (preferably drunk from the bottle through a straw) and tea and coffee should be safe. You should purify water for hygienic use. The easiest method is to purchase a pint-sized water purifier from a camping outfitter to take along. Otherwise, you can purify water by boiling it for twenty minutes. (Take a hot pot and, if necessary, an electrical current adapter, if you plan to boil water.) If this is not possible, treat water with Halazone tablets or mix in 10 drops of 2% tincture of iodine to one quart of water and let stand for 30 minutes. If the water is cloudy, filter it through a cotton cloth.

In Latin American countries, U.S. adoptive parents who stay in better hotels will have little to worry about regarding food and water. Luxury hotels post notices in each room explaining the purity of the water supply. However, if you stay in lower rate hotels, bottled water can be ordered. For all of the former Soviet Union, Eastern Europe, and all of Asia, except Japan, you must use bottled water at all times. This includes water for rinsing your toothbrush as well as for brushing.

Most parasites are transmitted in a human reservoir of a food-fecal cycle. Should you be unlucky enough to ingest contaminated food or water, your diarrhea may disappear in a few days, but you may still be harboring one or more parasitic organisms. Ask your doctor or the local health department for an antibiotic prescription such as Noroxin to take along for a serious case. Take Imodium A-D, which can be purchased over the counter, with you for milder cases.

Diarrhea drains salts and fluids from the body, causing the dehydration that accounts for the deaths of thousands of Third World babies. While an adult's diarrhea is not life threatening, grown-ups should replace the salts and fluids they are losing with almost any fluid. If diarrhea is severe (more than one stool every two hours), adults should use an oral rehydration solution (ORS) such as Pedialyte. An ORS powder to be mixed with boiled water is available over the counter at pharmacies around the world.

Be aware that many doctors in the United States believe that most cases of parasites are self-eliminating. Should you or your child feel ill within twelve to eighteen months after your trip, alert your doctor as to which country you visited. The doctor will then order the appropriate series of stool culture kits. Most diarrhea-producing parasites such as crypotosporidium or giardia are transmitted by contaminated water. Even if the diarrhea abates, you may still be harboring the parasite. Get rechecked at home if you are not completely back to normal. Tapeworms, flukes, etc., are transmitted by contaminated foods and, occasionally, by water. Some, like hookworms and schistosomiases, are acquired through the skin via swimming in contaminated water or walking barefoot outside. Most of these parasites require an intermediate animal host and are not contagious from person to person. These parasites typically do not give diarrhea and may be detected only weeks or months after travel.

Prior to leaving for Third World countries, try to find a doctor knowledgeable about health problems in developing countries. Arrange to visit this doctor as soon as you return. Since most parasites are transmitted in a food-fecal chain, consider each diaper a transmitter. Make certain that all members of your family keep up a scrupulous hand-washing ritual. All orphans and their new parents with symptoms should be tested for parasites every three months. Some worms and parasites have dormant periods and will not show up in each culture. (Chapter 13 provides a more detailed overview of the potential health problems of children from developing countries.)

Vaccinations and Immunizations

Adopters planning international travel may phone the Center for Disease Control hotline at (404) 332-4559 for information on epidemics, diseases, and the precautions as well as the inoculations necessary for travel to each country. Bear in mind that you will be in urban, not rural areas. A short stay in a foreign city requires fewer inoculations than a stay in a rural area or a long stay abroad or out in the country. At the minimum, individuals traveling abroad should update their tetanus vaccinations and should receive the vaccination series for Hepatitis A and B. This is best done one month prior to travel. In addition, all household members not traveling should also be inoculated for Hepatitis A and B. Adults traveling to Asia or Eastern Europe should also receive the one-time adult polio booster.

Malaria

Malaria is carried by certain kinds of mosquitoes in coastal and jungle areas, including parts of Mexico, Central America, some Caribbean Islands, and the northeastern half of South America. All three diseases are carried by mosquitoes in parts of Asia, including China. Since most adoption programs are in large cities where malaria outbreaks are rare, antimalarial drugs are not usually necessary, but check with your doctor at least one month before traveling to be certain, especially if you will be traveling outside of the city. Travelers may also call their state department of health or the Atlanta Center for Disease Control.

PACKING FOR HEALTH AND CONVENIENCE

Suitcases and Bags. For checked luggage, two pieces per passenger is the limit. One suitcase can be no larger than sixty-three inches; the other, no larger than fifty-five inches. In order to compute the size allowed by airlines, measure the height, length, and width and add them together. The two suitcases combined cannot weigh more than seventy pounds. You will be charged for overweight and oversized luggage.

In addition, each passenger is allowed one carry-on bag, forty-five inches wide, plus a purse or camera. If your bag is stowed overhead, it cannot weigh more than fifty pounds; if stowed beneath the seat, it can weigh no more than seventy pounds.

Be certain to get all of the documents for the adoption in your carry-on luggage. You may reach your destination, but your checked luggage may not arrive for another day or two. Plan for this emergency by placing nightwear and clothes for the next day in a soft-sided bag or folding garment bag that will fit under the seat ahead of you. Items for the child can be purchased abroad, such as handmade toys, national costumes, unique children's clothing, children's books and music tapes, fancy mosquito nets for beds, weavings, pictures, hats, baskets, and native jewelry. In major cities, you can also buy an inexpensive bag to bring them all home in.

What to Take

If your trip will only be for a few days, you won't need to take most of these items. For a trip of two weeks or more, you will need all of these items. However, if you stay with families most of the time, you won't need the hot pot or food items.

Camera: If your camera takes 35mm film, extra rolls can be purchased abroad. Other film is difficult to find.

Polaroid, with film: Good for making friends with children.

Video camera: As light in weight as possible.

Electrical current adapter: Ask your travel agent or consult a travel book to see if your hotel has outlets for A/C current. If not, you need the adapter for U.S. electrical appliances.

Water supply: Ask if the hotel has its own potable water supply. Water for the baby's formula must be boiled twenty minutes, regardless. Bottled water is available in most countries. Buy a supply as soon as you arrive overseas.

A hot pot is easily packed and handy for boiling water. Take a thermos to store the boiled water in. A water purifier is also a good idea. Pint-sized purifiers are available through camping outfitters.

Flashlight with extra batteries: Most countries have blackouts. Hotels provide candles, but a flashlight is better.

Instant foods: Many couples bring packets of foods–cocoa, instant coffee, cup-of-soup, Tang, etc.,–for their own use, making some meals convenient and less expensive than eating out or depending upon room service. Take a supply of drinking straws for carbonated beverages.

Entertainment: In countries where the wait is more than a week, you will have time to read, play board games, and do handiwork. Pack your favorites. Include a dictionary and phrase book of the native language.

Laundry aids: Try to be as self-sufficient as possible and also be prepared to do the baby's wash in the sink. Most hotels have laundry service, but your child may be using clothes faster than the hotel can wash them. A portable clothesline is helpful. Dryer sheets or other lightweight forms of fabric softeners are great in the rinse water; they make line-dried clothes softer. Also, bring a small bottle of liquid detergent and plastic bags with closures of assorted sizes.

Baby bottles: We suggest you buy the old fashioned baby bottles with the large nipples as close as possible to what the baby is using. The bottles with small nipples and plastic inserts are usually rejected by babies over five months old. Wait until you meet your baby before buying more. If your child is very young or of low weight, take "preemie" nipples, which are available at larger drug stores–it makes nursing much easier for the little ones. Also, remember to bring tongs for removing nipples from the boiling water.

Baby carrier: Canvas baby carriers, in which the baby is carried in front of you, can be purchased for babies under a year. Larger, older babies can be carried behind you where the weight is better distributed.

Baby stroller: "Century Light Weight" folds down for sleeping, folds up for storage in the overhead rack of the plane, and costs about $40.00. Buy stroller netting to keep insects off the child.

Booties, socks, and shoes: In Third World countries, persons without shoes are the poorest of the poor. Never take your baby outdoors without something on his or her feet.

Caps and bonnets: Summer caps and bonnets should have visors or brims. For winter, hats should cover the ears.

Baby soap and lotions: Bring mild baby soap for the baby's bath. (Tips for baby bathing: Babies react to changes in temperature. By lining the hotel basin with a towel and filling it with water, the bath should be accomplished fairly peacefully. Test the water with your wrist or elbow first before easing the baby in. For a sponge bath, uncover the baby slowly, one body part at a time. Start with the feet and work up. Wash and dry the first part before uncovering another part of the body. Most children are used to showers, usually cold ones in most countries. They may need to be gently coaxed into a warm bubble bath by floating some toys in it first.)

Baby food: Canned baby food and instant baby cereal are readily available overseas. Some restaurants will make it for you. Buy just a small supply to take along. Be sure to bring a can opener for food and formula.

Formula: Continue using the same formula while you are abroad. Generally, the switch from one formula to another should be made gradually, since many babies suffer stomach upsets from drastic changes in food. You may wish to take soy-based formula along in case the infant has a lactose intolerance. When traveling, put the prescribed amount of dry formula in as many bottles as you will need. Take about six extra preparations. Add sterile water to a bottle when the baby needs it.

Diapers: Be certain to take an adequate supply of disposable diapers–estimate ten per day. Diarrhea warrants an extra supply. If you bring too many, excess diapers are welcome gifts at the foster home as you leave and lifesavers for other American couples you will meet who may have not brought enough. Take a good supply of "Wet Ones" or other pre-moistened towelettes. Be sure to bring plastic bags for soiled diapers.

Diaper changing pads: Waterproof pads to put under the child, especially for messy jobs.

First aid kit: Instruments: tweezers, scissors (kept for this purpose only), thermometer (to take a baby's temperature, put the thermometer under the arm pit for three minutes), safety pins.

Medicine: Acetaminophen or soluble aspirin tablets, simple antiseptics like cetrimide or chlorhexidine in suitable dilution ready for use in stronger form with the instructions for diluting carefully marked on the bottle (ask your doctor or pharmacist), an antiseptic cream for spreading on dressings. Imodium and Noroxin for adult diarrhea. Kwell prescription lotion for lice and scabies. Dramamine for children.

Dressing: White gauze, absorbent cotton, paper tissues, 2-inch and 3-inch wide plain bandages, ready-to-apply sterile dressings, each packed singly in its protective covering (these are obtainable in various sizes), 2-inch and 3-inch wide adherent dressing strips which can be cut to size for covering simple wounds, 1-inch wide adhesive tape.

Infant salve: Diarrhea, because of strong bacteria, can sometimes result in extreme diaper rash, and at times bleeding ulcers can occur. Take along an anti-fungal ointment such as Mycolog (doctor's prescription only) and a dressing to put over it.

The above will cover most needs. It is better to keep a few standardized items than have a large mixed collection which can confuse. Items like absorbent cotton and gauze should not be put back for further use later. Anything you use from a box should be replaced with new items as soon as possible.

Insect repellent: Mosquito and insect body lotion and room spray. You may also want to bring roach spray for the kitchenette.

Sewing kit: Tiny size, with basics: threads, shirt buttons, needles, and several sizes of safety pins.

Wash cloths: Some foreign countries use natural or synthetic sponges. Thus, few hotels furnish wash cloths. Take some with you.

Hand puppets: (For children over one year). Bring enough for the whole family. "Actions speak louder than words," and puppets can help you break the language barrier. Also bring picture books of your state, pictures of your home, relatives, and pets, as well as a small, soft, stuffed toy animal to sleep with.

Stationery supplies: Writing pad, folder, pens, paper clips, tape.

Roll of nylon tape: To repair suitcases or close bottles, etc. Carry a roll in your pocket or purse.

Clothing for adults: Plan a coordinated wardrobe to cut down on the number of clothes and shoes you will need. Check travel book for climate. Most of the time you will be dressed in casual clothes. However, for business appointments, you should dress like the attorneys and social workers. Suits for men and a suit or modest dress for women are the acceptable clothing for appointments with government officials and lawyers. This will help make a favorable impression.

Dress conservatively but comfortably for your flight. Low heels for women—you never know how much running you may have to do when you change planes, especially if your flight schedule is changed at the last minute.

Foreign money: Take only American Express, Cook's, or Citi-Bank traveler's checks. Have some foreign money handy for the first taxi and probable expenses for your first day. You can obtain it at exchange houses in Miami, Houston, Los Angeles, and New York airports. It is helpful to inquire about the rate of exchange a day or two before traveling, and to make up your own rate-of-exchange chart in a notebook for $1, $2, $5, $10, etc. Pay attention to when your flight is arriving overseas to be sure that you will have access to a bank the following day. If you are arriving on a weekend or national holiday, you may need to take more foreign currency with you. Be certain to get small change for tips. We take $20 or $30, in $1 bills, for tips. American dollars are prized in most foreign countries.

U.S. EMBASSY AND CONSULATE SERVICES

In addition to issuing visas, embassies and consulates perform many other functions. The responsibility of the Department of State, as well as U.S. Consular offices overseas, is to do everything possible to protect the rights of U.S. citizens abroad while, at the same time, alerting the U.S. traveler to his or her responsibilities and obligations.

Few of us know exactly what services consular offices can provide. For example:

If you lose your passport, you can get an on-the-spot free temporary passport from the nearest U.S. Consulate. Keep a record of your passport number, some extra photos, and a photocopy of your original passport.

If you become seriously ill, destitute, die, or are arrested, a consular official can provide assistance.

If there is political turmoil in the country where you are headed, call the U.S. Consulate there for an on-the-spot analysis of the situation before you leave.

If you register at the U.S. Consulate upon arrival in a country of political unrest, you will be notified of an emergency evacuation. If you get into difficulties, the consulate will be aware of it.

The Office of Special Consular Services offers these recommendations for worry-free travel:

1. Provide family and friends with complete itinerary.

2. Take twice as many dollars and half as many clothes as you originally planned. Take a combination of cash, personal checks, credit cards, and world-wide brands of traveler's checks. Always take traveler's checks that can be cashed, or replaced if stolen, in the country of your destination.

3. Keep your documents and some of your money in the hotel safe. Or, split up money with your spouse. It is better to lose half rather than all of it. In a separate inner pocket, carry each other's passport numbers and the names and phone numbers of people to contact in an emergency.

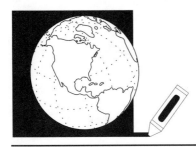

Chapter 11

Meeting Your Child

A doptive parents with high expectations are more likely to experience some initial disappointment with their child than new parents who have few expectations. The happiest parents have disengaged the dream child they carried around in their minds for so long. They have considered the fact that this child not only descends from different ancestors, but has survived in conditions that they have never experienced. They have opened their hearts and minds to let this real child enter their lives at a time and in a place they could never have imagined when they first thought of having children.

STEP 18

Meet your child.

You will usually be presented with your child the first or second day after your arrival. You will be expected to provide his or her going-home clothes and shoes, just as you would for a newborn birth-child. You must also be prepared to feed the child according to the directions given you. You may see your child for the first time at the adoption agency abroad, a foster home, or a hotel. If you are adopting through a lawyer, you may meet your child at the airport or in your hotel room.

Placements are joyous occasions. After so much longing, work, and struggle, the placement is climactic. But we express emotions differently. We look at the child with awe. Can this really be our child? Your joy is superimposed upon the birth parents' grief. I remember shedding a few tears. "They look just like I thought they would," I said. (We had not been sent pictures.) Heino said in a voice quavering with emotion, "They are lovely girls."

Your first moments together are cinematically recorded in your memory. Even newborns lock eyes with their new parents. A month later, they focus on faces and in response to your voice, will babble and coo. This is where differences in language and ways in which various cultures talk to babies begin to make a difference. For example, the Chinese clap their hands before they pick up a baby. Babies are distressed by extremely loud noises and soothed by quiet sounds. Unfortunately a quiet place is difficult to find in the frenzy and clamor of most cities.

Wear something soft the day you first meet your baby or child. Holding and rocking becomes an even more enjoyable experience when you feel soft and cuddly. Studies confirm that infants are more sensitive to developing attachment behaviors between four months and six months. Hard plastic baby carriers and infant seats should be used as little as possible. The child needs holding to promote bonding.

Between six and nine months, relinquished and abandoned children may not be fearful of strangers. Most likely, they have been cared for by many people, and try to keep a mother figure nearby with smiles and coos, since the urge for attachment is extremely strong. Adoptive parents at this stage must interact warmly with the baby, showing approval for this behavior, and must not reject clingy and whiny behavior. To reject this negative behavior will only intensify it. Your goal here is to promote attachment which in turn will help them relax. Then they can play and learn.

If your new child is between eighteen months and three years of age, she is able to recognize that she is a separate person. Institutionalized babies spend most of their lives cooped up in a box or crib, simply observing. When they finally climb out, they seek out adults, watching them work, and imitating their motions. They have learned there is no one to go to for comfort if they are hurt or afraid. One of your tasks is to win the child's trust and to prove that you are now there to give aid and comfort. Children are now able to talk and to understand most of what is being said in their native language. Suddenly they must learn a new language and a new routine in a new environment.

School-age children have all of these challenges and, in addition, must submit to the discipline required for a formal education. Formidable!

CARING FOR YOUR CHILD OVERSEAS

You will be caring for your child in his or her native country for two weeks or several months, depending on the country you are adopting from and the length of wait for the final adoption decree. Use this time to get to know your child and to begin to win his or her trust.

For children over one, use a hand puppet. The puppet can act out ideas for both of you as well as provide some comic relief. Be creative! And take a box of hypoallergenic bubble bath and a rubber ducky. Most orphans have been scrubbed under cold running water. If you can persuade your child to get in the warm, soapy water, he or she will be soothed and relaxed. If your child is too large to be carried and held a lot, giving the child smiles, pats, and light back massages when he or she is sitting or standing near you is an excellent way to give the child a feeling of closeness.

New children are usually fearful. Since they were rejected once, they may be again, or so they may reason. Boys and girls who have begged on the streets and lived in orphanages have learned some survival techniques, some of which will probably stay with them forever.

Older children need to believe that you will be there for support when they have problems–when something good happens or something bad happens. Be creative these first few days to start winning their trust. Attachment begins when you acknowledge their feelings and share their experiences. Shared laughter and shared tears are the glue of parent-child relationships.

We tend to treat Third World orphans as First World kids, overwhelming them with toys, furniture, and clothes. However, they have never had the luxury of making personal choices regarding style and color. And, if they had the leisure to play they probably made their own toys from stones, sticks, and paper. Your carefully chosen educational or trendy toys will probably be played with for five minutes and then carefully put back in the toy box. That was our experience with Omar, and countless other adoptive parents have reported similar behavior.

Your child has likely been eating the cheapest food available with little variety and no second helpings. Each child responds to this situation differently. They may eat the crumbs off the floor and hoard food. At home, your refrigerator and pantry will become a source of wonder and pride. The child may eat twice as much as you do, creating worries about obesity. Such concerns are unfounded. Let the child overeat for several months. You can control the calories by carefully shopping for meals and snacks. Children are no different than adults when it comes to seeing food as a comforter. Since their emotional needs have not been met, food soothes the soul, as well as the stomach. As children become more secure, food will lose its importance. Other children may eat very little and be suspicious of new foods. Introduce new foods a tablespoon at a time. Don't worry or fuss about it. In a few months, things will change. Concentrate on meal time as a happy family time. Turn off the TV and get to know your child. Struggles over food can hurt your relationship.

Many parents also report incidents of bedwetting. If you discover your child is a bedwetter (nocturnal enuresis), do not despair. Most Third World children are beaten for this problem, thus they will probably try to hide the evidence. Help is available as soon as you get home in the form of behavior modification, bed alarms available from Sears, or large size disposable diapers for nighttime for a while. See a doctor; the condition often responds to treatment within a few weeks.

ARE YOUR EXPECTATIONS FULFILLED? WHAT TO DO IF THEY ARE NOT

Many people feel rather let down when they first see the child they were assigned. Orphanage children often look too small for their ages, may have a runny nose or bad skin rash or both. On top of that, they are usually dressed in worn out, ill-fitting orphanage clothes, and often have shaved heads as a treatment for insects or lice. Babies may have bald spots on heads that are flattened on the back from spending too much time lying down. Disappointing. After all the work and all the waiting, the child does not match the dream child parents have been carrying around in their heads for so long. Some of this is normal. Mothers and fathers report similar let downs with biological children. What this tells you is that you don't have to fall in love with the child immediately. When you put your best efforts into being nurturing, the child will usually respond by showing appreciation and attentiveness. You suddenly feel more needed than you ever have in your life! Bonding, that much overused word, is a two-way feeling. A good adjustment takes place when the parents are able to overcome their initial disappointment and let their feelings and the child's feelings of love gradually develop.

If you can't stop emotionally rejecting the child, or the child seems to be rejecting you, what do you do? This depends on the kind of person or people you are. Mothers usually take the lead at a time like this, and fathers support them. Parents who do not have high expectations fare the best. If they believe they are good for the child and that the child has a lot of potential, they will show their admiration for the child and make him or her feel special. The parents will put a great deal of effort into building a loving relationship with the child. They realize that it may take years for the child to trust them completely and believe that they won't go away.

Prior to the adoption, most parents worry about the child's health; however, the major reason children are turned down is due to behavior. Orphanage children have learned to survive in what could be best described as a 24-hour big city public school. They have found ways to defend themselves. Children on the extreme ends of coping behavior worry parents the most–whether it be the depressed, withdrawn child who stays out of everyone's way or the high energy, aggressive child who kicks, hits, spits, and bites. If children have become attached to a caretaker or another child, they are confused as to why they have to leave their "home." They may not be able to trust this new relationship enough to show genuine affection or to depend on you for a long time. They have no concept of what you can do to make them happier, more comfortable, and secure.

The greatest difficulty in making a decision is that you have to make it so fast; usually, you are only given a few days before you must make up your mind about going ahead with the adoption. No one can really advise a parent caught in such a quandry. You can talk to doctors and psychologists abroad, or even by long distance here, but in the end, only you know whether you have the patience and tolerance to raise this child. Think about it as long as possible before making a decision that will affect both you and the child for a very long time.

If you are flooded with feelings that adoption is wrong for you or that this is not the right child for you, stop the legal proceedings. But be gracious. You may still want to adopt someday. Cooperate with all the authorities involved, in order that the child gets another chance for an adoptive home. Depending upon whether or not you have a final decree, you will need to communicate with your foreign agency or attorney, the U.S. consulate, the INS, your local adoption agency, and possibly ICPC to cancel the placement.

OTHER CHILD-PLACEMENT ISSUES

Unfortunately, the U.S.-based adoption agency does not have control over the referral information sent by the child-placing entity abroad. Attempts are constantly being made to make these entities more accountable and accurate with their records. Although cases occur in which an orphan has medical problems that are more severe or different than the referral information, parents rarely turn such a child down. The exception is if they suspect mental retardation or severe physical handicaps that would prevent the child from ever being self-sufficient. In this case, the U.S. embassy doctor typically will not give the child a medical classification to immigrate, and the agency will try to help the parents locate another child.

Once in a while, the child you were assigned is not the one placed with you abroad. If the authorities make a substitution, you can be assured it was for a good reason. Health concerns would be the usual reason for making the switch. Adopters who have had this happen have had to make some quick adjustments. Because of time constraints, the child you receive will probably have the documents of the child you were assigned. You can change the child's name during the readoption in the United States.

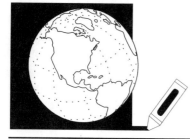

Chapter 12

Preparing for the Trip Home: Emigration and Immigration

GUARDIANSHIP AND
FINAL ADOPTION DECREES

In some countries, you will be given a temporary custody agreement when your child is placed with you. Placement usually occurs the first or second day after your arrival. As far as we know, Romania is the only country right now that will not allow you to have custody until the child is adopted in their country. You may have the child with you during the day, but still be required to return the child to the orphanage at night. Orphanage directors in other countries may also ask that you return older children at night in order to make the transition easier. Once you are granted a final adoption decree, the temporary custody agreement is no longer in effect.

While lawyers handle adoptions in Latin American countries and Romania, government welfare officals handle adoption in China, Vietnam, and Russia. If you are working through an adoption agency, the agency will engage a lawyer in countries where adoptions are handled by the courts. If you are adopting independently, you will need to contact your own foreign attorney or the national authority in charge of adoptions.

The foreign attorney or other designated official obtains the following set of birth documents for the foreign court. Neither the initiation of the adoption hearing abroad nor INS clearance for the orphan's U.S. visa can be accomplished unless these documents have been obtained. Before the court hearing and definitely before applying for the orphan visa, adoptive parents should make sure they have two sets of certified copies of:

STEP 19

Obtain the guardianship or final adoption decree.

Child's Birth Certificate, showing date and place of birth. Some countries record the child's original name and birth parents, if known. Other countries amend the certificate to show the child's new name and the names of the adoptive parents.

Birth Mother or Birth Parents' Release Form (under pending legislation, the release of two parents in some cases). The release must state the reason for relinquishing the child. The name of the biological father should be stated if known.

Certificate of Abandonment issued by the court after publishing for the child's relatives. The certificate grants custody to a legal child-placing entity or to the adoptive parents.

Decree issued in that particular country, such as initial adoption decree, final adoption decree, guardianship, or custody transfer, previously explained.

Although the process may vary slightly depending on the country, in most cases, the foreign attorney will prepare a presentation letter to the family welfare department of the child's country, if one exists. The presentation letter states the adoptive parents' identity according to the documents you have prepared; the parents' motives for adoption (that the only intention is to make the orphan a legal child and heir); that the adoptive parents will honor the adoption laws of the child's native country; that the adopted child will emigrate to your home address; and that you will notify the family welfare department of any change of address that might occur before you receive the final adoption decree. Adopters who travel abroad may be required to sign this document in the presence of a family welfare official.

Next, the attorney presents the case for preliminary review to the Civil Court for Minors, or a similarly named court. The attorney delivers your dossier of translated, notarized, verified, and authenticated documents to the court for legal consideration and secures a date on the court calendar. When the attorney presents the case, the court verifies that the documentation is legal and complete. Then, it either issues an initial adoption decree and a permanent custody agreement (which is effective until a final adoption decree is issued), or a final decree, or a permanent guardianship agreement (which is effective until the child is adopted in the country of the adoptive parents). Possibly, a family welfare department official may hold the adoption decree for one day to several weeks while he or she reviews the case. This person represents the orphan in court.

After this review, the attorney may direct the adopters to the judge's chambers. The judge may ask for a personal interview with the adoptive parents to study their dossier with them. Depending upon local procedures, the court may issue the final adoption decree anywhere from one week to one year after the case has been presented in court by your attorney. The law office will obtain notary seals for the final decree and present the decree to you in person or by registered mail. The attorney also obtains the child's travel documents and organizes and helps present them for the child's U.S. visa. The travel documents include a passport and photos, possibly a tax clearance form and a permit to leave the country, and any fees required.

The time needed to complete the foreign adoption process varies from country to country. When all of the required documents are provided, foreign attorneys can complete the adoption process. It may take anywhere from a few days to several months or more. Sometimes the adoptive parents can speed up the process by picking up and delivering the documents as directed by the foreign attorney.

Meeting and Communicating with Birth Mothers

In rare instances, in Guatemala and Honduras, for example, it is possible that you may meet the birth mother around the time of the court appearance in order to transfer custody. Naturally, this is an emotionally stressful time for everyone concerned. However, you must remember that the decision was made in the best interest of the child by the birth mother. Such meetings are very unlikely in most adoptions (with the exception of adoptions in Guatemala and Honduras). They are illegal in most countries, as well as prohibited by the Hague Convention Treaty.

It is important that you keep your last name and address confidential. Some families have received letters from their child's birth mother or relatives requesting money. These are impoverished people who have real needs; however, experience tells us that these requests for money will continue for the rest of your life. Your obligation to the child does not extend to the child's birth mother and her other children and relatives. We strongly recommend that you do not send gifts or money to the birth mother, during or after your trip. Your generosity could be interpreted as buying the baby. If you wish to correspond with the birth mother or family, let the orphanage or your international agency act as your post office.

OBTAINING THE ORPHAN VISA

After the child's adoption or guardianship has been granted, the adoptive parents must obtain an orphan visa before the child can enter the United States. An orphan's U.S. visa is obtained at the U.S. Embassy or Consular Section that has jurisdiction over the country in which the child resides. U.S. Embassies are usually located in the capital city of foreign countries. Your adoption agency will take the lead in coordinating most of this. If not, make an appointment at the visa section of the U.S. Embassy or, in some cases, the U.S. Consulate abroad. Since some consuls require additional documents, ask what is

STEP 20

Apply for the orphan visa and file the I-600 (Orphan Petition) if this was not filed earlier.

required before you appear. Usually, visas are issued the same day as the interview or the day after.

Depending on the country from which you are adopting, you will file the I-600 Orphan Petition either in the United States or while you are abroad. If you are supposed to file while in the United States, you will be sent a full set of the child's documents prior to your adoption trip. (See Chapter 9). If you are supposed to file while abroad, the orphan's documents will be transferred to you or your agency's representative. INS requires that the orphan's documents are in duplicate and are the originals or certified copies. The U.S. Consular Service Office abroad has the power to certify copies.

INS requires English translations of documents in foreign languages. For most adoptions, either the foreign child-placing entity or the U.S.-based adoption agency will arrange for translations. If not, contact the American Consulate for names of translators. The translation must be attached to the original or certified copy. To certify the competency of the translation, a brief statement signed by the translator must accompany the orphan's documents. This letter usually does not need to be notarized or authenticated for INS. (A sample of a statement of competency letter can be found at the end of Chapter 7.)

Required Documents

Show the U.S. Consulate abroad the certified set and file the copies with the consulate office, unless you have two sets of certified copies. After applying for the child's U.S. visa, be certain that the original set is returned to you. You will need the originals when you adopt or readopt, and apply for U.S. citizenship.

1. Form OF-230 (U.S. Visa Application). You can obtain this from the U.S. Consulate, Visa Issuing Post, when you apply for the orphan visa. (See sample at the end of this chapter.)

2. Child's birth certificate, as previously explained.

3. Decree issued in that particular country, such as initial adoption decree, final adoption decree, or guardianship.

4. Death certificates of the orphan's parents, if applicable.

5. Mother's or family welfare department's relinquishment form, previously explained. And/or

6. Certificate of abandonment, previously explained.

7. Medical report for the adopted child from the U.S. Embassy-approved doctor. If the child is fourteen years old or more, an HIV test is also required. (More information on arranging the medical evaluation is included later in this chapter.)

8. First page of your most recent 1040 Federal Income Tax return.

9. Letter from employer(s).

10. Statement of net worth.

11. Possibly, Form I-134 (Affidavit of Support), or a letter written by you stating that you are going to be responsible for the child. Such a letter must be authenticated by the U.S. Embassy. Form I-134 is not required by most U.S. visa issuing posts.

12. Child's foreign passport.

13. Three photos of the child. (See following section, for details on obtaining photos.)

14. I-600 (Orphan Petition), if the petition is completed abroad; or, a cable from the INS district office that your advance processing received a favorable determination (Form I-171H).

15. Evidence that your state's preadoption requirements have been met, such as a statement to that effect in your home study, or the Consent and Approval Form required by some states. (A sample of the consent and approval form can be found at the end of Chapter 6.)

16. Letter from U.S. international adoption agency, stating ICPC compliance (if applicable).

17. Visa fee of U.S. $200.00, or the equivalent in foreign currency to be paid in cash.

Photography for the Orphan Visa

Three photographs of the child in color with a white background must be presented for the orphan visa.

The U.S. Consulate will advise you regarding their approved photographers. An INS form, M-378 (Color Photograph Specifications), shows and explains the requirements (see sample at the end of this chapter).

Size of photograph: 4cm x 4cm (1 1/2 inch square).
Head size: 2.54 cm (about 1 inch) from chin to top of hair.
Subject should be shown in 3/4 frontal view showing right side of face with right ear visible.

Lightly print name on the back of each photograph and sign your name on the front left side of two photographs using pencil or felt pen.

Arranging a Medical Evaluation for the Orphan Visa

Every foreign child must have a physical exam conducted by a U.S. Embassy-approved doctor before departing for the United States. In some countries, adoptive parents can also request that the child be taken to a pediatrician for a more thorough evaluation before they obtain custody.

Waivers must be signed by U.S. citizens who adopt foreign orphans with certain disabilities, and this is the reason a medical report from the U.S. Embassy-approved doctor or clinic is required. Before approving the visa, the U.S. Consular service needs to know that the parents are aware of a child's disability and will take full responsibility for the child's care. Waivers must be applied for, but are not necessarily granted for, children diagnosed as Class A and Class B. No waiver is needed for those diagnosed as Class C.

The U.S. Embassy will direct you to an approved physician or clinic who will fill out a medical form. (See sample form at the end of this chapter.)

According to an article in the *American Journal of Diseases of Children*, March 1989, "International Adoption," by Margaret Hostetter, M.D. and Dana E. Johnson, M.D.:

> *"The quality of this visa medical evaluation is so extraordinarily variable that an assurance of health should be viewed by parents and their physician as confirming only that the child is alive rather than free of unsuspected medical problems. Parents may ask their physician to interpret the classification system (A, B, or C) used by the federal government in the examination. Class A includes psychiatric disorders, mental retardation, and dangerous contagious diseases, including chancroid (venereal ulcer), gonorrhea, granuloma inguinale (inflamed lesion of the groin), infectious leprosy, lymphogranuloma venereum (inflamed lymph nodes of the groin), infectious syphilis, active tuberculosis, and as of December 1, 1987, human immunodeficiency virus (HIV) infection."*

> *"Parenthetically, testing for HIV-seropositivity is not required in children younger than 15 years unless they have a history (hemophilia or an HIV-positive parent) or signs and symptoms suggestive of the disease. Therefore, few children will actually be screened for acquired immunodeficiency syndrome (AIDS) before their arrival in the United States. Class B is defined as physical defect, disease, or disability serious in degree or permanent in nature amounting to a substantial departure from normal physical well-being. Although this category sounds ominous, minor cosmetic defects, such as occipital hemangiomas or dark red birthmarks (stork bites), are often placed in Class B. Class C is defined as minor conditions. If the overseas investigation is successfully concluded, the child is issued a permanent resident's visa and can then be admitted to the United States."*

The Center for Disease Control in Atlanta, Georgia, is currently compiling a list of vaccinations that will be required for orphans immigrating to the United States.

When an orphan is so ill that he or she must travel to the United States immediately, adopters who have fulfilled their state and federal requirements may apply for a visitor's visa for their child that is specifically issued for medical emergencies. Before attempting to have the child emigrate for emergency medical reasons, adoptive parents should discuss the procedures with the appropriate U.S. Consular Service Office. They must present a statement from a doctor which describes the medical emergency and explains the need for that child to undergo medical treatment at once in the United States. Once in the United States, adopters must apply for permanent resident status for the child.

And when an orphan is not only critically ill but resides in a war-torn country, the potential adopters may apply for a humanitarian parole, with as much documented evidence as possible. The help of a member of Congress is essential, but does not guarantee success.

Orphan Visas IR-2, IR-3, and IR-4

Upon completion and submission of all of the required paperwork, your child will be issued one of three types of U.S. visas:

> *Visa IR-4. Orphan to be adopted in the United States by a citizen and spouse (or single parent). IR-4 is used in countries where the adoption process is not completed before the visa is filed. The court issues a guardianship agreement or an initial adoption decree. This visa is also issued if both adoptive parents have not observed the child prior to final adoption, since the child must be readopted in the United States.*
>
> *Visa IR-3. Orphan adopted abroad by a U.S. citizen and spouse (or single parent). IR-3 is used for orphan visas in countries where the adoption decree can be presented to the U.S. Consulate before the visa is issued. Both adoptive parents must observe the orphan prior to adoption in the foreign country to receive this visa.*
>
> *Visa IR-2. Applies to orphans who have lived abroad with their adoptive parents for at least two years.*

It should be noted here that you do not need a U.S. lawyer until three to six months after the child has immigrated with an IR-4 visa under a guardianship or initial adoption decree. Then you will need to consummate the adoption in your state of residence. If the child immigrates with an IR-3 visa, under a final adoption decree, your state may recognize this final decree. However, if you were unable to change the child's name abroad, you may still need to readopt, if that is the only means available in your county.

U.S. STATE REQUIREMENTS AND IMPORTATION LAWS

Since each of our fifty states has its own set of laws concerning adoptions, every adopter must take the responsibility for knowing and understanding his or her state's requirements concerning the importation of a foreign child into that state.

In some countries, a permanent guardianship decree is issued rather than a final adoption decree. This document permits a child to leave the country based on the adopter's promise of a future adoption at home. In all cases, adopters must have completed their home study, their state's preadoption requirements, and INS requirements. To discover which countries issue permanent guardianships or final decrees, see the adoption law summaries in the Compendium.

THE TRIP HOME

Once you have your child's visa, you are ready for the trip home.

Book your return trip before leaving the United States. Request bulkhead seats where there is more room. Also request a baby bed on your return flight. It cannot be reserved for you, as they are given on a first-come, first-serve basis.

Confirm your international return flight seventy-two hours before departure so as not to get bumped. Be at the airport at least two hours early. If you have a baby, prepare six bottles of the formula for the flight. Pour the amount of powdered formula needed into each bottle. Ask the cabin attendants to add water for one bottle at feeding time. Include pre-moistened towelettes to clean the child, since washing on board is difficult.

On the airplane during takeoff and landing, be certain the baby is sucking on a bottle or pacifier. This will prevent painful pressure on the delicate ear drum. Older children can be given candy to suck or gum to chew. You may consider taking children's Dramamine along, in case the child has motion sickness. Some kids fight being buckled in. Bring toys and activities for the flight.

The flight home is symbolic, recalled almost as a rebirth to children age two and up. Make it as pleasant as possible–the memory will be with them forever.

The Airport Tax

Have foreign cash ready at the airport to pay a departure tax for yourself and your child. People leaving foreign countries, regardless of whether they are citizens, adopted children, or travelers, usually have to pay the foreign governments this kind of tax. Find out how much it is when you buy your airline tickets. The tax must be paid in foreign currency or U.S. dollars. Traveler's checks are not accepted. You will need to have this amount with you when checking in for your trip home.

U.S. Immigration upon Arrival

At the same time that the child's passport and temporary visa is presented to you, the visa-issuing office will also give you a sealed envelope containing supporting documents for the child's visa. A list of the contained documents appears on the outside of the envelopes. (Officials in some countries must see this when you exit.)

When your flight arrives in the United States, present the sealed envelope to U.S immigration. INS will forward the papers to the office where you filed the application. If you were unable to retain a set of originals or certified copies, you can get them once they arrive at your district INS office. The alien card will be mailed to you.

OF-230 (U.S. Visa Application)

OMB APPROVAL NO. 1405-0015
expires: 00-00-00
ESTIMATED BURDEN: 30 MINUTES

APPLICATION FOR IMMIGRANT VISA AND ALIEN REGISTRATION

คำร้องขอวีซ่าประเภทเข้าเมือง และการจดทะเบียนคนต่างด้าว

PARTI-BIOGRAPHIC DATA
ชีวประวัติส่วนตัว

INSTRUCTIONS: Complete one copy of this form for yourself and each member of your family, regardless of age, who will immigrate with you. Please print or type your answer to all questions. Questions that are Not Applicable should be so marked. If there is insufficient room on the form, answer on a separate sheet using the same numbers as appear on the form. Attach the sheet to this form.
WARNING: Any false statement or concealment of a material fact may result in your permanent exclusion from the United States.
This form is Part I of two parts which, together with Optional Form OF-230 PART II, constitute the complete Application for Immigrant Visa and Alien Registration.

ข้อแนะนำ : ท่านและสมาชิกแต่ละคนในครอบครัวที่จะเดินทางเข้าสหรัฐฯ กับท่านไม่ว่าจะมีอายุเท่าใดจะต้องกรอกแบบฟอร์มนี้คนละ 1 ชุด โดยใช้พิมพ์ดีดหรือเขียนเป็นตัวพิมพ์เพื่อตอบคำถามทุกข้อ คำถามใดซึ่ง ไม่เกี่ยวข้อตกรุณาตอบว่าไม่เกี่ยวข้อง (Not Applicable) ด้วย หากเนื้อที่ในแบบฟอร์มไม่พอสำหรับกรอกข้อความให้ใช้กระดาษแผ่นอื่นแยกต่างหากโดยใช้หมายเลขเดียวกันกับที่ปรากฎในแบบฟอร์มนี้แล้ว เข้ากับแบบฟอร์มนี้
คำเตือน : การให้ข้อความอันเท็จ หรือการปิดบังอำพรางความจริงใด ๆ ที่เป็นสาระสำคัญ อาจมีผลทำให้ท่านถูกห้ามไม่ให้เข้าสหรัฐฯ ตลอดไป
แบบฟอร์มฉบับนี้ คือส่วนที่ 1 ในจำนวนสองส่วน ซึ่งเมื่อรวมกับแบบฟอร์ม โอเอฟ-230 ส่วนที่ 2 แล้ว จะประกอบกันเป็นคำร้องขอวีซ่าประเภทเข้าเมือง และจดทะเบียนคนต่างด้าวที่สมบูรณ์

1. FAMILY NAME นามสกุล   FIRST NAME ชื่อแรก   MIDDLE NAME ชื่อกลาง

2. OTHER NAMES USED OR BY WHICH KNOWN (If married woman, give maiden name) ชื่ออื่น ๆ ที่ใช้หรือเป็นที่รู้จัก (ถ้าเป็นหญิงมีสามีแล้ว ให้เขียนชื่อสกุลเดิมด้วย)

3. FULL NAME IN NATIVE ALPHABET(If Roman letters not used) ชื่อเต็ม ซึ่งเขียนเป็นภาษาพื้นเมือง (ถ้าไม่ใช่อักษรโรมัน)

4. DATE OF BIRTH วันเกิด (Day)(วัน) (Month)(เดือน) (Year)(ปี)	5. AGE อายุ	6. PLACE OF BIRTH สถานที่เกิด (City or town) (เมือง) (Province) (จังหวัด) (Country) (ประเทศ)

7. NATIONALITY (If dual national, give both) สัญชาติ (ถ้ามีสองสัญชาติ ให้ระบุทั้งสองสัญชาติ)

8. SEX เพศ
☐ Male ชาย
☐ Female หญิง

9. MARITAL STATUS สถานภาพสมรส
☐ Single (Never married) โสด (ไม่เคยสมรส) ☐ Married สมรสแล้ว ☐ Widowed เป็นหม้าย ☐ Divorced หย่าแล้ว ☐ Separated แยกกันอยู่

Including my present marriage, I have been married _____ times.
เมื่อรวมการสมรสในปัจจุบัน ข้าพเจ้าเคยสมรสมาแล้ว _____ ครั้ง

10. PERSONAL DESCRIPTION ลักษณะส่วนตัว
a. Color of hair สีผม _____   c. Height ส่วนสูง _____
b. Color of eyes สีตา _____   d. Complexion สีผิว _____

11. OCCUPATION อาชีพ

12. MARKS OF IDENTIFICATION ตำหนิหรือแผลเป็น

13. PRESENT ADDRESS ที่อยู่ปัจจุบัน

Telephone number: Home   Office
โทรศัพท์หมายเลข บ้าน   ที่ทำงาน

14. NAME OF SPOUSE (Maiden or family name) (First name) (Middle name)
ชื่อคู่สมรส (ชื่อสกุลเดิมหรือนามสกุล) (ชื่อแรก) (ชื่อกลาง)

Date and place of birth of spouse:
วันเกิด และสถานที่เกิดของคู่สมรส

Address of spouse (If different from your own):
ที่อยู่ของคู่สมรส (ถ้าแตกต่างไปจากที่อยู่ของท่าน)

15. LIST NAME, DATE AND PLACE OF BIRTH, AND ADDRESSES OF ALL CHILDREN ระบุรายชื่อ วันเกิด สถานที่เกิด และที่อยู่ของบุตรทุกคน

NAME ชื่อ	DATE AND PLACE OF BIRTH วันเกิดและสถานที่เกิด	ADDRESS (If different from your own) ที่อยู่ (ถ้าแตกต่างไปจากที่อยู่ของท่าน)

THIS FORM MAY BE OBTAINED GRATIS AT CONSULAR OFFICES OF THE UNITED STATES OF AMERICA
ขอรับแบบฟอร์มนี้ได้จากสถานกงสุลอเมริกันทุกแห่งโดยไม่ต้องเสียค่าใช้จ่าย
NSN 7540-00-149-0019
50230-106
Previous editions obsolete

OPTIONAL FORM 230 I (ENGLISH
REVISED 4-9
DEPT. OF STATE

OF-230 (U.S. Visa Application)

16. PERSON(S) NAMED IN 14 AND 15 WHO WILL ACCOMPANY OR FOLLOW ME TO THE THE UNITED STATES.
บุคคลที่มีรายชื่อในข้อ 14 และข้อ 15 ที่จะเดินทางพร้อมข้าพเจ้าหรือตามข้าพเจ้าไปยังสหรัฐฯ ในภายหลัง

17. NAME OF FATHER, DATE AND PLACE OF BIRTH, AND ADDRESS *(If deceased, so state, giving year of death)*
ชื่อ วันเดือนปีเกิด สถานที่เกิดและที่อยู่ของบิดา (ถ้าถึงแก่กรรมแล้ว ให้แจ้งว่าถึงแก่กรรมและให้แจ้งปีที่ถึงแก่กรรม)

18. MAIDEN NAME OF MOTHER, DATE AND PLACE OF BIRTH, AND ADDRESS *(If deceased, so state, giving year of death)*
ชื่อนามสกุลเดิม วันเดือนปีเกิด สถานที่เกิดและที่อยู่ของมารดา(ถ้าถึงแก่กรรมแล้ว ให้แจ้งว่าถึงแก่กรรมและให้แจ้งปีที่ถึงแก่กรรม)

19. IF NEITHER PARENT IS LIVING PROVIDE NAME AND ADDRESS OF NEXT OF KIN *(nearest relative)* **IN YOUR HOME COUNTRY**
ทั้งบิดาและมารดาถึงแก่กรรม ให้ระบุชื่อและที่อยู่ของญาติสนิทที่ใกล้ชิดลำดับถัดไป (ญาติสนิทที่สุด) ในประเทศบ้านเกิดของท่าน

20. LIST ALL LANGUAGES YOU CAN SPEAK, READ, AND WRITE ระบุภาษาต่าง ๆ ที่ท่านพูด-อ่านและเขียนได้

LANGUAGE ภาษา	SPEAK พูด	READ อ่าน	WRITE เขียน

21. LIST BELOW ALL PLACES YOU HAVE LIVED FOR SIX MONTHS OR LONGER SINCE REACHING THE AGE OF 16. BEGIN WITH YOUR PRESENT RESIDENCE. ระบุสถานที่ที่ท่านเคยพำนักอาศัยอยู่เป็นเวลาตั้งแต่หกเดือนขึ้นไป นับตั้งแต่ท่านมีอายุได้ 16 ปี เป็นต้นมาเริ่มจากที่อยู่ของท่าน ในปัจจุบัน

CITY OR TOWN เมือง	PROVINCE จังหวัด	COUNTRY ประเทศ	OCCUPATION อาชีพ	DATES (FROM-TO) วันที่ ถึง)

22. LIST ANY POLITICAL, PROFESSIONAL, OR SOCIAL ORGANIZATIONS AFFILIATED WITH COMMUNIST, TOTALITARIAN, TERRORIST OR NAZI ORGANIZATIONS WHICH YOU ARE NOW OR HAVE BEEN A MEMBER OF OR AFFILIATED WITH SINCE YOUR 16TH BIRTHDAY. ระบุรายชื่อองค์กรการเมือง องค์กรทางวิชาชีพ หรือองค์กรทางสังคมที่ท่านกำลังเป็นหรือเคยเป็นสมาชิกอยู่

NAME AND ADDRESS ชื่อและที่อยู่	FROM/TO จาก/ถึง	TYPE OF MEMBERSHIP สมาชิกภาพ

23. LIST DATES OF ALL PREVIOUS RESIDENCE IN OR VISITS TO THE UNITED STATES. *(If never, so state)* **GIVE TYPE OF VISA STATUS IF ANY. GIVE I.N.S. "A" NUMBER IF ANY.** ระบุ วัน เดือน ปี สำหรับช่วงที่ท่านเคยพำนัก หรือเดินทางไปท่องเที่ยวสหรัฐฯ (ถ้าไม่เคย-ให้ระบุว่าไม่เคย) และให้ระบุประเภท ของวีซ่าด้วย ถ้ามี เริ่งหมายเลข ไอ เอ็น เอส "เอ" (I.N.S. Number) ด้วย ถ้ามี

LOCATION สถานที่	FROM/TO จาก/ถึง	VISA วีซ่า	I.N.S. FILE NO. หมายเลขแฟ้ม (ถ้าทราบ)

SIGNATURE OF APPLICANT ลายมือชื่อของผู้ยื่นคำร้อง	DATE วันที่

NOTE: Return this completed form immediately to the consular office address on the covering letter. This form will become part of your immigrant visa and your visa application cannot be processed until this form is complete.

หมายเหตุ: กรุณาส่งแบบฟอร์มที่ได้กรอกข้อความเรียบร้อยแล้วคืนยังสถานกงสุลตามที่อยู่ที่ระบุในจดหมายประหน้าโดยทันที แบบฟอร์มนี้ถือว่าเป็นส่วนหนึ่งของวีซ่าประเภทเมืองของท่าน จะไม่มีการดำเนินการใด ๆ เกี่ยวกับคำร้องขอวีซ่าของท่าน จนกว่าท่านจะได้กรอกข้อความในแบบฟอร์มนี้ครบถ้วนแล้ว

*Public reporting burden for this collection of information is estimated to average 24 hours per response, including time required for searching existing data sources, gathering the necessary data, providing the information required, and reviewing the final collection. Send comments on the accuracy of this estimate of the burden and recommendations for reducing it to: Department of State (OIS/RA/DR) Washington, D.C. 20520-0264, and to the Office of Information and Regulatory Affairs, Office of Management and Budget, Paperwork Reduction Project (1405-0015), Washington, D.C. 20503.

จากรายงานของสาธารณชนที่ใช้เวลาเกี่ยวกับการเก็บรวบรวมข้อมูล ประเมินได้ว่าเรื่องนี้ใช้เวลาประมาณ 24 ชั่วโมง สำหรับคำตอบงานแบบสอบถามแต่ละชุด ซึ่งรวมถึงเวลาที่ต้องใช้ในการค้นหาข้อมูลจากแหล่งที่มีอยู่ การรวบรวมข้อมูลที่จำเป็น การให้รายละเอียดที่ต้องการ และการตรวจทานการรวบรวมข้อมูลชุดสุดท้าย กรุณาส่งข้อคิดเห็นของท่านเกี่ยวกับการ ประเมินการใช้เวลา นี้และข้อแนะนำของท่านที่จะช่วยลดเวลาของระบบสอบถามนี้ลงได้ด้วยไปที่ได้แก่ : Department of State (OIS/RA/DR) กรุงวอชิงตัน ดีซี 20520-0264 Office of Information and Regulatory Affairs, Office of Management and Budget, Paperwork Reduction Project (1405-0015) วอชิงตัน ดีซี 20503

M-370 (Color Photo Specs)

U. S. IMMIGRATION & NATURALIZATION SERVICE

COLOR PHOTOGRAPH
SPECIFICATIONS

IDEAL PHOTOGRAPH ◄

IMAGE MUST FIT INSIDE THIS BOX ►

THE PICTURE AT LEFT IS IDEAL SIZE, COLOR, BACKGROUND, AND POSE. THE IMAGE SHOULD BE 30MM (1 3/16IN) FROM THE HAIR TO JUST BELOW THE CHIN, AND 26MM (1 IN) FROM LEFT CHEEK TO RIGHT EAR. THE IMAGE MUST FIT IN THE BOX AT RIGHT.

THE PHOTOGRAPH

* THE OVERALL SIZE OF THE PICTURE, INCLUDING THE BACKGROUND, MUST BE AT LEAST 40MM (1 9/16 INCHES) IN HEIGHT BY 35MM (1 3/8IN) IN WIDTH.

* PHOTOS MUST BE FREE OF SHADOWS AND CONTAIN NO MARKS, SPLOTCHES, OR DISCOLORATIONS.

* PHOTOS SHOULD BE HIGH QUALITY, WITH GOOD BACK LIGHTING OR WRAP AROUND LIGHTING, AND MUST HAVE A WHITE OR OFF-WHITE BACKGROUND.

* PHOTOS MUST BE A GLOSSY OR MATTE FINISH AND UN-RETOUCHED.

* POLAROID FILM HYBRID #5 IS ACCEPTABLE; HOWEVER SX-70 TYPE FILM OR ANY OTHER INSTANT PROCESSING TYPE FILM IS UNACCEPTABLE. NON-PEEL APART FILMS ARE EASILY RECOGNIZED BECAUSE THE BACK OF THE FILM IS BLACK. ACCEPTABLE INSTANT COLOR FILM HAS A GRAY-TONED BACKING.

THE IMAGE OF THE PERSON

* THE DIMENSIONS OF THE IMAGE SHOULD BE 30MM (1 3/16 INCHES) FROM THE HAIR TO THE NECK JUST BELOW THE CHIN, AND 26MM (1 INCH) FROM THE RIGHT EAR TO THE LEFT CHEEK. IMAGE CANNOT EXCEED 32MM BY 28MM (1 1/4IN X 1 1/16IN).

* IF THE IMAGE AREA ON THE PHOTOGRAPH IS TOO LARGE OR TOO SMALL, THE PHOTO CANNOT BE USED.

* PHOTOGRAPHS MUST SHOW THE ENTIRE FACE OF THE PERSON IN A 3/4 VIEW SHOWING THE RIGHT EAR AND LEFT EYE.

* FACIAL FEATURES **MUST BE IDENTIFIABLE.**

* CONTRAST BETWEEN THE IMAGE AND BACKGROUND IS ESSENTIAL. PHOTOS FOR VERY LIGHT SKINNED PEOPLE SHOULD BE SLIGHTLY UNDER-EXPOSED. PHOTOS FOR VERY DARK SKINNED PEOPLE SHOULD BE SLIGHTLY OVER-EXPOSED.

SAMPLES OF UNACCEPTABLE PHOTOGRAPHS

INCORRECT POSE

IMAGE TOO LARGE

IMAGE TOO SMALL

IMAGE TOO DARK
UNDER-EXPOSED

IMAGE TOO LIGHT

DARK BACKGROUND

OVER-EXPOSED

SHADOWS ON PIC

Immigration & Naturalization Service
Form M-378 (6-92)

Medical Examination for U.S. Visa

MEDICAL EXAMINATION OF APPLICANTS FOR UNITED STATES VISAS	PLACE
	DATE OF EXAMINATION *(Mo., Day, Yr.)*

At the request of the Amercian Consul at	CITY		COUNTRY	

I certify that on the above date I examined	NAME *(Last in CAPS)* *(First)* *(Middle)*	DATE OF BIRTH *(Mo., Day, Yr.)*	SEX ☐ F ☐ M
	WHO BEARS PASSPORT NO.	ISSUED BY	ON

GENERAL PHYSICAL EXAMINATION

I examined specifically for evidence of the conditions listed below. My examination revealed:

☐ No apparant defect, disease, or disability
☐ The conditions listed below were found *(Check boxes that apply)*

CLASS A CONDITIONS *(Give pertinent details under remarks)*   **CLASS B CONDITIONS**

☐ Chanorold   ☐ Hansen's Disease, Infectious   ☐ Tuberculosis, Active   ☐ Tuberculosis, Not Active
☐ Gonorrhea   ☐ Lymphogranuloma Venereum   ☐ Human Immunodeficiency   ☐ Hansen's Disease, Not Infectious
☐ Granuloma Inguinale   ☐ Syphilis, Infectious   Virus (HIV) Infection   ☐ Other Physical Defect, Disease or Disability:

☐ Mental Retardation   ☐ Previous Occurance of One or   ☐ Mental Defect   _____
☐ Insanity   More attacks of Insanity   ☐ Narcotic Drug Addiction
☐ Sexual Deviation   ☐ Psychopathic Personality   ☐ Chronic Alcoholism   _____

EXAMINATION FOR TUBERCULOSIS   **TUBERCULIN SKIN TEST** *(See USPHS Instructions)*

CHEST X-RAY REPORT   ☐ No Reaction

☐ Normal   ☐ Abnormal   ☐ Not Done   ☐ Reaction _____ mm

Describe findings: ☐ Not Done

DOCTOR'S NAME *(Please print)*

DOCTOR'S NAME *(Please print)*	DATE READ	DATE READ

SEROLOGIC TEST FOR SYPHILIS   **SEROLOGIC TEST FOR HIV ANTIBODY**

☐ Reactive Titer (Confirmatory test performed - Indicate treatment under Remarks)   ☐ Positive (Confirmed by Western Biot or equally reliable test)
          ☐ Negative
☐ Nonreactive   ☐ Not Done
☐ Not Done   TEST TYPE:
TEST TYPE:

DOCTOR'S NAME *(Please print)*	DATE READ	DOCTOR'S NAME *(Please print)*	DATE READ

OTHER SPECIAL REPORT(S) *(When needed)*

DOCTOR'S NAME *(Please print)*

REMARKS

APPLICANT CERTIFICATION

I certify that I understand the purpose of the medical examination and I authorize the required tests to be completed. The information on this form refers to me.

Signature   Date

DOCTOR'S NAME *(Please type or print clearly)*	DOCTOR'S SIGNATURE	DATE

OPTIONAL FORM 157
Revised 2-88
DEPT. OF STATE

Chapter 13

A Parent's Guide to Health Problems of Third World Orphans

The general health of children adopted internationally depends a great deal upon the condition of the child at the time of relinquishment and how much information the birth mother is able to relate at that time. We have seen children in excellent health, but more often, they have a degree of malnutrition, some intestinal parasites, and colds. These are most quickly remedied with a loving home and medical attention. Babies and children come from impoverished environments and often arrive at orphanages and foster homes with malnutrition, lice, scabies, skin problems, worms or parasites, diarrhea, and infectious diseases. Although treatment is usually begun, it is not always possible to have the problems cleared up by the time the child is placed.

Most U.S. health insurance policies cover adopted children–sometimes even while the children are still abroad. Federal law and some state laws mandate that certain employer-provider insurance policies cover adopted children despite preexisting conditions.

Third World children get all diseases U.S. children do with an important difference. Many foreign children have never had the series of vaccinations commonly administered to U.S. children. Consequently, complications and disabilities are sometimes caused by cases of the more serious children's diseases, such as hard measles and infantile paralysis. Their effects, as well as birth defects, burns, and fractures, often go untreated since the poor cannot afford medical care. In addition, simple conditions are often complicated by the effects of poor nutrition and the lack of medical attention. Disabled orphans face a bleak future in these countries. As adopted children, they have made some spectacular recoveries.

In the United States adopted foreign-born children are eligible for free orthopedic correction or surgery for burns. Middle income families whose quality of life will change if they must pay for a child's expenses themselves may apply to the nearest Shriner's Hospital for Crippled Children. Donations from the Shriners make it possible for these hospitals to serve newborns and children up to sixteen years of age. The Shriners maintain twenty-one hospitals on the U.S. mainland, one in Hawaii, and two others: one in Mexico City and one in Manitoba. Families apply to the Shriner's Medical Board and Board of Governors, who review and accept applications within two to three weeks.

The following sections include introductory information about common and more severe illnesses.

IMMUNIZATIONS

Immunizations do not begin until an infant is two months of age. If your child has not been immunized, wait until you are home to begin the series of inoculations, since they can cause fevers and stomach upsets. If there is any doubt as to whether a child has been immunized, you should consult your pediatrician about reimmunizing upon your return home.

DETERMINING THE AGE OF CHILDREN

In the case of abandoned children, or those without records, a doctor must make an educated guess as to the child's age. Malnourished children are usually quite short for their age and, generally, are determined to be younger than they actually are. This is to the child's benefit since he has a lot of catching up to do, both physically and socially. U.S. doctors and dentists can also make educated guesses by looking at the teeth and bone x-rays, although the variation in these tests is great, typically plus or minus six to twelve months.

MALNUTRITION

Most foreign children immigrated into the United States have mild caloric deprivation or mild to serious psychosocial dwarfism. Given love, nourishment, and medical care, they rapidly develop into normal little kids. Prospective adoptive parents may fear that malnutrition will lead to brain damage and diminished intellectual ability. People who have these concerns should visit with parents who have adopted foreign children who were once in this condition. Although the relationship of severe malnutrition in infancy to brain damage is a well established fact, its effects among Third World children may have been exaggerated. Seriously affected children are not typically selected for adoptions. Long-term studies of malnourished children show generally good outcomes, especially if the child is adopted before the age of three years.

Newly adopted children usually have phenomenal appetites. Children over two usually gain ten pounds the first month, then level off as they begin growing taller. Serve them well-balanced, high-protein meals and snacks.

U.S. pediatricians use a growth chart that shows the scales of normal growth that produces average-sized (50th percentile), tall (95th percentile), or short (5th percentile) adults. By plotting the child's growth, the doctor knows what size is normal for this child, and can also see if the patient's growth has slowed down. In normal growth, the child's measurements follow along one of the scales on the chart. If growth slows, the measurements fall below the scale. The doctor can see if the child has recovered by plotting his return to normal. This system depends on taking repeated measurements in order to establish the normal patterns of growth.

Malnourished children, of course, do not have a normal pattern. Adoptive parents are usually very disappointed at their first appointment with a pediatrician because their child does not measure up to ideal U.S. standards. Upon placement in a nurturing adoptive home, however, the children's sizes change dramatically, due to the advent of "catch-up" growth. Catch-up growth may continue for two to three years after placement. Your child's recovery from malnutrition is complete when height and weight are in proportion to each other, and the child is growing at a steady pace in a typical growth diagram.

COMMON WORMS AND PARASITES

Adopted orphans have had as many as five varieties of parasites at once, some active, some in a cyst-like stage, or in an ova (egg) stage. Most chronic parasite infections produce no symptoms at all. The child's stool should be tested two or three times, two to three weeks apart after arrival. For diaper changes, be certain to lay the baby on a washable or disposable surface and wash your hands thoroughly afterwards. Most antiparasite drugs can be special-ordered by your pharmacy or from the Parasitic Drug Division of the Center for Disease Control and Prevention in Atlanta at (404) 639-3311.

Adoptive parents and siblings also should be tested several times three or four months after arrival of the foreign child. Drugs for some varieties not available in local pharmacies can be ordered by your physician from the Tropical Disease Center of the Medical School of Tulane University in New Orleans, Louisiana.

If an infant or child has profuse diarrhea (more than one stool every two hours), or there is obvious blood or pus in the stool, seek help immediately. Begin an oral rehydration solution (ORS) such as Pedialyte, while taking the child to the nearest medical care.

The most common worms and parasites found among adopted children are amoebas, round worms, pin worms, giardia, hookworm, lice, and scabies.

Amoebas (one-celled organisms): The symptoms of amoebas are dysentery, dizziness, nausea, weight loss, or failure to gain weight. Left untreated, amoebas can cause colitis, bleeding ulcers, and in rare cases a liver abscess. The treatment is iodoquinol or metronidazole.

Ascaris (round worms): There are usually no symptoms. Infection is often discovered when the child passes a large, white, pencil-sized worm. Treatment is mebendazole.

Enterobious (pin worms): Pin worms are tiny thread-like worms in the stool. They may cause the child to scratch around the anus. Treatment is mebendazole.

Giardia (one-celled protozoa): Stomach cramps, nausea, vomiting, weight loss, bloating, and fatigue are some symptoms, as well as foul-smelling gas. Children often have no symptoms at all. Nonsymptomatic giardia can multiply and cause the above problems. The treatment is metronidazole, furazoli done, or quinacrine.

Hookworm: Symptoms are iron deficiency anemia, abdominal and pulmonary symptoms. Treatment is mebendazole.

Hymenolepsis Nana (small tropical tapeworm): Treatment is Niclosamide or Proziquantel.

Lice: Detected by looking for white eggs at the base of the hair in a good light. It is a good idea to take Permenthrin shampoo and a fine-tooth comb along just in case. Some toddlers and older children have had them and have infested their new families and schools.

Scabies: Adoptive parents who did not read this section have infected their friends and family with scabies by not treating the baby and by passing him or her around for everyone to hold. Scabies is caused by tiny mites that lay eggs under the skin. Symptoms include blistering of the skin and intense itching. The treatment is a bath and applications of Elimite (permethrin lotion).

Schistosomiasis (Bilharziasis): Schistosomiasis are microscopic blood flukes (worms) present in fresh-water lakes and streams of northeastern and eastern South America and the Antilles, and Asia and Africa. Snails are the intermediate hosts for these worms, which penetrate human skin and later develop into larger worms in the abdominal blood vessels. Symptoms are not usually present. Treatment is praziqantel.

Trichuris (whip worms): These are contagious. Symptoms include nausea, stomach pain, diarrhea, anemia, and, infrequently, rectal prolapse. This is treated with mebendazole.

OTHER HEALTH CONCERNS

Shigellosis (Bacillary dysentery): This acute bacterial disease occurs world-wide wherever malnutrition and poor sanitation exist, such as crowded institutions for children. Two-thirds of the cases and most of the deaths are in children under ten years of age. Symptoms include diarrhea, fever, vomiting, cramps, and tenesmus (straining). In severe cases, stools contain blood, mucus, and pus. The treatment includes fluid and electrolyte replacement. Antibiotic treatment is trimethoprim/sulfamethoxazole.

Salmonella: The symptoms are severe abdominal pain, nausea, vomiting, and diarrhea, often with blood in the stool. The treatment is trimethoprim/sulfamethoxazole.

Abnormally high hemoglobin: Children over four years old who have been living in high altitudes may have a hemoglobin higher than normal and yet be anemic. This is determined by small red blood cell size. Abnormally high hemoglobin in and of itself is not a problem. Anemia in most children is due to iron deficiency; it should be treated and followed.

ACQUIRED IMMUNE DEFICIENCY SYNDROME (AIDS) AND ADOPTION

William E. Crowder, Jr., M.D.

AIDS is a virally induced defect in the immune system of the human, acting on what is known as the T-cells and causing a serious problem in fighting infection. It has been recognized for just less than ten years and has become one of the most dreaded diseases of humans. People who are considering adoption desire to know the status of the health of the adopted child and fear diseases such as AIDS. This disease is particularly uncomfortable because it may lay in a dormant state for years after the infection.

Current testing for AIDS is based on two methods. One is a test for an antibody to the virus, the other a test for the viral protein. Neither test confirms the presence of the disease, but rather an infection by the virus, which may remain dormant for a long period. The antibody test (usually done by a method called ELISA) is the simplest and least expensive. False positive tests (positive tests without an infection by the virus) do occur, however. For this reason, the test for the viral protein (called a Western Blot) is used to confirm infection (but not disease). The Western Blot is a difficult and expensive test that requires an expert laboratory technician, good equipment and multiple high quality lab reagents. Therefore, today we usually see antibody testing (ELISA) as the first line test followed by viral protein tests (Western Blot) only for those with positive ELISA tests.

One serious drawback is the lack of absolute reliability of the test in infants less than 18 months of age. This is partly because the immune system of the infant is immature and not always capable of producing antibodies to the virus. Thus despite infection by the virus, the ELISA test may show a negative result in the infant prior to development of a competent immune system. This can be overcome at times either by testing the birth mother or by testing multiple times over the course of time. Each of these methods improves the reliability of the test to predict infection by the virus.

Particular concerns of AIDS are seen in international adoptions, especially when the country of origin has a high incidence of AIDS in their population. Often, these countries are also burdened by poor economic conditions and lack of appropriate medical facilities to do sophisticated testing. This makes the decision process difficult for the adopting family. It should be the goal to obtain an appropriate amount of information about the child to allow an informed decision before the adoption. For some adopting families, this may mean the need to obtain absolute information about the potential of infection, making adoption of infants from countries which have a high incidence of AIDS not advised. For other adopting families, testing multiple times over a two or three month period may supply adequate reassurance (though not absolute). It is recommended that potential adopting families discuss these issues with their physicians prior to an adoption to make an informed decision. The adoption agency may make children available who have had reasonable testing. The agency cannot guarantee that negative testing absolutely precludes rare cases of the disease. The adopting family should be aware of this small but present risk when attempting an infant adoption (less than 18 months) from a country where AIDS is endemic (seen in relatively high frequency).

Infants can be medically cleared with high (but not absolute) accuracy with appropriate testing over a few month period. These infants can then be made available for adoption. The prospective adoptive parents should be aware of the small but present risk of undiagnosed infection. If this is a particular concern, they should seek additional medical advice, additional testing, or possibly consider alternatives to this situation.

Acquired Immune Deficiency Syndrome (AIDS): All children should be evaluated for the presence of HIV infection after arrival in the adoptive home. Tests in other countries are not reliable and should always be repeated. A positive test in a baby under eighteen months of age may indicate the mother's infection, rather than the baby's. Fortunately, specialized testing in the United States can determine within weeks if the baby is truly infected. (More detailed coverage of AIDS and adoption can be found in the nearby box.)

Circumcision: Most of the world does not routinely circumcise. Ask your doctor if this operation is really necessary for your particular boy. The risks include possible mutilation of the penis, hemorrhage, and local infection. However, emerging evidence suggests that uncircumcised male infants may be more prone to urinary tract infection, although this remains controversial.

Lactose intolerance: Lactose intolerance is the inability to digest the milk sugars found in formula and cow's milk and is fairly common in all dark-skinned populations and in Asia. Mother's milk, soybean formulas, or yogurt are substituted. Tolerance to cow's milk may eventually be attained, especially if the lactose intolerance was due to infection or malnutrition rather than inherited.

Hepatitis: There are two common strains of the hepatitis virus.
Hepatitis A–Prevalent in all countries, including American day care centers, Hepatitis A is transmitted in a food-fecal cycle. Fifty percent of all children under the age of six who immigrate to the United States are asymptomatic and many of the remaining children have mild symptoms that are not recognized as Hepatitis A. Fewer than five percent of children under three and ten percent of children under six develop jaundice.

Hepatitis B: Hepatits B is prevalent in all Third World countries and is transmitted by mother to fetus or through the exchange of body fluids. One to two percent of Asian and Eastern European children test positive for this disease prior to adoption. Both Hepatitis A and B tests done in another country should be considered unreliable.

   INS does not prevent a child who tests positive for this disease from immigrating, even if the child is accutely ill with flu-like symptoms. Medical problems are highly unusual for most children with Hepatitis B. Most of the intervention in the first twenty years of life is merely monitoring for possible clearing of infection or the rare early complication. Because Hepatitis B is also found in the American population, newborns here are inoculated.

Malaria: Malaria is carried by certain kinds of mosquitoes in coastal and jungle areas, including parts of Mexico, Central America, some Caribbean

Islands, the northeastern half of South America, south and southeast Asia, China, parts of Africa, and the southern countries of the former Soviet Union. Malaria may not be apparent in the adopted child for weeks to months after arrival. Symptoms are often confusing (fever, malaise, diarrhea, etc.). Malaria should always be considered in any febrile illness that is not responding to bed rest as expected.

Mongolian spots: Adoptive parents who do not read this section are aghast when they change their baby's first diaper and see what looks like bruises. Most babies of Asian, Indian, or Black ancestry have blue/black spots on their bottoms and along their spines called Mongolian spots. These spots gradually disappear as the baby grows older.

Poliomyelitis (Infantile paralysis): This disease no longer exists in North or South America, but is still prevalent in all parts of Asia except Japan, the former Soviet Union, and Eastern Europe. Paralysis in a Latin American child is more likely to be due to cerebral palsy or other neurologic conditions. Acute paralysis in Asia is most likely to be due to polio. However, the diagnosis should always be confirmed after arrival in the United States by physical examination.

Sickle-cell disease: Sickle-cell disease is a serious anemia due to a recessive gene and is found in African, Latin American, Mediterranean, as well as other non-Caucasoid groups. Other hemoglobin or red blood cell diseases are very common in Asians. Anemia not responding to iron is often the first clue to the condition.

Skin pigmentation: Cuts and scrapes on dark skin heal at the same rate as on light skin, but may require many more weeks for the pigmentation to return. Brown, black, or olive children may have delicate complexions that sunburn and windburn easily. In addition, malnutrition can cause a genetically olive-skinned, black-haired child to be pale and blond or red-haired. With a balanced diet, the pigment gradually becomes normal.

Teeth: Some orphans need a lot of expensive dental work. Others have perfect teeth. Most dentists believe the birth mother's diet has a great influence over her child's first set of teeth. The practice in lower classes of weaning babies with bottles of sugar water contributes to tooth decay. Orphans with yellowed teeth have probably been treated with tetracycline, a drug that can cause this kind of side effect.

Tuberculosis (TB): In all countries except in North America, a BCG (tuberculosis vaccine) is given at birth or soon after. The BCG scan looks like an old smallpox scan, on the shoulder, back, or upper thigh. All children, regardless of BCG scan history, need an evaluation for tubercu-losis after arrival, usually a PPD or Mantoux test. Occasionally, a chest

X-ray is also needed. The four-prong "tine" test is not appropriate for immigrant children.

U.S. bacteria and viruses: Foreign babies should be protected from well-meaning U.S. visitors who have colds and flu. These illnesses can become critical in babies already weakened from malnutrition and/or parasites.

PREADOPTIVE MEDICAL CONSULTATIONS

Several international adoption clinics will review the medical information and videos of the child you have been assigned. They will let you know the fee or donation required for each record and/or video. Send a self-addressed, pre-paid envelope if you want the information returned.

Dr. Laurie Miller
    The International Adoption Clinic
    The Floating Hospital for Children
    750 Washington St., Box 286
    Boston, MA 02111
    (617) 636-8121

Dr. Dana Johnson
    International Adoption Clinic
    University of Minnesota
    (612) 626-2928

    Mailing Address: *Courier delivery address:*
    Box 211   Mayo Building, Room C432
    420 Delaware St. NE   420 Delaware St. NE
    Minneapolis, MN 55455 Minneapolis, MN 55455

Dr. Jerri Jenista
    Children's Hospital
    University of Michigan
    551 2nd St.
    Ann Arbor, MI 48103
    (313) 668-9492

SCREENING TESTS

About two weeks after children arrive home, the American Academy of Pediatrics recommends that the following screening tests be administered, even if the child appears healthy and normal.

1. Hepatitis B profile, to include hepatitis B surface antigen, hepatitis B surface antibody, and hepatitis B core antibody

2. PPD (mantoux) with skin test

3. Fecal examination for ova and parasites, three times at least one week apart

4. VDRL–screen for syphilis

5. HIV screen

6. Complete blood count with erythrocyte indices

7. Urinalysis

8. Review and update of immunizations

9. Assessment of development*

10. Assessment of growth and nutrition*

11. Dental health assessment for all older children

To be followed closely at one- to three-month intervals for the first year after arrival.

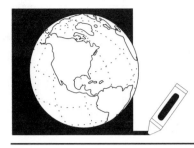

Chapter 14

After You Return Home: Postplacement, Readoption, and Citizenship

POSTPLACEMENT SUPERVISION

After you return home with your child, your adoption agency will send you a set of forms to fill out and return. These will likely include a postplacement supervision contract, five or more monthly progress reports to fill out on your child after the first month, a publicity release form, a form confirming your child's date of U.S. citizenship, and possibly other forms as well.

Each state has its own requirements regarding the frequency and length of postplacement supervision. Some states require supervisory contacts over a period of six months to one year. Three to six contacts may be required during this time period.

TABLE 14-1	NUMBER OF POSTPLACEMENT REPORTS REQUIRED BY SELECTED COUNTRIES

Country	Number of Social Worker Reports Required (depends on state)	Number of Adoptive Parents Reports Required by Country	Translation Needed
Bolivia	Yes, 3-6		Yes
China, Mainland	Yes, 3-6	Agencies provide these although they are not requested at this time.	Yes
Colombia: Private agencies	Yes, 3-6		No

Country	Number of Social Worker Reports Required (depends on state)	Number of Adoptive Parents Reports Required by Country	Translation Needed
Colombia: National Welfare System	Yes, 3-6		No
Ecuador	Yes, 3-6	One per year for 4 years.	Yes
Ethiopia	Yes, 3-6	At one year and then annually until child is 18.	No
Guatemala	Yes, 3-6		Yes
Honduras	Yes, 3-6	One per month for the first year and then 1 quarterly during the second year. After the second year, 1 per year until the child is 14.	Yes
India	Yes, 3-6	Quarterly for the first year, plus semi-annual reports for five years.	No
Korea	Yes, 3-6	Three over a period of six months.	Yes
Romania	Yes, 3-6	At 2, 4, 6, 18 and 24 months.	Yes
Russia	Yes, 3-6	At 6, 12, 24 and 36 months.	Yes
Vietnam	Yes, 3-6	One per year until child is 18.	Yes

In addition, the national child-placing authorities in each foreign country have specific requirements as to the kind of information they wish to see, as well as how often and for how long. Your social worker will coordinate your state requirements with those of the foreign country. The nearby table shows a sample of postplacement requirements for some of the child-sending countries.

Depending upon your state requirements and those of the foreign country, your social worker will make one to six postplacement contacts. If you are having any problems, tell the social worker. One of the tasks that this person has been schooled for is helping families make satisfactory adjustments. The social worker will summarize the information she gathers at the interviews as well as referral information in postplacement reports. These are needed for the adoption or readoption in the U.S. courts and may also be translated and sent to your child's foreign agency. (A sample of a typical postplacement supervision report guide is included at the end of this chapter.)

Adoption agencies are licensed in their states under the child-placement standards in that state. The agencies must follow regulations governing the standards for the placement of a child in an adoptive home. The intent of state licensing departments is to cover the pre- and postplacement studies written by a social worker. The legal adoption in court is governed by the legal code on adoption procedures in the child's new county of residence.

STEP 21

Participate in postplacement supervision.

The requirements for pre- and postplacement studies by the state licensing department and the requirements set down in the state legal code do not necessarily match. This causes a lot of confusion for the adoptive parents. Judges and lawyers inexperienced in international adoption usually request a new home study, and handle the adoption or readoption of a foreign-born child as they would a private adoption.

In such a case, once the situation has been discussed, the judge may write a waiver for the additional home study. Your adoption agency will be requested to send the existing home study and postplacement reports to your lawyer or to the court for the adoption or readoption of your child.

If your health insurance company needs a letter to confirm the date of your child's placement, ask your agency to send it on your behalf.

ICCC POSTPLACEMENT REQUIREMENTS

International Concerns Committee for Children (ICCC), Report on Foreign Adoption, 1996, has more to say on postplacement supervision.

Many countries require that follow-up documentation be returned to the foreign courts to monitor the child's progress for a designated length of time. This is not pure whimsy or curiosity. If these children were left in their birth-countries it is likely that they would be "sold" as servants, or "encouraged" to augment their family's income, or simply to survive by themselves, becoming shoe-shine boys or prostitutes of either sex. The documents and reports required allow the placing organizations to provide to the courts that this is not the case in the child's adoptive country, and that the child is, in truth, being loved and cherished for the unique person he is, and not being exploited.

Failure to comply with these various postplacement requirements means it is entirely possible for foreign governments to shut down further foreign adoptions because no assurance is forthcoming that the children are in any better circumstances or their future is any more favorable than if they were left in their birth countries. In short, it is essential these requirements be followed to the letter if future adoptions are going to be allowed at all!

Even when postplacement documentation is not required it is strongly encouraged. Not only would pictures, letters, etc., be greatly appreciated by the placing organization who–let's face it–are themselves not only the cause of your dear child being yours, but are very possibly the reason he is alive at all. Former caretakers exult in seeing the rosy face and sturdy limbs of a child who may have arrived to them on literally the edge of death. All of these caretakers live with children's death every day and it is never easy and never without anguish.

If you have adopted a child from another country, please write to the source from which you adopted and tell them, with photographs if possible, how your child is doing. Apparently some really wild rumors surface from time to time about the reasons U.S. citizens want children. Medical experimentation is not the most far-out example. Write every six months if you can, especially if you adopted from an independent source rather than from one of the well-established orphanages or government agencies. Even if you adopt from the latter, it is an extremely good idea to correspond, especially for a single person. You will do a real favor to all hopeful adoptive parents who come after you, and to your child, who may wish to visit them some day.

ADOPTING OR READOPTING IN YOUR COUNTY OF RESIDENCE

Not only is there no national adoption law in the United States, adoption procedures are not even consistent among the counties in each state. The Clerk of Court in your county of residence and a civil lawyer with experience in foreign adoption can advise you on the best way to procede.

STEP 22

Readopt your child in your county of residence.

At this point, you may engage a lawyer to handle the adoption or readoption, or, if local laws allow it, you may handle your own case. The latter is called a *pro se* adoption. If you do hire a lawyer, try to find a family practice attorney with international adoption experience.

Readoption in the child's state of residence can be important for a number of reasons, including future custody disputes, distribution of property, survivor's benefits, and child support. And, a state court decree would also be entitled to full faith and credit in other states, an advantage not available to decrees of foreign nations.

Pro Se Adoption

Pro se adoptions procedures vary from state to state and probably from county to county. *Pro se* adoption may be applied by parents who received a permanent guardianship or custody transfer. Children with final foreign adoption decrees may also be readopted *pro se* as may children brought into the United States under guardianships or custody arrangements held by international adoption agencies.

The best source of information on how to adopt your child without a lawyer is the Clerk of Court. Your social worker may also have this information, or he or she may know a postadoptive parent who will advise you.

State Adoption Procedures

Ask your social worker to send the necessary adoption papers to you or your lawyer after your last postplacement meeting. From an office form supply company, purchase the forms required by your court. You can contact the Clerk of Court to determine what forms are necessary.

Send the completed and notarized court-required form to the Clerk of Court. (If you are conducting a *pro se* adoption, enter *pro se* in the blank for the name of the lawyer.) With the form, enclose the filing fee (usually about $150.00). If you are conducting a *pro se* adoption, you will also need to enclose a letter to the Judge of the District Court, Juvenile Division explaining why you wish to represent yourself. (For example, you wish to exercise your constitutional right, and you need to save the lawyer's fee.) You may wish to add that you are adequately prepared because you have read your state adoption laws and you have discussed them with your social worker.

The adoption hearing takes about ten minutes. If possible, ask the Clerk of Court for a photocopy of the questions to be asked at the hearing. Be prepared to pay about $150.00 in court costs in addition to the filing fee and $25.00 for a new birth certificate (in some states). At the hearing, you or your lawyer will attest to the legality of the foreign adoption, guardianship, or other legal arrangement made for your child abroad. Under oath, you will verify all of the facts listed on the adoption forms. You will state that your child has been examined by your family physician and that you are satisfied with the child's mental and physical health. You may also be asked if you are responsible for any other minors living in your home, as well as other questions the judge may decide to ask. In most states, a new birth certificate is issued. If you have second thoughts about the child's name, now is the time to change it.

FILING FOR U.S. CITIZENSHIP

STEP 23

File for U.S. citizenship for your child.

Immediately after adopting or readopting a foreign-born child in your state of residence, you may apply for your child's U.S. citizenship.

If both parents are U.S. citizens, order form N-643 ($80.00) from your INS office. (See sample at the end of this chapter.) If only one parent is a citizen, order N-600 ($100). After receiving your completed form and fee by money order, INS will notify you of an interview. Take your identification and passports along, as well as all documents pertaining to the adoption and/or guardianship of the child. Children must have a final adoption decree prior to application for citizenship.

Once your documents are in order, you will be notified of the hearing. The child's alien card is surrendered in lieu of the Certificate of Citizenship. Keep the Certificate of Citizenship in a safe place. This document cannot be photocopied. The entire process of applying for and receiving citizenship can take anywhere from three to twelve months, depending on the INS office workload.

If your child does not have a U.S. birth certificate, apply for a social security card and a U.S. passport for your child so that he or she has some form of identification readily available.

Forward information regarding your child's date of citizenship to your U.S.-based international agency. Both the U.S. agency and the foreign child-placing entity need this information to close their files.

Required Documents

Certified copies or originals of the following documents will be required:

1. Adoptive parents' birth certificate(s)

2. Adoptive parents' marriage license, if applicable

3. Child's birth certificate

4. Child's adoption decree

5. Child's passport

6. Child's alien registration card

Take your identification and passports along, as well as all documents (both foreign and U.S.) pertaining to the child's adoption or guardianship, in case the court wishes to examine them.

Once citizenship is awarded, be certain to store the child's documents in a safe place. A safe-deposit box would probably be best. Type the citizenship number and the name and location of the bank where the safe-deposit box is located on a sheet of paper and file it elsewhere.

Celebration

Once you have obtained citizenship for your child, you have completed the adoption requirements from A to Z. Now is the time to unfurl the Stars and Stripes! Decorate cakes in red, white, and blue for this day and on every anniversary of this memorable occasion. Take pictures of these activities for your child's life book.

Postplacement Supervision

REPORT GUIDE

Unless otherwise indicated, one report per month, written by a social worker, will be required for five months. For children under the age of two, these reports should be based on two face-to-face interviews with the entire family, one of which has to be in the home, and three telephone interviews. For special needs children and children ages two or older, monthly face-to-face interviews are required for the first six months, two of which must take place in the home with the entire family.

Contact #____: State whether the contact is made in the home with all members present, face-to-face, or by telephone.

Date: _____   Date contact was made.

Child's name: _____

Date of birth: _____

Date of placement: _____

Name of child-placing entity abroad: _____

Adoptive Parents: Name: _____
                          Address: _____
                          Telephone numbers (home & work) _____
                          _____
                          _____

INFANT

1. Describe the child's appearance.
2. List the child's habits, behavior, and personality characteristics.
3. List the child's favorite games and toys.
4. Cite new developmental milestones or new skills acquired.
5. What was the date last checked by a physician? Include any changes in height and weight and immunizations. Include any reports from physician, therapist, or psychologist.
6. Are there any changes in the number of household members?
7. Are there any changes in the health of members of the household?
8. Have there been any changes in the financial condition of the household?
9. What are the adjustments, changes, and concerns of the adoptive parents?
10. Is the family bonding? What is the attachment of the adopter(s) to the child and vice versa?
11. What are the social worker's impressions and recommendations. (Please comment upon the manner in which the child is being raised. Also state whether you recommend we continue postplacement supervision until adoption is consummated.)

State the Social Worker's Name and Credentials: _____
_____
_____

See **OLDER CHILDREN & FUTURE ISSUES** on the back of this sheet.

Postplacement Supervision

POSTPLACEMENT SUPERVISION REPORT GUIDE (Continued)

OLDER CHILDREN & FUTURE ISSUES

Child's Adjustment

* Language and cultural differences.
* Emotional, social and physical changes since placement (include height and weight).
* Child's personality and integration of past experience with present living situation (the older child's memories or lack of them). Explain how parents see and respond to the manifestations of separation trauma (for example, withdrawal, not eating, screaming, bedwetting, regression in toilet training).

Family Adjustment

* Emotional and social adjustments.
* Methods of coping with increased responsibility and changing roles.
* Parent's ability to individualize the special needs of birth child(ren) and adoptive child.
* Interpreting racial differences to the child. Handling racial prejudice—both positive and negative.
* Child rearing development. How do the parents apply their theories regarding discipline, setting limits, and understanding of how children grow and learn.

Changes in Family Structure or Dynamics

* Residence, homemaking responsibilities, and community involvement.
* Child's enrollment and adjustment to school, and/or readiness for school.
* Changes in parents' employment.

Evaluation

* Family's feelings about their preparation for this experience—is the child as they visualized? How have their ideas changed?
* Child's preparation for placement in the United States. Does the family and/or social worker feel it was adequate?
* General appraisal of the placement.
* Local worker's role as a helping person.

Impressions and Recommendations

* Prognosis for the future—how has placement changed the family?
* Discuss helping the child understand the meaning of adoption.
* Social worker's recommendation for legal adoption. Request a waiver and citation of consent to adoption.

N-643 (U.S. Citizenship)

U.S. Department of Justice
Immigration and Naturalization Service

OMB No. 1115-0152
Certificate of Citizenship on Behalf of Adopted Child

START HERE - Please Type or Print

Part A.   Information about adopted child.

Last Name	First	Middle

Address:

Street Number and Name		Apt. #
City	State or Province	
Country	ZIP/Postal Code	

Date of Birth (Mo/Day/Yr)	Place of Birth (City, Country)
Social Security #	A#

Personal Description:

Sex ☐ M ☐ F   Height   Ft. _____ In. _____

Marital Status	Visible Marks or Scars

Information about Entry:

Name of Entry (If different from Item A)

Date of Entry	Place of Entry
Date of Adoption (Mo/Day/Yr)	Place of Adoption (City, Country)

Part B.   Information about the Adoptive Parents (If there is only one parent write "None" in place of the name of the parent which does not apply.)

Last Name of Adoptive Father	First	Middle

U.S. Citizen by: ☐ Birth in the U.S.

☐ Birth abroad to USC parents (List certificate of citizenship number or passport number)

☐ Naturalized or derived after birth (List naturalization certificate number)

Last Name of Adoptive Mother	First	Middle or Maiden

U.S. Citizen by: ☐ Birth in the U.S.

☐ Birth abroad to USC parents (List certificate of citizenship number or passport number)

☐ Naturalized or derived after birth (List naturalization certificate number)

Form N-643 (rev. 5/10/93) N   *Continued on back.*

FOR INS USE ONLY

Returned	Receipt
Resubmitted	
Reloc Sent	
Reloc Rec'd	
☐ Applicant Interviewed	

Action Block

Recommendation of Officer:

Approval ☐   Denial ☐

Concurrence of District Director or Officer in Charge:

I Do ☐   do not ☐   concur

Signature

Certificate # _____

To Be Completed by
Attorney or *Representative*, if any

☐ Fill in box if G-28 is attached to represent the applicant

VOLOG#

ATTY State License #

N-643 (U.S. Citizenship)

Part B.   Continued.

Date and Place of Marriage of the Adoptive Parents

Number of Prior Marriages of Adoptive Father	Number of Prior Marriages of Adoptive Mother

Is residence of parents' the same as the child's?   ☐ YES ☐ NO   (If no, explain on a separate sheet of paper.)

If the residence address is different from Item A, list actual residence address.   Daytime Telephone #
( )   -

Part C.   Signature. *(Read the information on penalties in the instructions before completing this section.)*

I certify that this application, and the evidence submitted with it, is true and correct. I authorize the release of any information from my records, or that of my child, which the Immigration and Naturalization Service needs to determine eligibility for the benefit I am seeking.

_____   _____   _____
Signature   Print Name   Date

Part D.   Signature of person preparing form if other than above. *(Sign below.)*

I declare that I prepared this application at the request of the above person and it is based on all information of which I have knowledge.

_____   _____   _____
Signature   Print Name   Date

Firm Name
and Address

DO NOT COMPLETE THE FOLLOWING UNTIL INSTRUCTED TO DO SO AT THE INTERVIEW.

AFFIDAVIT.   I, the (parent, guardian) _____ do swear or affirm, under penalty of the perjury laws of the United States, that I know and understand the contents of this application signed by me, and the attached supplementary pages number (   ) to (   ) inclusive; that the same are true and correct to the best of my knowledge, and that corrections numbered (   ) to (   ) were made by me or at my request.

Signature of parent or guardian _____   Date _____

_____   _____   _____
Person Examined   Address   Relationship to Applicant

Sworn or affirmed before me on _____ at _____

Signature of interviewing officer _____ Title _____

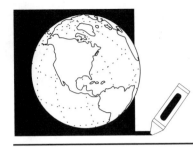

Chapter 15

Parenting the Adopted Child

This chapter includes an overview of what you might expect as you and your child begin to adjust to one another. Many social workers and child psychologists have much experience and expertise to offer on the issues of bonding and attachment in families. These professionals are able to help adoptive parents through the critical first months of an adoptive adjustment and can be called upon later if further help is needed. Prospective parents can help prepare themselves for the first few months of the adoptive adjustment by reading and talking to postadoptive parents of children of the age group and nationality in which they are interested. Recommended books on adoption and adoptive parent magazines are listed in the Bibliography.

Third World abandoned children, who have usually been malnourished over an extended period, are usually small for their ages and physically weak. Unfortunately, their early (birth to three months) emotional and developmental needs were probably never met. Typical orphanage infants and children are normal in their mental development, yet lag behind in gross motor skills. Children like these overcome their physical problems quite rapidly in adoptive homes. At the same time, however, the adoptive parents must temporarily forget their child's chronological age and tend to their child's emotional needs, just as they would to a baby's physical and emotional needs. Thus, parents nurture their children and establish mutual trust, love, and cooperation.

Bonding, the process of attachment to a family, gives children the chance to grow and to change within a family over an extended period of time. In bonding, adoptive children decide to trust their parents to not disappear. Bonding is a process that can take up to five years. Working adoptive couples and singles must plan on one parent spending at least six months at home to carry on this bonding process with the child before returning to a career. Yet, keep in mind, it is quality of attention given to the child rather than the quantity of time that leads to a strong bond.

Parenting children culturally and ethnically different from ourselves is a unique challenge, especially when the child is past the baby stage and already has a personality, memories, habits, and a different language.

HOUSEHOLD RULES FOR OLDER CHILDREN

Before you emigrate your child, think about age-appropriate household rules. List what the child will and will not be allowed to do. This is particularly important for school-age children who are accustomed to rules and schedules and feel insecure without them. All children feel more relaxed when they know what their new parents expect of them.

Explain these rules the first day your child moves in. A weekly family meeting to highlight each member's progress, to plan family activities, and to maintain or revise the rules is beneficial to everyone, even if it has to be conducted in hand and body signals because of language barriers.

Help from someone who speaks the child's native language is usually seen as threatening to a child under six. They have found security and loving attention with you. They don't know what the native speaker's motives are and may interpret it to mean that they are about to be moved again. A native speaker usually makes the child feel insecure.

SIBLINGS

Brothers and sisters are either happy or neutral when they hear about a new sibling. Many adoptive parents take their children along on the adoption trip. This helps some children feel important, especially if they took responsibility for entertaining the new sibling, in order to give their parents a break. Other children have immediately become jealous and difficult, which has added to the stress of the adoption experience. A family meeting should be held before the new child comes home to establish everyone's responsibilities with the new sibling. Household rules should be developed with everyone's ideas making a contribution. Most orphans are used to a structured environment in an institution. The new child will feel more comfortable with a household routine. Siblings will be able to feel important by their cooperation.

Toys should be sorted out by siblings and decisions made regarding what the newcomer can play with. Perhaps some favorites should be put out of sight for a while, as well as other items precious to the siblings. Most problems with new children have to do with the destruction of possessions that are important to the established children. The inability to share toys may be a symptom of the inability to share parental attention. The happiest children are those who are taken out individually for an ice-cream cone or a walk. They feel that they are a valued member of the family. And you can enjoy each other's company away from the demands of the house and the rest of the family.

The oldest child of a large adoptive sibling group needs special attention in this respect, since this child has carried the responsibility of the family on his or her small shoulders. The child needs to let go of this responsibility as soon as he or she can trust you. Then the child can relax and be a child.

STAGES IN AN ADOPTIVE ADJUSTMENT

Once your child has arrived, you may notice some puzzling behavior. Various stages occur in the adoptive adjustment of a child, in varying degrees, depending upon the age, sex, and history of the child.

Compliant: Children's initial presence in an adoptive setting is one of submission. The parent has little to complain about as the child is good.

Curious: Children leap into our culture and imitate the fads of children around them. Children may tell their new mother or father by words or actions, "You're not my parent, you can't tell me what to do."

Disoriented: Children's new culture is in conflict with their old culture concerning what is expected of them. They may reject the new family or become aggressive. The child is frightened and defensive.

Experimental: Children try to cope. They acquire the more appropriate behaviors of peers, become involved with the family, friends, and school work.

The All-American Boy or Girl: At this stage, children reject their old culture more vehemently than in stage three. They don't want to talk about their past. They say that they are a regular American kid. Adoptive parents must create a climate of acceptance of all kinds of people since the children need a connection with their past. Adoptive parents should continue to check on how the child feels about his or her origins.

Adjustment: Children achieve a balance by knowing who they were and who they are in order to function in the United States, in their new family structure, and with their new language.

ADOPTIVE ADJUSTMENTS: THINGS THAT PARENTS GO THROUGH

Like children, parents also go through an adjustment process. The number one factor in the adoptive adjustment of parents is their expectation of what the child will be like and the degree to which the child is like or different from that dream. Often the adoptive parent feels somewhat disillusioned. The ability of the parent to resolve feelings of disappointment is the key in bonding with the child.

Adoptive parents must realize that their child will always be different from his or her North American friends and classmates because their child:

was raised under a different set of child-raising beliefs.

was born in a foreign country.

spoke another language.

does not match the adoptive parents racially.

has had more than one set of parents.

experienced a disrupted family.

has learned a different way to act with adults.

has experienced serious emotional or physical trauma.

has national loyalties to another country.

All of these problems are potential concerns to the adoptive parents and to a child, depending somewhat on his or her age and history. To achieve a good adjustment within the adoptive family, the children must handle these concerns and ultimately resolve them. Your attitude toward the child's history is key. Nothing is more important to a child's self-esteem than their adoptive parent's high esteem of their birth mother. The adoptive parents' first job is to explain that their child was placed for adoption with the authorities because the birth mother trusted them to provide the care that she could not. There was nothing wrong with the child, and he or she was not rejected.

The possibility that the family can never adjust is higher when the child is handicapped, more than two years old, or part of a sibling group. Parents should not blame themselves too harshly if they have to ask to have the child removed from their home when they believe another family can do a better job. (Further information on disrupted adoptions can be found at the end of this chapter.)

Adoptive parents can learn about the child-raising beliefs of other cultures by talking to adult immigrants from their child's homeland. Unfortunately, not every Third World immigrant is aware of how their poverty-stricken countrymen raise children. Another possible way is to search the anthropology (study of the people) department of the library for books on your child's native land.

HELPFUL ACTIVITIES FOR ADOPTED CHILDREN

1. If possible, work through your U.S. international adoption agency to have your child draw a picture to send to his or her foster mother or orphanage.

2. Help the child save money to send to an orphanage or church in the child's native land.

3. Find a pen pal for your child in the native land.

4. Read some relevant books together, such as *Why Am I Different* by Norma Simon or *Filling in the Blanks: A Guided Look at Growing Up Adopted* by Susan Gabel. (See Bibliography for other books.)

5. Discuss minority Americans you admire. You can talk about the good qualities of color; think of all the good things that are the color of brown, yellow, red, etc. You can discuss children you know, along with their good and bad traits and point out that the traits have nothing to do with color.

6. Go to the children's department of your public library and check out some books on the child's country with pictures. Plan an imaginary trip to that country and talk about what you would see and do there together.

7. Help your child design a Life Book (described below).

THE LIFE BOOK

One of the best ways to help a child maintain a sense of identity is to create and maintain a Life Book for your child. Design the book to reflect both cultures. A large scrap book is a good background for placing a copy of your child's birth documents, pictures of the people and places where the child stayed, and pictures and memorabilia connected with the child's first moments with you.

While you are abroad, buy picture postcards for the book, small maps, a small flag, and save some change to tape into the Life Book. Tickets, menus, and any other paper tourist-type items will fascinate the child later on as you look through the book together.

Add pictures of the child's journey home, the first meeting with other new family members, the readoption, and the ceremony of citizenship. This Life Book is the most meaningful baby book an adopted child can possess since the book gives a child a sense of continuity regardless of the changes in his or her life.

Above all, start a journal once you have made the decision to adopt. Keep this as an open letter for the child to read later on. This record will help the child understand that your waiting time was a very important and meaningful period in your lives.

Your cover letter and the response from your foreign child-placing source should also be saved for the child, as well as the foreign stamps.

YOU AND YOUR CHILD

The challenge ahead is one of adjustment for both parent and child. Foreign-born orphans, regardless of which country they are from, have similar adjustment patterns. There is information available on building close parent-child relationships. You may also find studies on adopted foreign orphans at your public library or perhaps at some adoption agencies.

One important, but often overlooked, part of the adoption adjustment involves vocabulary. "The Language of Adoption," a research paper by Marietta E. Spencer, ACSW, Children's Home Society of Minnesota, begins by saying one important aspect in developing close parent-child relationships is the use of correct terminology.

> *"A vital part of education for adoption must include an inspection of the words we use. Vocabulary helps give meaning to the sensitive human process. One should choose words with care. Alternatives to 'put up for adoption' might be the following:*
>
> *"To arrange for an adoption.*
> *To make a placement plan for the child.*
> *To find a family who will adopt the child, and so on.*
>
> *"Adoption holds out the promise of the fullest realization of the child's (and family's) potential. Such full potential can only be reached if society provides a benign and supportive climate for both the adopted person and for his family."*

Unfortunately, our society is not yet benign or supportive. From kindergarten through adulthood, adopted foreign children, as well as adoptive parents, need a lot of answers to a lot of questions that the children ask, those that strangers ask, and those that we ourselves ask.

Consider joining a support group of adoptive families or starting one. Together, you can help your children learn about their cultures with other adopted children and adults of their ethnic origin. As a group, you can also discover resources to aid you in planning transracial, cross-cultural workshops for adoption agency staff and prospective adoptive parents.

RACIAL PREJUDICE

In retrospect, Heino and I realized that our personal experience with minorities in this country had been very limited before we adopted our foreign children. We entered into a transracial, cross-cultural adoption believing that by the time our children grew up there would be less racism. Now we know that they will not see the end of prejudice and discrimination in their lifetime. Nevertheless, our lives were enriched by transracial adoption. Our family befriended people we would not have otherwise met. And we experienced a richly varied lifestyle.

Yet as social workers, we soon discovered that most childless couples preferred to adopt baby girls. Was it because mothers wanted to reexperience the joys of their childhood with a little girl? Or, should we believe the reason advanced by cynics–that boys carry on the family name, sire future generations and, therefore, should look like a member of the family?

Prospective adoptive parents who inquired about adoption almost always mentioned their relatives as either being supportive or dead set against a transracial, cross-cultural adoption. After months of hearing some of these callers complain that they could not consider adopting a foreign child because of their relatives, I began asking them how they personally felt about Asian, Black, or the other minority groups in the United States. Now that we are placing white children from Eastern Europe, we must look at political hatreds, as well.

Not until several years after we adopted our foreign children did we realize that we had been thinking of adoption as a single event, done once and for all. We began talking about the additional responsibility of adoptive parents of foreign children as we helped organize their paperwork. We needed to help parents help their children to develop feelings of self-esteem and a sense of identity with both their old culture and their new culture.

One way to accomplish this is to find friends within the minority groups in our communities to provide adult role models for our middle-school-age children. The prospective adoptive parents who are unwilling to mingle with minorities or foreigners are not likely to feel comfortable in future social situations with their adopted children. Postadoptive parents tend to neglect this important aspect of their children's lives.

Most of our inquirers usually mentioned whether they already had, or planned to have, biological children. Had the couple already decided how to handle the problem if a grandparent showed a preference for their genetic grandchildren? Or, had they given some thought to the opposite problem: the foreign adopted child might be given too much attention by everyone and the biological child would feel left out?

Some of the parents considering adoption wondered if the school teachers in their communities might believe that children from certain minority groups were intellectually inferior. Other prospective parents confided that minority children were such a rarity in their communities that teachers might overindulge a foreign adopted child.

Most of the time, adoptive parents gave a great deal of thought to their transracial, cross-cultural adoptions. And, usually, once they understood the prospective adoptive parent's feelings, the relatives were emotionally supportive. If their relatives were truly against the idea, the prospective adopters had to ask themselves if they were strong enough to function well without the emotional support and the child care that their extended family would have provided. Fortunately, very few parents considering adoption had to make such a difficult decision. The children were welcomed into loving, extended families. And, some of the grandparents even flew overseas with their children to help with the care and the adoption of their new grandchild.

Whether your extended family supports your adoption plan or not, you do need to make some arrangements concerning your will as well as who shall care for the child should you and your spouse die before the child reaches adulthood. If you have a relative or friend who agrees to accept this responsibility, a letter to this effect can be attached to your will. If you do not have anyone to assume your parental duties, consider writing a letter to your adoption agency who may agree to re-place your child in a permanent home. Without these provisions, your child could, upon your death, become a ward of the state and be placed in long-term foster care.

CROSS-CULTURAL AND INTERRACIAL WORKSHOPS

To help widen their own awareness and to continue to help other parents and children learn more about the child's country of origin, some parents have volunteered to organize cross-cultural and interracial workshops on an annual or even quarterly basis. Some ideas for similar workshops are listed below.

Purpose: To grow in awareness and understanding of cultural differences. Adoptive parents need to discover some links to the people and culture of their child's native country.

Organization: Gather educational materials from most of the categories in the Bibliography for a display. Include a map, posters of children, and other book and non-book materials. Those from UNICEF are colorful, informative, and inexpensive.

Preworkshop reading: Have the workshop participants read some of the anthropological studies of families in Asia, Africa, Europe, or Latin America and discuss the book they chose with the group (see Bibliography).

Music: Play folk music indigenous to these countries. You can probably find tapes and records at the public library.

Featured guest: Present a pro-adoption foreigner from a Third World country who is willing to answer questions concerning the conditions which lead to child abandonment and adoption. Prepare a list of questions about the conditions in the guest's country to discuss before his or her presentation concerning child raising.

Films: Present a slide show or rent a film. Slide presentations complete with scripts showing children struggling for survival in Third World conditions are available through UNICEF at very low cost.

Group leaders: Ask the foreign featured guest, a social worker, and a postadoptive couple who have at least three years experience as adoptive parents to answer questions during the group discussion sessions.

Group discussion: Discuss the following questions:

How can we be one another's teachers:
in researching foreign cultures?
in finding immigrants who are willing to teach us culture and customs?
in seeking awareness and understanding of racial and cultural differences?
in learning child-raising methods of other cultures as a comparison?
in discovering how children are taught in other cultures?

Adopted children's interest in these groups may drop off when children are in elementary school. At this point, the family is involved in church and athletic activities and the child just wants to fit in and be an American kid.

DISRUPTIONS OF ADOPTIVE FAMILIES

Not every adoptive placement succeeds. In our agency's history of more than 1600 placements, only nine have disrupted. Other agencies cite similar statistics. The reasons have been varied. One child had a serious hearing loss, which was not noticed by the U.S. Embassy-approved doctor. The adoptive parents did not wish to deal with the handicap. Another was an eight-year-old beggar girl who was not easy to transform into a Girl Scout. Another neglected and abused eight-year-old Panamanian boy was uncivilized at home and unruly at school. Another child turned up with Hepatitis B and was rejected. A sibling set of three pubescent boys proved impossible for their mother to control. And we were forced to remove an infant when the adoptive parents split up and neither was capable of raising the child alone. On three separate occasions, Romanian and Russian boys of three years old were returned by their first set of adoptive parents for hyperactive, destructive behavior. Each boy adjusted well in his new family, probably because the new families were more tolerant, and their expectations were not as high.

Keep your social worker informed of any concerns. Get counseling. Most problems can eventually be resolved. However, if your family agrees that the placement can never succeed, you will need to make plans. If you do not have a final foreign decree, your agency must be contacted. If they hold managing conservatorship, they will take the child into foster care until they can arrange a new placement. The agency must be given all the child's original documents, passport, and alien registration card in order to re-place the child and notify the authorities of the child's change of address.

If you have a foreign decree or U.S. adoption decree, you will need to enlist the assistance of your agency, or another private or public agency, depending upon the needs of the child. If you are able to secure the help of an adoption agency in order to re-place the child in a new home, you must give them the child's previously listed documents. In addition, you will need to sign relinquishments of parental rights in order to terminate your parental rights in court. Only then can the child be placed in an adoptive home.

In our experience, second placements have been successful. The new adoptive parents are already aware of the child's problems and are ready, willing, and able to help the child overcome them. A family meeting held before the child moves in is mandatory in order to establish household rules. The children, unfortunately, blame themselves for having been rejected again. They are generally eager to comply with a new living arrangement in the hope of permanence. If at all possible, the first adoptive family should make a pre-placement visit with the new adoptive family prior to the placement. They should be there when the transfer is made. If the first family has other children, they should be part of the process so that they don't worry after the transfer is made.

If a family cannot be found for the child, you or your agency will need to call your state agency to obtain a list of public and private church-run residential homes.

However, the majority of adoptive parents know their limitations and have the right motives: love for children. To them, children are worth all the paperwork, the expense, and the waiting. They feel enriched by their racial and cultural diversity and pleased that succeeding generations will probably be of mixed ethnicity.

Figures from the U.S. State Department show that approximately 10,000 foreign children are being adopted annually by U.S. citizens. According to sociologists researching this type of adoption, the odds are in favor of happy cross-cultural, transracial families. And we Erichsens, along with 140,000 others in our great nation, say, Amen.

Compendium

Compendium of Adoption Information for Participating Countries

Information in this Compendium is based on the responses received from worldwide questionnaires sent out from 1995 to 1996.

Statistical data is from *Report of the Visa Office 1995-1996* released in October 1996 by the Department of State Publication, Bureau of Consular Affairs. Figures are from the U.S. Government State Department, October 1995-September 1996 and Key Officers of Foreign Service Posts, Spring 1996, available through the U.S. Government Printing Office, Washington DC 20402. Foreign sources selected for this book were based on the current political situation at the time of writing. Political and legal situations for individual countries are subject to rapid change.

The U.S. State Department Office of Visa Processing distributes a list called "Significant Source Countries of Immigrant Visas." 1996 visa statistics in the Compendium reflect these figures between October 1995 and September 1996. The world total for that time period is 11,340 foreign orphans adopted by U.S. citizens.

The U.S. State Department Office of Children's Issues may be contacted for adoption information on specific countries at 202-736-7000 or the World Wide Web at http://travel.state.gov.

For each country listed, available information is provided concerning the number of orphan visas issued, adoption procedures, key contacts for adoption authorities, location of the U.S. Embassy or Consulate, and the issuing post for U.S. visas (if visas are issued at a location other than the listed embassy). In addition, the Compendium includes summary information on each country's geography, capital city, demography, language, currency, and major religion.

If information is not available or is not relevant to that particular country, the section is omitted. For example, not every country has an adoption agency or even a government authority in charge of adoption. In such a case, write to the

U.S. Consulate in that country for a list of attorneys who practice family law and speak English. You should also write to the Consulate to learn about any recent changes in adoption practices for a particular country. The world of adoption changes constantly. As you are contacting countries overseas, keep in mind that time zones are 12 to 24 hours ahead of U.S. time zones, and that the work week in Islamic countries is Sunday through Thursday.

Note that as many as four different modes of child placement are used in many countries. The methods used in each country, such as granting an initial decree, a final decree, or guardianship are stated when known.

When evaluating the following prospectuses, keep in mind that the personal philosophy and policies of foreign judges, attorneys, and child-placing entities are as important as the national adoption laws concerning foreign adoption. Whether a foreign adoption proceeds quickly, slowly, or not at all depends upon the judge, the lawyer, and the child-placing entity, in that order. Few countries have adoption laws written specifically for international adoption. To date, eleven countries have signed and ratified the Hague Convention: Costa Rica, Cyprus, Burkina Faso, Ecuador, Mexico, Philippines, Peru, Poland, Romania, Spain, and Sri Lanka; eleven other countries (including the United States) have signed the convention, indicating that they are working towards ratification.

Instructions for the dossier of documents generally required by foreign child-placing entities and courts can be found in Chapter 7. Additional requirements might be a psychological evaluation as well as a letter from your adoption agency stating the agency's commitment to supervise the child for a specific period of time, a copy of the agency's license, a letter of their authorization from your state, and possibly a set of your state adoption laws.

Prospectuses on a few countries and/or states within some countries indicate residency requirements. Full information on types of residency permits is available at local consulates or tourist offices of the country in which you are interested. Your public library will be able to provide their addresses and telephone numbers.

DIVISIONS OF THE COMPENDIUM

The organization of the Compendium is based on the geographic designations used in the Report of the Visa Office. The geographic designation Oceania, which includes Australia and the Pacific Islands, is not included in the Compendium because international adoption activity in this part of the world is almost nonexistent.

Africa – We list the few countries that place orphans abroad. Islamic religious law or other restrictions hamper international adoptions in many African countries.

Asia – The geographic designation of Asia includes the countries of Asia as well as the Middle East.

Those countries not listed have no history of orphan visas because of Islamic religious laws or other such restrictions. Israel does not permit adoption of their children by anyone living outside of Israel.

Europe – Most of the sources listed are in Eastern Europe. Western European countries are not listed due to a shortage of babies available for adoption.

For the most part, the countries of Europe are presented in alphabetical order. However, Russia and other members of the Commonwealth of Independent States are grouped together, as are republics of the former Yugoslavia.

Latin America – This section of the Compendium includes Mexico and the countries of Central America, South America, and the Caribbean.

INDEX TO COUNTRIES IN COMPENDIUM

AFRICA
Cape Verde
Ethiopia
Mali
Mauritius
Morocco
Sierra Leone

ASIA
Cambodia
China
Hong Kong
India
Indonesia
Japan
Jordan
Korea
Laos
Lebanon
Macao
Malaysia
Nepal
Pakistan
Philippines
Singapore
Sri Lanka
Taiwan
Thailand
Vietnam

EUROPE
Albania
Bulgaria
Cyprus
Czech Republic
Estonia
Germany
Greece
Hungary
Ireland
Latvia
Lithuania
Poland
Portugal
   *Azores
Romania
Russia
   *Armenia
   *Belarus
   *Georgia
   *Kazakhstan
   *Moldova
   *Ukraine
   *Uzbekistan
Yugoslavia (former republic)
   *Bosnia-Herzegovina
   *Croatia
   *Macedonia
   *Serbia-Montenegro

*Slovenia
Slovak Republic
Spain
Turkey

LATIN AMERICA
Argentina
Bahamas
Barbados
Belize
Bermuda
Bolivia
Brazil
Chile
Colombia
Costa Rica
Cuba
Dominican Republic

Ecuador
El Salvador
Grenada
Guatemala
Haiti
Honduras
Jamaica
Mexico
Nicaragua
Panama
Paraguay
Peru
Puerto Rico (U.S. Possession)
Suriname
Trinidad and Tobago
Virgin Islands of the United States
Uruguay
Venezuela

Africa

According to Cheryl Shotts, Director of Americans for African Adoptions, Islamic laws have an impact on the adoption laws and procedures in each country. In countries such as Sudan where the religious law and the law of the nation are the same, adoption by persons who are non-Muslims and non-residents is impossible. In countries where adoption is possible, such as Ethiopia, Mali, Morocco, and Sierra Leone, adoptive parents can be of any religion. However, since the adoption takes place under Islamic law, the final adoption decree is granted with the child's original family name. The decree does not allow children to inherit from their adoptive parents. After immigrating to the United States, however, these terms can be changed when the children are readopted under the laws of their new state of residence.

In 1996, only 96 orphans from the entire African continent were adopted by U.S. citizens.

CAPE VERDE

Geography: A nine-island group of 1,557 square miles, 300 miles off Senegal, Africa. Cape Verde is a former Portuguese colony.

Capital: Praia

Demography: 302,000 persons, mainly of mixed Portuguese and African descent

Languages: Portuguese

Currency: Cape Verde Escudo

Major Religions: Roman Catholic

Orphans Admitted into the United States
Fiscal year 1996: 0
Fiscal year 1995: 0

Adoption Information: Cape Verdean authorities are involved in the adoption process by issuance of a final adoption decree and a new birth certificate through the civil registry. For adoption information and a list of Cape Verde lawyers, contact the U.S. Embassy at the address below.

U.S. Embassy/Visa Issuing Post
Rua Abilio Macedo 81
C.P. 201
Praia, Cape Verde
Tel: [238] 61-56-16
Fax: [238] 61-13-55

Mailing Address:
Department of State
Washington, DC 25201-2060

ETHIOPIA

Geography: East African country of 1,221,918 square kilometers bordered by Sudan, Somalia, and Kenya

Capital: Addis Ababa

Demography: Population 4,200,000

Language: Amharic

Currency: Birr

Major Religions: Christianity, Islam, Judaism

Orphans Admitted into the United States
Fiscal year 1996: 44
Fiscal year 1995: 63

Adoption Information: Most adoptions are handled by proxy through international adoption agencies. When the final decree is issued, the international adoption agencies arrange for the child to be escorted to the adoptive parents, usually by airline personnel.

Ethiopian authorities require the usual documents, as well as two passport-size photos of each spouse and a statement explaining why you prefer to adopt an Ethiopian child. Another form, called "Obligation of Adoption or Social Welfare Agency," must be signed by your local adoption agency. With this form, the adoptive parents promise to submit progress reports to the Ethiopian Children and Youth Affairs Organization (CYAO).

These documents are authenticated at the Ministry of Foreign Affairs in Ethiopia. Then they are submitted to the Adoption Committee of the CYAO for approval. Upon approval, a child may be located for the adoptive parents. A Contract of Adoption is signed between the CYAO and the adopting parents or their legal representative, after which they file for a court date. The adoption may be initiated by power of attorney and consummated by the prospective parents or their representative. The CYAO issues a final decree.

Adoption Authority
Children's Youth Affair Office
Addis Ababa, Ethiopia
Tel: [215] (1) 55-22-00 ext. 28

U.S. Embassy/Visa Issuing Post
Entoto Street
P.O. Box 1014
Addis Ababa, Ethiopia
Tel: [215] (1) 550-666
Fax: [215] (1) 551-191

Mailing Address:
Department of State
Washington, DC 20521-2030

MALI

Geography: African country of 464,873 square miles bordering Algeria, Mauritania, Senegal, Guinea, Ivory Coast, Burkina Faso, and Niger

Capital: Bamako

Demography: Population of 5,800,000 is made up of people of African and Arabic descent

Languages: Bambara, Senufo, Fulani, Soninke, French

Currency: Mali Franc

Major Religions: Islam, tribal religions

Orphans Admitted into the United States
Fiscal year 1996: 1
Fiscal year 1995: 0

Adoption Information: Most adoptions are handled by proxy through an adoption agency. When the final decree is issued, the child is escorted to the adoptive parents by approved airline personnel. Current adoption information may be obtained from the American Consulate.

U.S. Embassy/Visa Issuing Post
Rue Rochester NY
  and Rue Mohammed V
BP 34
Bamako, Mali
Tel: [223] 225470
Fax: [223] 223712

Mailing Address:
Department of State
Washington DC 20521-4210

MAURITIUS

Geography: An island group of 1,865 square kilometers in the Indian Ocean, 934 miles southeast of the Seychelles. This former British and French colony includes Mauritius and several dependencies, Rodriquez Island, as well as scattered coral islands.

Capital: Port Louis

Demography: The population of 1,082,000 are descendants of French colonists and the East Indian laborers they imported; the majority are East Indians.

Languages: English, French, Creole, Hindi, Tamil, Chinese

Currency: Mauritian Rupee

Major Religions: Christianity and East Indian faiths

Orphans Admitted into the United States
Fiscal year 1996: 0
Fiscal year 1995: 0

Adoption Information: The National Adoption Council Act of 1984 regulates adoption. A final adoption decree is issued.

Adoption Authority
National Adoption Council
Ministry of Women's Rights, Child Development
 and Family Welfare Manory Bldg.
St. George Street
Port Louis, Mauritius

U.S. Embassy/Visa Issuing Post
Roger House, 4th Floor
John Kennedy Street
Port Louis, Mauritius
Tel: [230] 208-9763
Fax: [203] 208-9534

Mailing Address:
Department of State
Washington, DC 20521-2450

MOROCCO

Geography: Northwest African country of 172, 413 square miles with coastlines both on the Atlantic Ocean and Mediterranean Sea. Morocco is bordered by Algeria and Western Sahara.

Capital: Rabat

Demography: 16,800,000

Languages: Arabic, French, and Berber

Currency: Dirham

Major Religions: Islam, Judaism, Christianity

Orphans Admitted into the United States
Fiscal year 1996: 7
Fiscal year 1995: 3

Adoption Information: The adoptions of Moroccan children appear to be "parent-initiated" at this time. The U.S. Consulate may be contacted for adoption information and a list of lawyers.

U.S. Embassy/Visa Issuing Post
2 Ave. De Marrakech
Rabat, Morocco
Tel: [212] (7) 76-22-65
Fax: [212] (7) 76-51-61

Mailing address:
PSC 74, Box 003
APO AE 09778

SIERRA LEONE

Geography: A small African country of 27,925 square miles on the Atlantic coast. Sierra Leone is bordered by Guinea, Libera, and the Ivory Coast.

Capital: Freetown

Demography: 3,100,000

Languages: Mende, Temne, Vai, English, Krio (pidgin)

Currency: Leone

Major Religions: Tribal religions, Islam, Christianity

Orphans Admitted into the United States
Fiscal year 1996: 10
Fiscal year 1995: 5

Adoption Information: Most adoptions are handled by proxy through an adoption agency. When the final decree is issued, the child is escorted to the adoptive parents by approved airline personnel. Current adoption information may be obtained from the American Consulate.

U.S. Consulate
Corner of Walpole and Siaka Stevens Streets
Freetown, Sierra Leone
Tel: [232] (22) 226-481
Fax: [232] (22) 225-471

Mailing Address:
Department of State
Washington DC 20521-2210

Asia

The geographic designation of Asia is used by the U.S. Visa Office to describe the countries of Asia and the Middle East. Countries not listed, particularly in the Middle East, either do not permit or do not encourage intercountry adoptions. Islamic countries usually do not allow adoptions by foreigners except in the case of adoption by relatives. Thus, information on these countries is sparse.

CAMBODIA

Geography: A southeast Asian country of 181,035 square kilometers, bordered by Thailand, Vietnam and Laos

Capital: Phnom Penh

Demography: Population of 8,500,000 is made up of people of Cambodian and Thai descent

Languages: Cambodian (Khmer), French

Currency: Riel

Major Religion: Buddhism

Orphans Admitted into the United States
Fiscal year 1996: 32
Fiscal year 1995: 10

Adoption Information: Contact the U.S. Embassy in Bangkok, Thailand for detailed information on foreign adoption.

U.S. Embassy/Visa Issuing Post

U.S. Embassy
27 EO Street 240
Phnom Penh, Cambodia
Tel: [855] (23) 426436
Fax: [855] (23) 426437

Mailing Address:
APO AP96546

*U.S. visas are issued at the U.S. Embassy in Bangkok, Thailand.

CHINA

Geography: Land mass of 9,561,000 square kilometers bordering Mongolia, Russia, Korea, India, Nepal, Burma, Laos, and Vietnam

Capital: Beijing

Demography: Population of 1,300,000,000, of which 93 percent are Han (ethnic Chinese). The remaining 68 million are distributed among 55 minority groups ranging in size from the 12 million Zhuang to some groups numbering less than 1,000.

Languages: Mandarin, Cantonese, Chuang, Uigar, Yi, Tibetan, Miao, Mongol, Kazakh

Currency: Yuan (Renmin)

Major Religions: Confucianism, Buddhism, Taoism, Islam

Orphans Admitted into the United States
Fiscal year 1996: 3,333
Fiscal year 1995: 2,130

Adoption Information: Singles and couples must be between 35 and 45 years of age and childless to qualify for normal, healthy, abandoned babies who are wards of the state. A new adoption law, passed in December 1991, took effect on April 1, 1992. This established a special provision for the adoption of orphans with no living parent and handicapped children for adoption by foreigners who already have children. Most of the children are females, born in one of five central and southern provinces.

The national child-placing authority is the China Adoption Centre in Beijing. The approval of applications, the assignment of abandoned children, and the formal invitation to travel to China for the adoption are handled by the Centre. Adoptive parents then travel to the child's home province for adoption, and then to Guanzhou to obtain the orphan visa.

Adoption Authority	*U.S. Embassy/Visa Issuing Post*
China Centre for Adoption Affairs	U.S. Consulate-General
No. 103 Beiheyan Street	No. 1 South Shamian Street
Dongcheng District	Shamian Island 20031
Beijing 100006	Guanghzou, China 510133
China	Tel: [86] (20) 8188-8911
Tel: [86] (10) 6428-0607	Fax: [86] (20) 8186-2341
Fax: [86] (10) 6428-0604	

Mailing Address:
PSC 461, Box 100
or FPO AP 96521-0002

HONG KONG

Geography: Hong Kong is a British Crown Colony comprising the Kowloon Peninsula on the Chinese mainland and Hong Kong Island, plus a number of smaller islands and the leased New Territories.

On July 1, 1997, Hong Kong will become a part of the People's Republic of China. According to the Sino-British joint declaration of 1984, the transfer of control should allow for the current social and economic policies of Hong Kong to continue for 50 years.

Capital: Victoria (694,500), an island of only five square miles

Demography: Population of 4,400,000, the majority of which are of Chinese descent, with East Indian and European minorities.

Languages: Chinese and English

Currency: Hong Kong Dollar

Major Religions: Confucianism, Buddhism, Christianity

Orphans Admitted into the United States
Fiscal year 1996: 36
Fiscal year 1995: 40

Adoption Information: The Social Welfare Department accepts applicants between the ages of 25 and 45, married long enough to determine their probability of childlessness, and able to show an income sufficient to ensure financial stability. Unmarried individuals and persons less than 25 years of age are considered for adoption under exceptional circumstances. Those over 45 must be willing to accept older children. Most children are at least two years of age and have medical disabilities.

U.S. citizens may apply through approved agencies. Children may be escorted. Either a final adoption decree or guardianship is issued.

Adoption Authority
Social Welfare Department
38 Pier Road and 4/F Harbour Blvd.
Hong Kong
Tel: 8523105

U.S. Embassy/Visa Issuing Post
American Consulate General
26 Garden Road
Hong Kong
Tel: [852] 2523-9011
Fax: [852] 2845-1598

Mailing Address:
PSC 464, Box 30
or FPO, AP 96522-0002

INDIA

Geography: A republic of southern Asia that was once a British colony. With 1,261,482 square miles, India covers most of the land mass of the Indian subcontinent.

Capital: New Delhi (324,283)

Demography: The population of 853,100,000 consists of six major ethnic groups and millions of tribal people.

Languages: Hindi is the official language, and English is widely spoken by educated people; however, a total of 141 different languages and dialects are spoken in India.

Currency: Rupee

Major Religions: Hinduism, Islam, Sikhism, Buddhism, Jainism, Zoroastrianism, Animism, and Christianity

Orphans Admitted into the United States
Fiscal year 1996: 380
Fiscal year 1995: 371

Adoption Information: International agencies must be accredited by Central Adoption Resource Agency (CARA). After that they must link up with an Indian licensed adoption agency which places children domestically. An Indian agency can only place as many children internationally as they have already placed domestically. Children leave India with a guardianship unless the adopters are Hindus since Indian law only allows Hindus to adopt. Other children will be adopted in their new country of residence.

Adoption Authority
CARA (Central Adoption Resource)
Ministry of Welfare
West Block 8
Wing 2
R.K. Puram
New Delhi, India 110001
Tel: [91] (11) 605346
Fax: [91] (11) 384918

U.S. Embassy/Visa Issuing Post
American Embassy
Shanti Path
Chanakyapuri 110021
New Delhi, India
Tel: [91] (11) 688-9033
Fax: [91] (11) 687-2028

American Consulate General
Lincoln House
78 Bhulabhai Desai Road
Bombay, India 400026
Tel: [91] (22) 363-3611
Fax: [91] (22) 363-0350

American Consulate General
5/1 Ho Chi Minh Sarani
Calcutta, India 700071
Tel: [91] (33) 242-3611
Fax: [91] (33) 245-1616

American Consulate General
220 Mount Road
Madras, India 600006
Tel: [91] (44) 827-3040
Fax: [91] (44) 825-0240

INDONESIA

Geography: An island republic surrounded by the South China Sea, the Java Sea, and the Indian Ocean, covering 735,264 square miles

Capital: Jakarta (3,429,000)

Demography: 185,000,000, primarily of Malaysian descent

Languages: Bahasa Indonesian, Papuan languages and local Indonesian languages

Currency: Rupiah

Major Religions: Islam, Hinduism, tribal religions, Christianity

Orphans Admitted into the United States
Fiscal year 1996: 1
Fiscal year 1995: 0

Adoption Information: Adoption in Indonesia is handled by the Department of Social Affairs.

Adoption Authority
Drs. Muchrodji
Direktur Jenderal
 Bina Kesejahteraan Social
Jalan Salemba Raya 28
Jakarta, Indonesia
Tel: [62] (21) 310-3740, Ext. 4042

Dra. Istikana Soepardo
Direktur Kesejahteraan Anak,
 Keluarga & Lanjut Usia
(Child Welfare, Family, and Old Age Development)
Department Social
Jalan Salemba Raya 28
Jakarta, Indonesia
Tel: [62] (21) 310-3740, Ext. 2502

U.S. Embassy/Visa Issuing Post
Medan Merdeka
Selatan 5
Jakarta, Indonesia
Tel: [62] (21) 344-2211
Fax: [62] (21) 386-2259

Mailing Address:
APO AP 96520

JAPAN

Geography: An island empire consisting of four large islands, eight small islands, and two island groups, covering 142,798 square miles

Capital: Tokyo (11,350,000)

Demography: 123,500,000

Language: Japanese

Currency: Yen

Major Religions: Shintoism, Buddhism, Christianity

Orphans Admitted into the United States
Fiscal year 1996: 34
Fiscal year 1995: 63

Adoption Information: The law does not prohibit foreigners from adopting, and no specific government requirements exist. Either a final decree or guardianship may be obtained. One or both parents may travel to Japan to immigrate the child, or the child may be escorted.

Adoption Authority
According to the Tokyo Metropolitan Government, there is no national child-placing authority in Japan. Rather, each prefecture is authorized to handle adoption cases independently.

U.S. Embassy/Visa Issuing Post
10-5 Akasaka 1-chome
Minato-ku (107), Unit 45004
Tokyo, Japan
Tel: [81] (3) 3224-5000
Fax: [81] (3) 3505-1862

Mailing Address:
APO AP 96337-0001

JORDAN

Geography: The Kingdom of Jordan is bordered on the west by Israel, on the north by Syria, on the northeast by Iraq, and on the east and south by Saudi Arabia.

Capital: Amman

Demography: 2,700,000 of Arab ethnicity

Language: Arabic

Currency: Jordanian Dinar

Major Religion: Islam

Orphans Admitted into the United States
Fiscal year 1996: 0
Fiscal year 1995: 0

Adoption Information: Since this is an Islamic country, only Muslims are usually able to adopt. A few U.S. citizens posted abroad have been successful in obtaining a final decree or guardianship.

U.S. Embassy/Visa Issuing Post
U.S. Embassy, Consular Section
Amman, P.O. Box 354
Amman, Jordan 11118
Tel: [962] (6) 820-101
Fax: [962] (6) 824-102

Mailing Address:
APO AE 09892-0200

KOREA

Geography: The Republic of Korea, commonly referred to as South Korea, occupies the southern half of the Korean peninsula, covering 38,452 square miles.

Capital: Seoul (4,100,000)

Demography: 31,683,000

Language: Korean

Currency: Won

Major Religions: Confucianism, Buddhism, Chondogyo, Christianity

Orphans Admitted into the United States
Fiscal year 1996: 1,516
Fiscal year 1995: 1,666

Adoption Information: All international adoptions in Korea must be arranged through one of the adoption agencies listed below, which are authorized by the Korean government. These Korean agencies have child-placing agreements with many adoption agencies in North America and Western European countries.

Adoption Authority

Family Welfare Bureau
Ministry of Health and Social Affairs
Republic of Korea
#77 Sejongro, Jongro-gu
Seoul, Korea

Adoption Agencies

Eastern Child Welfare Society, Inc.
(Korean Christian Crusade)
#493, Changchun-Dong,
  Seodaemun-Ku
Seoul, Korea
Tel: (2) 332-3941-5

Social Welfare Society, Inc.
#718-35, Yuksam-Dong
Kangnam-Ku
Seoul, Korea
Tel: (2) 552-1015/8 or
(2) 555-0810

Holt Children's Services
#382-14, Hapjong, Dong
Mapo-Ku
Seoul, Korea
Tel: (2) 322-7501-4 or 322-8102-3

Korea Social Service
533-3 Ssangmun-Dong
Dobung-Ku
Seoul, Korea
Tel. (2) 908-9191-3

U.S. Embassy/Visa Issuing Post

U.S. Embassy, Consular Section
82 Sejong-Ro, Chongro-Ku
Seoul, Korea
Tel: [82] (2) 397-4114
Fax: [82] (2) 738-8845

Mailing Address:
Unit 15550
APO 96205-0001

LAOS

Geography: A country in southeast Asia, formerly a part of French Indochina, with 236,789 square kilometers

Capital: Vientiane

Demography: Population of about 4,000,000

Languages: Lao, French

Currency: Kip

Major Religions: Buddhism, tribal religions

Orphans Admitted into the United States
Fiscal year 1996: 0
Fiscal year 1995: 1

Adoption Information: The Ministry of Justice notified the U.S. Embassy of the Laos government's suspension of adoption of Laos children by foreigners, pending review of the Lao adoption law. (The suspension will not be lifted until the Laos National Assembly completes its review; the Embassy has received no indication that such a review has even begun, much less been completed.)

U.S. Embassy/Visa Issuing Post

Rue Bartholonie, BP. 114

Vientiane, Laos

Tel: [856] (21) 212581

Fax: [856] (21) 212584

Mailing Address:

Box V, APO AP96546

*Visas are issued in Bangkok, Thailand.

LEBANON

Geography: A republic on the Arabian peninsula which borders Turkey and covers 4,015 square miles

Capital: Beirut

Demography: 2,800,000, the majority of whom are of Arab descent. Most of the rest are Turk and Armenian minorities.

Languages: Arabic and French

Currency: Lebanese Pound

Major Religions: Christianity and Islam

Orphans Admitted into the United States
Fiscal year 1996: 15
Fiscal year 1995: 20

Adoption Information: The Lebanese civil war has prevented the country from instituting international adoption procedures for orphans. Adoptions are governed by the laws and regulations of the religious communities. No civil laws on adoption exist. Each religious community appears to have its own court. Couples as well as singles are eligible to adopt. A final decree is issued. For current adoption information, contact the U.S. Consulate.

U.S. Embassy/Visa Issuing Post

American Embassy

Antelias

P.O. Box 70-840

Beirut, Lebanon

Tel: [961] 417-774

Fax: [961] 407-112

Mailing Address:

FPO AE 09836-0002

MACAO

Geography: Portuguese island colony 40 miles from Hong Kong

Capital: Macao

Demography: 300,000 persons, mainly of Chinese descent

Languages: Chinese and Portuguese

Currency: Pataca

Major Religions: Confucianism, Buddhism, Taoism, Christianity

Adoption Information: Single persons or married couples over 35 years of age, Chinese or non-Chinese, may adopt Chinese children in Macao. There is no upper age limit for adoptive parents. The procedure requires the adoptive parents to sign a power of attorney to enable a lawyer in Macao to act in court on their behalf. Macao will go under the control of China soon after Hong Kong becomes a part of China. For more adoption information, contact the American Consulate General in Hong Kong.

*Visas are issued by the American Consulate General in Hong Kong.

MALAYSIA

Geography: An independent country of Southeast Asia occupying the southern part of the Malayan Peninsula

Capital: Kuala Lumpur

Demography: 17,900,000, including Malay (Orang Malayu) Malaysians, Sumatrans, Javanese, Chinese, and Indians

Languages: Malay, Chinese, English, Tamil, Dayah, Kadayan

Currency: Malaysian Dollar

Major Religions: Islam, Confucianism, Buddhism, Hinduism, Taoism, Christianity, Sikhism, and tribal religions

Orphans Admitted into the United States
Fiscal year 1996: 3
Fiscal year 1995: 0

Adoption Information: The Adoption Act of 1952 states that applicants must be residents, natives, or foreigners posted there for several years. A final adoption decree is issued.

Adoption Authority
Director, Social Welfare Department
Att: Children's Division
Ministry of National Unity
  and Social Development
14th Floor Wisma Shen
Jalan Masjid, India
50564 Kuala Lumpur
Tel: [60] (3) 292-5011 ext. 1406
Fax: [60] (3) 293-4270

U.S. Embassy/Visa Issuing Post
American Embassy
376 Jalan Tun Razak
50400 Kuala Lumpur
Malaysia
Tel: [60] (3) 248-9011
Fax: [60] (3) 242-2207

Mailing Address:
P.O. Box 10035
50700 Kuala Lumpur, Malaysia

NEPAL

Geography: Mountain kingdom in the Himalayas between China and India

Capital: Kathmandu

Demography: More than 13 million of Nepalese and Tamang descent

Languages: Nepali, Maithili, Tamang, Newars, and Than

Currency: Nepalese Rupee

Major Religions: Hinduism, Buddhism

Orphans Admitted into United States
Fiscal year 1996: 16
Fiscal year 1995: 8

Adoption Information: Adoption has reopened after a moratorium. A final adoption decree is issued.

Adoption Authority
> Mr. Deepak Sapkota, Chief
> Nepal Children's Organization
> P.O. Box 6967
> Bal Mandir
> Kathmandu, Nepal
> Tel: [977] (1) 411202
> Fax: [977] (1) 414485

U.S. Embassy/Visa Issuing Post
> U.S. Embassy
> Pani Pokhari
> Kathmandu, Nepal
> Tel: [977] (1) 411179
> Fax: [977] (1) 419963

PAKISTAN

Geography: Located on the Arabian Sea, and bordered by Iran, the former Soviet Union, and India

Capital: Islamabad

Demography: 122,600,000 of Pathan, Baluch, Brahui, Rajput and Jat

Languages: Urdu, English, Punjabi, Pashto, Sindhi, Baluchi, Brahui, Saraiki

Currency: Pakistani Rupee

Major Religions: Islam, Hinduism, Sikhism, Christianity, Buddhism

Orphans Admitted into the United States
Fiscal year 1996: 17
Fiscal year 1995: 6

Adoption Information: Pakistan is basically an Islamic country and adoption is not recognized by the Muslim family laws in Pakistan. However, a non-Muslim can adopt a non-Muslim child through court procedure. The U.S. Embassy, Consular Section, can provide a list of lawyers handling adoption.

U.S. Embassy/Visa Issuing Post
> U.S. Embassy
> Diplomatic Enclave
> Ramna 5; P.O. Box 1048
> Islamabad, Pakistan
> Tel: [92] (51) 826161 through 79
> Fax: [63] (51) 214222

Mailing Address:
> PSC 1212, Box 2000
> APO AE 09812-2000

PHILIPPINES

Geography: An island republic covering 115,707 square miles in the Malay

Archipelago Island group. The Philippines became independent from the United States in 1946.

Capital: Manila, on the island of Luzon (2,000,000)

Demography: 62,400,000 people of Indonesian and Malayan ethnic backgrounds

Languages: Filipino (Tagalog), English, Spanish, Bisayan, Ilocano, Bikol, and many other dialects

Currency: Piso

Major Religions: Roman Catholic, Islam, Protestant, and tribal religions

Orphans Admitted into the United States
Fiscal year 1996: 229
Fiscal year 1995: 298

Adoption Information: Effective August 4, 1988, Executive Order No. 209, the revised Family Code of the Philippines, took effect. The new code made several significant changes in the laws governing adoption of children by foreigners in the Philippine courts.

Article 184 provides that aliens may not adopt children in the Philippines except in the following circumstances: Former Filipinos who seek to adopt a relative by consanguinity, or who seek to adopt the legitimate child of their Filipino spouse, or who are married to Filipino citizens and seek to adopt a relative jointly with their spouse.

Aliens not included in the foregoing exceptions may adopt Filipino children in accordance with the rules on intercountry adoptions as may be provided by law. In general, to process an intercountry adoption, a U.S. citizen must be physically outside the Philippines and process the adoption through a licensed agency in conjunction with the Philippine Department of Social Welfare and Development. It will no longer be possible for American citizens living in the Philippines to identify a child and adopt through the Philippine courts, except as noted above. Either a guardianship or final adoption decree is issued.

Adoption Authority
U.S. Adoption
Department of Social Welfare
and Development
389 San Rafael Street
Legarda Metro Manila
Manila, Philippines
Tel: [63] (2) 741-0785

U.S. Embassy/Visa Issuing Post
Embassy of the United States
Consular Section
1201 Roxas Blvd.
Manila, Philippines
Tel: [63] (2) 521-7116
Fax: [63] (2) 522-4361

Mailing Address:
APO AP 96440

SINGAPORE

Geography: A republic on the tip of the narrow peninsula in Southeast Asia occupying 226 square miles

Capital: Singapore (1,930,000)

Demography: 2,700,000

Languages: Chinese, Malay, Tamil, English, Hindi

Currency: Singapore Dollar

Major Religions: Confucianism, Buddhism, Taoism, Hinduism, Islam, Christianity

Orphans Admitted into the United States
Fiscal year 1996: 1
Fiscal year 1995: 0

Adoption Information: According to our American Consul in Singapore, "babies for adoption are extremely difficult to obtain. Family planning is effective; abortions are readily available, and the babies which are born to unwed mothers are often accepted into extended families."

Adoption Authority
The Social Welfare Department
of the Ministry of Social Affairs
Pearl's Hill Terrace
Singapore 3

U.S. Embassy/Visa Issuing Post
American Embassy
   Consular Section
30 Hill Street
Singapore 0617
Tel: [65] 338-0251
Fax: [65] 338-4550

Mailing Address:
FPO AP 96534

SRI LANKA

Geography: An island republic at the tip of the Indian subcontinent covering 25,332 square miles

Capital: Colombo (551,200)

Demography: 12,300,000

Languages: Sinhala, Tamil, English

Currency: Ceylonese Rupee

Major Religions: Buddhism, Hinduism, Christianity

Orphans Admitted into the United States
Fiscal year 1996: 4
Fiscal year 1995: 8

Adoption Information: Married couples over the age of 25 and not less than 21 years older than the child they wish to adopt may apply. The personal attendance of both spouses is required during the court proceedings, unless special dispensation is granted by the court. This dispensation is only granted on the grounds of documented instances of ill health.

Formal application to adopt in Sri Lanka should be made to the government authority listed below. The dossier should include two copies of the home study, a formal letter of request for a child, two certified copies of the birth certificates, marriage certificate, any divorce certificates, and two passport photos, as well as "Documents required by Foreign Adoption Sources." Either a guardianship or final adoption decree is issued.

The National Directory of Social Welfare Organizations in Sri Lanka, from the Department of Census and Statistics, P.O. Box 563, Colombo 7, Sri Lanka, lists all children's homes in Sri Lanka. An approach to one of the private homes listed may result in a private adoption in the courts in Sri Lanka.

Adoption Authority
Commissioner
Department of Probation
 and Child Care Services
P.O. Box 546
Chatham Street
Colombo 1, Sri Lanka

U.S. Embassy/Visa Issuing Post
American Embassy
210 Galle Road
Colombo 3
P.O. Box 106
Colombo, Sri Lanka
Tel: [94] (1) 448007
Fax: [94] (1) 437345

TAIWAN

Geography: An island off the coast of China, which is claimed by China as a "renegade province"

Capital: Taipei (1,604,543)

Demography: 14,577,000

Languages: Chinese and Formosan

Currency: New Taiwan Dollar

Major Religions: Confucianism, Buddhism, Taoism, Christianity

Orphans Admitted into the United States
Fiscal year 1996: 19

Fiscal year 1995: 23

Adoption Information: Since the United States recognized the People's Republic of China as the official government of all China, we no longer have consular representation. The American Institute in Taiwan (A.I.T.) acts as a U.S. liaison office. Childless couples or those with one child, who have been married three years, and are under 42 years of age may apply. Either a guardianship or final adoption decree is issued. Contact the A.I.T. for names and addresses of orphanages. All visas are issued by the U.S. Consulate in Hong Kong.

The American Institute in Taiwan
7 Lane 134
Hsin Yi Road, Section 3
Taipei, Taiwan
Tel: [886] (2) 709-2000
Fax: [886] (2) 702-7675

THAILAND

Geography: A kingdom in Southeast Asia on the gulf of Siam. This country, which was formerly named Siam, covers 198,445 square miles.

Capital: Bangkok (2,000,000)

Demography: 55,700,000 persons of Thai and Chinese descent

Languages: Thai, Lao, Chinese, Khmer, Malay

Currency: Baht

Major Religions: Buddhism, Islam, and tribal religions

Orphans Admitted into the United States
Fiscal year 1996: 55
Fiscal year 1995: 53

Adoption Information: The Minor Adoption Act of 1979 is in the stages of implementation. The law contains provisions for a "trial raising" for a period of no less than six months (Section 23). However, since clear provisions for adoption by foreigners who do not reside in Thailand are included in the new laws, it is expected that the intent of the law is to encourage legal foreign adoptions.

The adoptive couple must be over 25 and married at least five years. The time between the assignment of a child and the issuance of a guardianship can be between six and nine months. Then one or both prospective parents must travel to Thailand for a stay of about one week until a guardianship is issued and the child's visa is obtained. The child must be readopted in the United

States.

All adoptions in Thailand are managed by the Department of Public Welfare. The first step in the process is direct communication with that office. For complete information and appropriate forms, write to the address below.

Adoption Authority
Child Adoption Center
Department of Public Welfare
Rajvithee Road
(Rajvithee Home for Girls)
Bangkok 10400, Thailand
Tel: [66] (2) 577-1172

U.S. Embassy/Visa Issuing Post
American Consulate
120 Wireless Road
Bangkok, Thailand
Tel: [66] (2) 252-4000
Fax: [66] (2) 254-2990

Mailing Address:
APO AP 96546

VIETNAM

Geography: A country in Southeast Asia of 329,566 square miles, which shares borders with China, Laos, and Cambodia

Capital: Hanoi

Demography: Population of 66,693,000

Languages: Vietnamese, Thai, Muong, Chinese, French, Khmer

Currency: Dong

Major Religions: Buddhism, Taoism, Confuscianism

Orphans Admitted into the United States
Fiscal year 1996: 354
Fiscal year 1995: 315

Adoption Information: The authority in Vietnam lies with the local People's Committees, the Department of Justice in the Province, and the Welfare Centers in the province. Vietnam has approved U.S. agencies to place children in the United States. After a final decree is issued, the new family proceeds to Thailand for appointments with the Orderly Departure Program (ODP) and the U.S. Consulate in order to obtain the orphan visa.

U.S. Embassy/Visa Issuing Posts
7 Lang Ha Road
Bu dinh District
Hanoi, Vietnam
Tel. [84] (4) 431500
Fax. [84] (3) 1510

Mailing Address:
PSC 461
FPO, AP 96521-0002

*All visas are issued by the U.S. Consulate in Thailand.

Europe

As sources have opened in Eastern European countries and as U.S. Embassies are being established, new possibilities may arise. We are listing U.S. Embassies in all countries where information has become and may become available. Please note that although some of the countries, formerly a part of the Soviet Union and now the Commonwealth of Independent States or C.I.S., are located in Asia, they are listed here because if orphan visas for children from these countries can be obtained, they will still be issued by the U.S. Embassy in Moscow. However, visas for Latvia, Lithuania, Belarus, and Ukraine will be issued by the U.S. Embassy in Warsaw, Poland. Visas for Estonia will be issued by the U.S. Embassy in Helsinki, Finland, and visas for Moldova are issued in Bucharest, Romania.

ALBANIA

Geography: A small Balkan country bordering the former Yugoslavia and Greece

Capital: Tirana

Demography: 3,200,00 mainly descendants of the Illyrians of Cental Europe. The rest are Greek.

Language: Albanian (Tosk and Gheg)

Currency: Lek

Major Religions: Islam, Eastern Orthodox, and Roman Catholic

Orphans Admitted into the United States
Fiscal year 1996: 7
Fiscal year 1995: 3

Adoption Information: A law passed in January 1993 regulates all foreign adoption to be overseen by the Albanian Adoption Committee (AAC). The authority of this Committee began in July of 1995. A register of children eligible for adoption exists. Children are kept for six months on the list for Albanian citizens, residing in Albania. After such a period, they become eligible for overseas adoption. Adoptions can only be handled through a foreign agency licensed by the Adoption Committee. Prospective adoptive families are not allowed to go to an orphanage to select a child without authorization by the committee. In general, the Adoption Committee will work through a licensed foreign agency. Contact the U.S. Consulate or the U.S. State Department for names of U.S.-based international agencies working in Albania.

Adoption Authority
Albanian Adoption Committee
Ms. Ilmije Mara
Komiteti Shqiptar I Biresimeve
Kryeministria
Tirana Albania

U.S. Embassy/Visa Issuing Post
U.S. Embassy, Consular Section
Rruga E. Labinoti 103
Tirana, Albania
Tel: [355] (42) 32875
Fax: [355] (42) 32222

Mailing Address:
PSC 59
Box 100 (A)
or   APO AE 09624

BULGARIA

Geography: A Balkan country of 110,911 square kilometers

Capital: Sofia

Demography: 9,000,000. The majority of the population consists of ethnic Bulgarians; ten percent are mainly Turk, with lesser minorities of Macedonians and Gypsies.

Languages: Bulgarian and Turkish

Currency: Lev

Major Religion: Eastern Orthodox

Orphans Admitted into the United States
Fiscal year 1996: 163
Fiscal year 1995: 110

Adoption Information: Adoptive parents must be at least 15 years older than the child. Parent-initiated and agency-initiated adoptions are permitted. In addition to the documentary requirements, there are other conditions of foreign adoptions in Bulgaria to keep in mind. Bulgarian regulations prohibit foreign adoptions of orphans under one year of age or by parents who have previous natural or adopted children.

The Ministry of Justice can waive these prohibitions, but prospective adoptive parents should not count on waivers. In practice, most children adopted by Americans are three or four years old. For children under three, the orphanage must certify that three Bulgarian families have refused to adopt the child before it can be given to a foreigner. This means that most children adopted by foreigners in Bulgaria either have a medical problem (which may be very slight in terms of treatment in the U.S.) or are from one of the Bulgarian ethnic minorities, usually Turkish or Gypsy.

There are many orphanages in Bulgaria, and there is no central organization for identifying available children, through photographs or videotapes. If adoptive parents insist on identifying an orphan personally, they should plan on either making at least two trips to Bulgaria, or delegating power of attorney to a lawyer or agent in Bulgaria to complete the case, as the process always takes several months.

After the child has been identified and the U.S. preadoption requirements have been met, a packet containing all the documents is submitted simultaneously to the Bulgarian Ministry of Justice and the Ministry of Health (for children 0-3 years old) or the Ministry of Education (for children 3-6 years old). The Ministry of Justice must give permission for the adoption to take place, with advisory opinions only from the other ministries. When the Ministry of Justice has given approval, the case is turned over to the court for the final adoption decree and the amendment of the birth record. Foreigners must retain a Bulgarian lawyer for the court case, and must also pay court costs of 160,000 Bulgarian leva (approximately $2,050 at the current rate of exchange).

Adoption Authority

The Ministry of Public Health (children ages 0-3)
The Ministry of Education (children over 3)
The Ministry of Justice (approves adoption)

All three ministries are located at the district center of each town and at the district center for Sofia.

U.S. Embassy/Visa Issuing Post

U.S. Embassy, Consular Section
1 Saborna Street
Sofia, Bulgaria
Tel: [359] (2) 980-5241
Fax: [359] (2) 963-2859

Mailing Address:
Unit 1335
APO AE 09213

CYPRUS

Geography: The third largest island in the Mediterranean Sea

Capital: Nicosia

Demography: 639,000; 80 percent of the population is of Greek descent

Languages: Cypriot (Greek), Turkish, and English are all widely spoken

Currency: Cypriot Pound

Major Religions: Greek Orthodox and a minority of Sunni Muslim

Orphans Admitted into the United States
Fiscal year 1996: 0
Fiscal year 1995: 0

Adoption Information: Cypriot law requires that the adoptive parent(s) reside in Cyprus for two years before applying for a Cypriot child.

Adoption Authority	*U.S. Embassy/Visa Issuing Post*
Director	U.S. Embassy, Consular Section
Department of	Metochiou and Ploutarchou Streets
Social Welfare Services	Engomi, Nicosia, Cyprus
Nicosia, Cyprus	Tel: [357] (2) 47611
	Fax: [357] (2) 465944

Mailing Address:
APO AE 09836

CZECH REPUBLIC

(Czechoslovakia split into the Czech and Slovak Republics in 1996. Information on the Slovak Republic is included toward the end of this section.)

Geography: A small country bordered by Poland, Slovakia, Austria, and Germany

Capital: Prague

Demography: The population of approximately 10 million consists mainly of Czechs, Slovaks, and Poles.

Languages: Czechoslavak, Slovak

Currency: Koruna

Major Religions: Roman Catholic, Protestant

Orphans Admitted into the United States
Fiscal year 1996: 0
Fiscal year 1995: 0

Adoption Information: Due to the falling birthrate, the current adoption needs of Czech citizens is not met, much less candidates for international adoption.

The Legal Advice Bureau No.1 at Narondni trida, Prague 1, has been designated to provide assistance in international legal matters and has the capability of corresponding in English.

There is no central authority for adoption. A private lawyer must be engaged.

U.S. Embassy/Visa Issuing Post

American Embassy, Consular Section
Trziste 15
11801 Prague, 1
Prague, Czech Republic
Tel: [42] (2) 2451-0847
Fax: [42] (2) 2451-1001

Mailing Address:
Unit 25402
APO AE 09213-1330

ESTONIA

Geography: A Baltic republic of 45,1000 square kilometers, which was part of the former Soviet Union. Estonia is now independent.

Capital: Tallin

Demography: 1,600,000 Finno-Ugric people, 2/3 Estonian, 1/4 Russian, with Ukranian, Finnish, and Belarussian minorities

Languages: Estonian, Russian

Currency: Ruble, Kroon

Major Religions: Eastern Orthodox, Protestant

Orphans Admitted into the United States
Fiscal year 1996: 6
Fiscal year 1995: 0

Adoption Information: Those wishing to adopt a child in Estonia must first contact a U.S.-based adoption agency approved by the Ministry of Social Welfare (MSW) in Tallin. That agency will prepare the application, assist the applicants with their own local legal prerequisites, obtain all the necessary civil documents, and forward them to the MSW. The MSW will have a list of children in Estonia who are currently available for international adoption. A commission consisting of representatives from the ministries of Social Welfare, Foreign Affairs, and Culture will identify a child on that list and offer the prospective parent(s) the choice of adopting that particular child. If a prospective parent declines three successive offers, his or her application will be terminated. Contact the U.S. Embassy for more detailed adoption information.

U.S. Embassy
U.S. Embassy
Kentmanni 20
EE 0001
Tallin, Estonia
Tel: [372] (6) 312-021
Fax: [372] (6) 312-025

Mailing Address:
Department of State
Washington, DC 20521-4290

U.S. visas are issued at
U.S. Consular Section
Itainen Puistotie 14A
Helsinki, Finland
Tel: [358] (0) 17193
Fax: [358] (0) 174681

GERMANY

Geography: A federal republic in Central Europe with 130,412 square miles. Reunification with "East Germany" (formally known as the German Democratic Republic—GDR) occurred on October 3, 1990.

Capital: Berlin

Demography: 79,000,000, as well as four million refugees and guest workers

Language: German

Currency: Deutsche Mark

Major Religions: Christian; southern Germany is Roman Catholic, northern Germany is Protestant.

Orphans Admitted into the United States
Fiscal year 1996: 2
Fiscal year 1995: 0

Adoption Information: Adoptions by foreign nationals fall into three major categories:

1. Foreign adopters residing in Germany who adopt a German child. Adopters petition the court for an adoption. The local Jugendamt (youth office) will conduct a home study. The court may require the submission of the adopter's state laws pertaining to adoption. The foreign adopters obtain a final adoption degree in Germany. The consent of the child is required as well as that of the guardian. The judge will examine whether the best interests of the child are being served by this adoption. It is usually verified that the adopted child will receive citizenship by the adoptive parents since German citizenship is automatically revoked when a foreign citizenship is granted.

2. Foreign adopters living outside of Germany wanting to adopt a German child. The adopters may obtain the consent of the child and the approval of the Vormundschaftsgericht (Court of Chancery) and, with a guardianship, emigrate the child. They complete the adoption in their home state/country and forward the adoption decree to the German court.

When foreign adopters living outside of Germany adopt a German child in Germany, the proceedings can be held at the court in the city where the child resides or at the court at Berlin-Schoeneberg. The latter applies if the adoptive parents are already residing abroad with the child during the completion of the adoption. A selection can be made since foreign law is also taken into consideration. The Court of Chancery approval is required.

3. Foreign adopters living abroad who adopt a foreign or stateless child who was born in Germany or who is residing in Germany

No legal status has been created for these cases. Foreign nationals may find it easier to complete the adoption in Germany if legal difficulties for the completion exist abroad. Or, they may adopt under the laws of their state or country.

Different citizenships of the adopting couple is no longer a problem. A new law eases restrictions in cases where one spouse is German and living abroad. When German law has been observed, the requirements are deemed met.

There is no central adoption agency in Germany. Although some regional adoption referral centers exist, they tend to discourage foreign applicants. In actuality, each community is responsible for the care of its youth. We recommend that you or a personal acquaintance of yours who is living or visiting in Germany visit the Jugendamt in large cities. If children are available for adoption, the Jugendamt should have a list of their names.

Since there are over four million refugees and guest workers (migrant workers) in Germany who have come from the Middle East, the Balkan countries, and North Africa, Germany has some enormous social problems, including some orphaned and abandoned children. Some have been fathered by the guest workers and others have been fathered by the African American soldiers stationed there, according to articles that frequently appear in German magazines and newspapers.

Adoption Authority

Unterministerium fuer Jugend, Familie und Gesundheit.
(Federal Ministry for Youth, Family, and Health)
Kennedyallee 105
5300 Bonn 2, Germany

U.S. Embassy/Visa Issuing Post

U.S. Embassy, Consular Section
Deichmanns Aue 5300 Bonn 2
Bonn, Germany
Tel: [49] (228) 3391
Fax: [49] (228) 339-2663

Mailing Address:
Unit 21701
APO AE 09080

GREECE

Geography: A republic of 131,955 square miles in the southern part of the Balkans, including the islands of Crete, the Aegean, and Dodecanese Islands. Greece is bordered by Turkey, Bulgaria, Macedonia (former Yugoslavia), and Albania.

Capital: Athens (627,564)

Demography: 10,000,000 persons of European descent

Languages: Greek, Turkish

Currency: Drachma

Major Religion: Greek Orthodox

Orphans Admitted into the United States
Fiscal year 1996: 9
Fiscal year 1995: 8

Adoption Information: Greek children can only be adopted by persons who are either Greek citizens or of Greek origin and residents in Greece. Exceptions are made for children with health problems, at the discretion of the institution sheltering the child. The only condition in such a case is that the adoptive parents be the same religion as the child. A Greek lawyer is needed to obtain a final adoption decree. There is no central adoption authority.

Greek Orphanages
Metera Foster Home
65 Democratias Street
GR-131 22 Athens
Tel: [30] (1) 262-1911

(Demotrika Urefokomeica)
Municipal Home for Foundlings
Painoniou and Domokou, No. 2
Stathmos larissis 10440
Athens
Tel: [30] (1) 882-2500

Patriotic Institution for Social Welfare
  and Assistance (PIKPA)
5 Tsoha Street Ambelokipi
GR-115, 21 Athens
Tel: [30] (1) 642-7856

U.S. Embassy/Visa Issuing Post
U.S. Embassy, Consular Section
91 Vasilissis Sophias Blvd.
10160 Athens, Greece
Tel: [30] (1) 721-2951
or 721-8407
Fax: [30] (1) 645-6282

Mailing Address:
PSC 108
Box 56
or   APO AE 09842

HUNGARY

Geography: A landlocked country covering 25,000 square miles, bordered by Romania, Moldova, the Czech Republic, Austria, and the former Yugoslavia

Capital: Budapest

Demography: 10,600,000 people of Hungarian and Gypsy heritage

Language: Hungarian

Currency: Forint

Major Religion: Christian

Orphans Admitted into the United States
Fiscal year 1996: 51
Fiscal year 1995: 28

Adoption Information: Parent-initiated and agency-initiated adoptions are permitted. Children in Hungary are available for adoption from institutions. Nineteen such institutions are located in Hungary. The U.S. Embassy can provide a list. Adoption from private sources (from parent to parent) is no longer possible. People who are interested in adopting a child from Hungary should write to one of the Children Care and Welfare Institutes (GYIVI) for information. The GYIVI provides information in writing regarding the procedure and the documentary requirements for adoption.

Once a request for adoption with the supporting documents is received, the GYIVI enters the request on a waiting list and the adopting parents must wait until a child becomes available. This waiting period might be five to six years, because the demand for children (especially under age 3) is much higher than the number of children available for adoption in Hungary. However, the waiting period for older children or those of non-ethnic Hungarian background is much shorter, perhaps six months to two years.

When the desired child or children are located, the GYIVI notifies the prospective parents and they must come to Hungary to see the child. If they accept the offered child, the GYIVI makes an official record of intention to adopt . At the same time, up-to-date documents must be presented if the original documents, which are generally required, were submitted more than a year earlier (see below). Original documents and/or certified copies with Hungarian translations are required. If translations are done in the United States, the Hungarian Embassy in Washington, D.C. must authenticate the official translations.

Although there are no fees for the adoption itself, expenses for obtaining documents and translations, and paying lawyer's fees, if any, can be high. The embassy usually advises adoptive parents to seek the assistance of a lawyer if no friends or relatives are available to help in Hungary since the adoption procedure is time consuming and complex.

Adoption Authority

In Budapest
Public Authority of the Municipality of Budapest
Administrative Office (Budapest Fovaros Kozigazgatasi Hivatala,
   Hatosagi Osztaly)
1056 Budapest
V. Vaci u. 62-64

In surrounding areas

County Public Authority of the Municipality Hivatala
Administrative Office (Megyei Kozigazgatasi Hatosagi, Osztaly)

U.S. Embassy/Visa Issuing Post

American Embassy, Consular Section
1054 V. Szabadsag Ter 12
Budapest, Hungary
Tel: [36] (1) 267-440
Fax: [36] (1) 269-9326

Mailing Address:
American Embassy
Unit 25402
APO AE 09213

IRELAND

Geography: The republic of Ireland occupies all but a small part of Ireland in the north (North Ireland or Ulster), covering 27,136 miles.

Capital: Dublin

Demography: 3,700,000

Languages: English, Gaelic

Currency: Irish Pound

Major Religion: Roman Catholic

Adoption Information: A communique from the Irish Consulate explains that under the provisions of the Adoption Act of 1988, adoptions are administered by Adoption Societies. Almost all Irish children eligible for adoption are now being adopted by residents of Ireland.

Adoption Authority

The Department of Justice
Adoption Board
72-76 State Stephen's Street
Dublin 2, Ireland

U.S. Embassy/Visa Issuing Post

U.S. Embassy, Consular Section
42 Elgin Road
Ballsbridge, Dublin, Ireland
Tel: [353] (1) 6688777
Fax: [353] (1) 6689946

Mailing Address:
Department of State
Washington, DC 20521-5290

LATVIA

Geography: A Baltic small republic of 63,700 square miles, which was part of the former Soviet Union. Latvia is now independent.

Capital: Riga

Demography: Approximately 2,700,000; over half are ethnic Latvians, the rest are Lithuanians and ethnic Russians

Languages: Latvia, Russian

Currency: Ruble, Lat

Major Religions: Catholic, Protestant, some Eastern Orthodox

Orphans Admitted into the United States
Fiscal year 1996: 82
Fiscal year 1995: 59

Adoption Information: Latvia's new intercountry adoption law has been in effect since July 1, 1992. Pursuant to the law, the Ministry of Justice and the Ministry of Welfare will be jointly responsible for administering intercountry adoptions.

Adoption of Latvian children is allowed by singles and couples if: The persons adopting are relatives of the child; or the child is ill, and will receive medical treatment which is unavailable in Latvia; or no Latvian citizens have expressed a willingness to adopt the child during the first three months of its life (applies only to children available for adoption from birth); or the child has been rejected by at least two persons who had applied for adoption (applies to children available for adoption for one year). The fact that the child was rejected twice must be verified by records in the child's adoption file.

Adoption Authority
The Ministry of Welfare
Orphans Department
28 Skolas Street
Riga, LV 1050
Tel: 371-2277468
contact: Ms. Norina Meksa

Foreigners interested in adopting a Latvian child should also express their interest in writing to the Ministry of Justice of Latvia at the following address:

Civil Registration Department
Latvian Ministry of Justice
Kalku Iela
24 Riga
Latvia LV1050

Address:

ent of State

on, DC 20521-2340

nd.

ers, which was part of

anian and Russian

Fiscal year 1995: 96

Adoption information: Agency-initiated and parent-initiated adoptions are allowed. Beginning in mid-1995, the Children's Rights Protection Service (Vaiku teisiu apsaugos tarnyba) created a register of foreign families wishing to adopt in Lithuania. Prospective parents must register on this list before beginning any adoption proceedings. As children become available, the CRPS contacts parents according to their position on the list. Prospective parents may register with the CRPS in person or in writing at the address listed below. Representatives of prospective adoptive parents may register on their behalf, if they have a power of attorney. Applicants should also provide a statement in which they specify the age, health condition, sex, or other qualities they are seeking in an adopted child. Along with the statement, prospective adoptive parents must present to the Children Rights Protection Service the documents generally required. All documents must be accompanied by certified and authenticated Lithuanian translations.

Adoptive parent(s) or their representative must present the documents to
 Mr. Ramelis
 Chairman of Civil Cases Department
 Vilnius District Court
 Domaseviciaus Street 9
 Tel: 61 49 23

There is a 20-day waiting period after the adoption hearing. During that time, the child remains in the institution.

Adoption Authority
 Vaiku teisiu apsaugos tarnyba
 (Children's Rights Protection Service)
 Juozapavicias 10A
 Vilnius, Lithuania

U.S. Embassy, Consular Section
 Akmenu 6 232600
 Vilnius, Lithuania
 Tel: 370-223-031
 Fax: 370-670-6084

 Mailing address:
 APO AE 09723

*Visas are issued by the U.S. Embassy in Warsaw, Poland.

POLAND

Geography: Eastern European Republic occupying 120,725 square miles, bordering Germany, the Czech and Slovak Republics, the Ukraine, Belarus, Lithuania, and the Russian region of Kaliningrad

Capital: Warsaw

Demography: 38,400, 000. Most of the population are ethnic Poles; 2 percent are European minorities from bordering countries, as well as Jews and Gypsies.

Language: Polish

Currency: Zloty

Major Religion: Roman Catholic
Orphans Admitted into the United States
Fiscal year 1996: 64
Fiscal year 1995: 30

Adoption Information: Infants and children may be adopted directly from their parents or from an orphanage. A central adoption authority maintains a list of children available for adoption. A final adoption decree is issued after which there is a two-day waiting period. Catholics of Polish descent are preferred in private adoptions. Polish citizens are given preference.

Adoption Authority
Director, Elzbieta Podczaska
Publiczny Osrodek
  Adopcyjno Opiekunczy
ulica Nowogrodzka #75
02-018 Warszawa
Tel: [48] (2) 621-1075

U.S. Embassy/Visa Issuing Post
U.S. Embassy, Consular Section
Aleje Ujazdowskie 29/31
Warsaw, Poland
Tel: [48] (2) 628-3041
Fax: [48] (2) 628-8298

Mailing Address:
APO AE 09213-1340

*Visas for Belarus, Ukraine, Latvia, and Lithuania are also issued here.

PORTUGAL

Geography: A republic of western Europe occupying the western part of the Iberian peninsula plus the Azore Islands and Madeira, covering 35,441 square miles

Capital: Lisbon (828,000)

Demography: The population of 10,300,000 is the most homogenous population in Europe. Almost everyone is of Mediterranean heritage.

Language: Portuguese

Currency: Escudo

Major Religion: Roman Catholic

Orphans Admitted into the United States
Fiscal year 1996: 0
Fiscal year 1995: 0

Adoption Information: In the case of infant placements, preference is given to young couples. Adopters must be personally interviewed. The adoption agency will maintain contact with the adoptive parents and the child.

Portuguese law does not prohibit adoption by foreigners, but in practice it is not easy since waiting lists for adoptive children exist and preference is given to Portuguese citizens. Portugal grants a formal final adoption decree or a simple adoption. The simple adoption does not qualify a child for an orphan visa under the United States immigration laws.

Adoption Authority
Ministerio da Justica
Direccao-Geral dos Servico
  Tutelares de Menores
Praca do Comercio
1100 Lisbon, Portugal

Adoption Agencies
Instituto da Familia e Accao Social
Largo do Rato
Lisbon, Portugal

The Instituto has about 200 small agencies in Portugal and is under the Ministry of Social Affairs.

U.S. Embassy/Visa Issuing Post

U.S. Embassy, Consular Section
Avenida das Forcas Armadas
1600 Lisbon, Portugal
Tel: [351] (1) 726-6600,
   726-6659, 726-8670
Fax: [351] (1) 726-9109

Mailing Address:
PSC 83
APO AE 09726

*AZORES

Geography: An archipelago of three island groups in the Atlantic Ocean and a refueling base for the U.S. Air Force

Capital: Ponta Delgada, on the island of Sao Miguel

Demography: The population of 334,300 is predominantly Portuguese.

Languages: Portuguese; English is spoken in the larger cities.

Currency: Escudo

Major Religion: Roman Catholic

Orphans Admitted into the United States
Fiscal year 1996: 3
Fiscal year 1995: 0

Adoption Information: A list of attorneys may be obtained through the American Consulate (see address below). They will also send you a long list of orphanages. However, almost all of the children in these orphanages have relatives who have not relinquished them for adoption. Therefore, the best approach appears to be through an Azorean English-speaking attorney who is able to locate a relinquished or orphaned baby. A final decree is issued.

There is no central adoption authority.

U.S. Embassy/Visa Issuing Post

U.S. Embassy, Consulate Section
Avenida D. Henrique
Ponta Delgada
Sao Miguel, Azores
Tel: [351] (96) 22216
Fax: [351] (96) 27216

Mailing Address:
PSC 76
Box 3000
APO AE 09720-0002

*Visas are issued at the U.S. Consulate in Lisbon, Portugal.

ROMANIA

Geography: A country whose coast is the Black Sea and is bordered by Moldova, Hungary, the former Yugoslavia, Ukraine, and Bulgaria

Capital: Bucharest

Demography: 23,300,000, the majority of whom trace their origins to the early Romans. 9.4 percent are minorities of Magyars, Szeklers, and Gypsy descent.

Languages: Romanian, Hungarian

Currency: Leu

Major Religion: Eastern Orthodox

Orphans Admitted into the United States
Fiscal year 1996: 565
Fiscal year 1995: 275

Adoption Information: An adoption law passed in July of 1991 gave control of all adoptions to the Romanian Committee for Adoption. The committee has child-placing agreements with a number of U.S.-based international agencies. Private adoption through attorneys is not legal. A list of approved agencies is available through the U.S. State Department and the American Consulate in Bucharest.

Birth mothers may no longer place their children directly with adoptive parents. However, institutionalized orphans can be placed for adoption after they have been listed by the committee for six months. This gives Romanians the first chance to adopt.

Adoptive couples must be married for at least three years and there must be no more than 35 years between the adoptive mother and child and no more than 40 years between the adoptive father and child. Single women will be considered for handicapped or special needs children. No more than two children can already be in the adoptive family.

Adoption Authority
Romanian Committee
for Adoption
c/o Ministry of Health
Bucharest

U.S. Embassy/Visa Issuing Post
U.S. Embassy, Consular Section
Strada Tudor Arghezi 7-9 Unit 1315
Bucharest, Romania
Tel: [40] (1) 210-4042
Fax: [40] (1) 210-0395

Mailing address:
Unit 25402
APO AE 09213

RUSSIA, COMMONWEALTH OF INDEPENDENT STATES (CIS)

(Other members of the Commonwealth of Independent States are marked with an asterisk and include Armenia, Belarus, Georgia, Kazakhstan, Moldova, Ukraine, and Uzbekistan. Tajikistan and Kyrgyzstan did not respond to requests for information and are not listed in the compendium. Both are Muslim countries and are, therefore, unlikely to allow adoption by foreigners.)

Geography: With 17,025,000 square kilometers, Russia is the largest of the former republics of the Soviet Union and is now part of the Commonwealth of Independent States. Russia reaches from the Baltic republics, Belarus, and the Ukraine in the west, to the Pacific Ocean in the east, and borders Finland in the north, Georgia and Kazakhstan to the south.

Capital: Moscow

Demography: 147,386,000. The majority call themselves "Great Russians" (Causasians). The rest are Mongols, Jews, Kazakis, and other ethnicities from the former Soviet Union.

Languages: Russian, plus many of the languages of the other republics

Currency: Ruble

Major Religions: Russia has been officially atheist for more than 70 years; however, the Eastern Orthodox church, some Protestant religions, and Judaism are experiencing a revival. There are some Muslim temples, as well.

Orphans Admitted into the United States
Fiscal year 1996: 2,454
Fiscal year 1995: 1,896

Adoption Information: Some U.S. agencies require that you meet with the child prior to making a final decision (thus necessitating two trips to Russia); others do not. Russian law, however, does require that both parents be physically present in Russia before the local court responsible for the child to accept the adoption certificate and take custody of the child.

Russia issues a final adoption decree at the end of a process which takes about two weeks. The adopters need to be there for the last 14 days. Since political upheavals are still likely, it is highly recommended that travelers register with the U.S. Embassy at the time of arrival.

What follows is a more detailed explanation of what steps must take place in order to complete the adoption of a Russian child by foreigners, once that child has been identified by the prospective parents.

(1) The regional educational authorities responsible for the child must enter the child into the Federal Data Base of the Ministry of Education in Moscow. Children must be on the register of the Bank for three months from the date of entry.

Suggestion: Ask your agency to ascertain the specific date the child was entered into the national data base.

(2) On or about the date when the child you are interested in has been on the register of the data base for the length of time required by Russian law, the regional educational authorities responsible for the child must send a written inquiry to the Minister of Education (ZAPROS) in Moscow asking if the child may now be made available to foreigners. According to the September 1995 implementing regulations, the Ministry has ten days within to respond to this inquiry.

Suggestion: As you get closer to the date your child's name can come off the data base, your agency needs to ensure that the regional educational authorities send the inquiry to Moscow in as timely a fashion as possible. You should ask your agency what date the inquiry was sent.

(3) The Ministry, in response to step two, responds to the local educational authorities with a numbered letter. The Ministry sends the letter through a governmental mail system which, according to the Ministry, should take no more than three days to reach the appropriate local authorities. The Ministry will not release these letters to either agents or parents.

Note: Your agency should stay in close contact with regional authorities to learn when the letter has been received. The Embassy advises parents not to travel to Russia until this letter has been issued, as the adoption and immigrant visa processing cannot proceed without this document. Also, agencies should contact the U.S. Embassy to schedule a visa interview date, once they have confirmed that the Ministry has issued the letter.

(4) The local Expert Commission, a joint body of child welfare and health authorities, sits to consider the adoption case and present its conclusion to the chief of administration for the region (or, in certain cases, to the mayor of the city).

(5) The Chief Administration of the region, after reviewing the Expert Commission's findings, turns the case over to the courts. The adoption decree is granted by the courts.

(6) The local Registrar of Public Records (ZAGS) issues the adoptive certificate and the new birth certificate.

Adoption Authority
Russian adoptions are handled by region, rather than by a central authority. The Federal Data Base of the Ministry of Education is the only central resource.

U.S. Embassy/Visa Issuing Post
U.S. Embassy, Consular Section
Novinsky Bal'var 19/23
Moscow, Russia
Tel: [7] (095) 252-2451 through 59
Fax: [7] (095) 205-2813

Mailing Address:
Unit 25402
APO AE 09213

*ARMENIA (CIS)

Geography: Small republic of 29,800 square kilometers, bordered by Georgia, Azerbaijan, Turkey, and Iran

Capital: Yerevan

Demography: 3,283,000 Armenians and Russians

Languages: Russian, Armenian

Currency: Ruble

Major Religion: Eastern Orthodox

Orphans Admitted into the United States
Fiscal year 1996: 5
Fiscal year 1995: 4

Adoption Information: Orphans fall under the jurisdiction of the Ministry of Education. There is no child-placing authority. The Ministry of Education and the President of the Republic must approve adoptions by foreigners.

U.S. Embassy/Visa Issuing Post
   U.S. Embassy, Consular Section
   18 Gen Bagramian
   Yerevan, Armenia
   Tel: 7-3742-151-144
   Fax: 7-3742-151-138

*Visas are issued by the U.S. Embassy in Moscow, Russia.

*BELARUS (CIS)

Geography: Republic of 207,600 square kilometers bordered by Lithuania, Poland, Latvia, Ukraine, and Russia

Capital: Minsk

Demography: Population of 10,200,000.

Languages: Russian and White Russian (a dialect)

Currency: Ruble

Major Religion: Eastern Orthodox

Orphans Admitted into the United States
Fiscal year 1996: 36
Fiscal year 1995: 7

Adoption Information: A moratorium on adoption was still in effect as of early 1997. A new process is under discussion according to the State Department. The Ministry of National Education in Minsk is responsible for foreign adoptions.

Located north of the Ukraine, Belarus bore the brunt of the Chernobyl nuclear explosion. Radiation-related illnesses have affected a large part of the population.

U.S. Embassy/Visa Issuing Post

U.S. Embassy, Consular Section
Starovilenskaya 46
Minsk, Belarus
Tel: (375) (172) 31-50-00
Fax: (375) (172) 34-78-53

Mailing Address
Department of State
Washington, DC 20521-7010

*Visas are issued by the U.S. Embassy in Warsaw, Poland.

*GEORGIA (CIS)

Geography: A small republic on the Black Sea bordered by Russia, Armenia, and Azerbaijan

Capital: Tbilisi

Demography: 5,449,000 people of Georgian and Russian descent

Languages: Georgian and Russian

Currency: Ruble

Major Religion: Eastern Orthodox

Orphans Admitted into the United States
Fiscal year 1996: 77
Fiscal year 1995: 52

Adoption Information: The Republic of Georgia continues to adhere to the legal procedure for adoption that was set forth in the Code of Marriage and Family of the Georgian SSR. Agency-initiated and parent-initiated adoptions are permitted.

If the child's parents retain parental rights, a notarized certificate of consent to adoption must be obtained from the parents or guardians. When the natural parents have been deprived of these rights due to negligence, the orphanage should have taken the case to court and been issued a document indicating the court's decision. With this document, the orphanage has the right to issue consent to adoption in lieu of the natural parents. The orphanage also retains this right when the child has no surviving parents or guardians.

Once a child is located, the adopting parents, or, in the case of foreigners, the adoption agency, must apply to the State Council Advisory on Education with several documents, including an announcement addressed to the state minister stating their intention to adopt a specific child.

The process of finding a child and presenting these documents may be done through a lawyer if the adopting parents grant power of attorney.

Based on the required documents and the home study, the Georgian government forwards its approval of the adoption to the district government of the child's residence. The local government may also provide a new birth certificate with the child's new name, or the adopting parents may choose to wait and obtain a birth certificate in the United States.

Adoption Authority

In the Republic of Georgia, both the Ministry of Education's Agency for Orphanages and the Ministry of Health's Agency for Motherhood and Childhood are responsible for adoptions. The first will assist primarily with children three years and older, and the latter will assist with infants.

> Mr. Guram Jumbaridze
> Ministry of Education's Agency for Orphanages
> 52 Uznadze Street
> Tbilisi, 380002
> Tel: (8832) 95-99-81

> Mr. Jojua Dazmir
> Ministry of Health's Agency for Motherhood and Childhood
> 30 Gamsakhurdia Avenue
> Tbilisi, 38002
> Tel: (8832) 38-98-67
> Telex: 212223
> Lazer SU

> Ms. Lamara Gagua
> Leading State Advisor (on Education)
> State Building 7 Dzerjhinski Street
> Tbilisi
> Tel: (8832) 98-39-06

U.S. Embassy/Visa Issuing Post

U.S. Embassy, Consular Section
#25 Antoneli St.
380026 Tbilisi, Georgia
Tel: 995-32-98-99-67
Fax: 995-32-93-37-59

Mailing Address:
Department of State
Washington, DC 20521-7060

*Visas are issued by the U.S. Embassy in Moscow, Russia.

KAZAKHSTAN (CIS)

Geography: A large republic of 2,717,300 square miles bordered by Russia, China, Kyrgyzstan, Uzbekistan, and Turkmenistan

Capital: Alma Ata

Demography: Population of 16,538,000 Kazakhs and Russians

Languages: Russian and Kazakh

Currency: Ruble

Major Religions: Islam and Eastern Orthodox

Orphans Admitted into the United States
Fiscal year 1996: 1
Fiscal year 1995: 16

Adoption Information: Until recently, the adoption of Kazakhstani children by foreigners was expressly forbidden by law. However, in July of 1996, the U.S. Embassy in Almaty, Kazakhstan received diplomatic note from the government of Kazakhstan stating that foreign adoption is now legal. Unfortunately, beyond this statement, there has been no clarification of Kazakhstan's stance on foreign adoption, nor has any information on adoption procedures become available.

The only organization that seems to be involved in handling adoption cases is the Ministry of Education (see address below).

Adoption Authority
Ms. Sembayera Gulmira
Ministry of Education
   of the Republic of Kazakhstan
Almaty 4800100
25 Dzambul Street

also

Ms. Aparbekova Nadezhda
Almaty City Administration
Tel: 63-82-43 or 62-56-98

U.S. Embassy/Visa Issuing Post
U.S. Embassy, Consular Section
Farmanova Street
Alma Ata, Kazakhstan
Tel: [7] (3272) 63-39-05
Fax: [7] (3272) 63-38-83

*Visas are issued by U.S. Embassy in Moscow, Russia.

*MOLDOVA (CIS)

Geography: A small republic of 33,7000 square kilometers bordered by the Ukraine and Romania

Capital: Chisinau (Kishinev)

Demography: Approximately 4,341,000, the majority of whom are Moldovans of Russian and Romanian descent

Languages: Moldovan, Russian, and Romanian

Currency: Ruble

Major Religion: Eastern Orthodox

Orphans Admitted into the United States
Fiscal year 1996: 44
Fiscal year 1995: 40

Adoption Information: In order to be eligible for adoption, a Moldovan child must first be registered on the official list of orphaned or abandoned children. Moldovan citizens are given first priority in adopting children; if after six months the child has not been adopted by a Moldovan family, he or she is then eligible to be adopted by foreign parents, working through a registered adoption agency. In practice, it is impossible for a foreigner to adopt a child who is less than six months old. All adoption agencies that wish to operate in Moldova must register with the Committee for Adoption by presenting credentials which establish the agency's right to operate in its country of origin. Once an agency has successfully registered with the Committee, it will be allowed to petition to adopt eligible Moldovan children. Only registered agencies will be given permission to visit these children in orphanages and/or hospitals.

Once an agency has matched a prospective family with an eligible child, the agency must submit documentation to the Committee showing that the family has met all legal requirements for adoption in their own country. The Committee will then review all documentation and make a final decision on the adoption. The Committee will meet on an as-needed basis to consider cases. Those approved to adopt a Moldovan child must pay $1000.00 and the equivalent of a round-trip ticket to the adoptive country, so that Moldovan authorities would be able to visit the child to monitor the home environment, should the need arise.

In 1993, the Moldovan Parliament created the Committee of the Republic of Moldova for Adoption, which is responsible for overseeing and approving all adoptions by foreigners. The Committee is a division of the Ministry of Science and Education and, as chairperson of the Committee, the Vice-Minister of Science and Education has the sole authorization to sign documents of adoption. In addition to the permanent staff of five people, the Moldovan State Chancery and the Ministries of Health, Justice, Internal Affairs, and Foreign Affairs are represented on the Committee. Adoptions will be approved or rejected by a majority of votes.

Adoption agencies already registered or seeking registration, along with prospective adoptive parents, should know the following: Every American notarized document submitted in support of an application to adopt a Moldovan child must be authenticated. Authentication of American notarized documents is a time-consuming process which can only be accomplished in the United States. The Embassy in Moldova cannot authenticate American notarized documents. Arriving in Moldova without authenticated American notarized documents may mean a long and costly trip to Moldova in vain.

Adoption Authority
Ministry of Science
and Education
Kishinev, Moldova

U.S. Embassy/Visa Issuing Post
American Embassy
Strada Alexei Mateevicie #103
Kishinev, Moldova
Tel: [373] (2) 23-37-72
Fax: [373] (2) 23-30-44

*Visas are issued by the U.S. Embassy in Warsaw, Poland.

UKRAINE (CIS)

Geography: A republic of 603,700 square kilometers bordered by Poland, Belarus, Slovakia, Romania, Russia, and Moldova

Capital: Kiev (Kiyeu)

Demography: 51,704,000, ethnic Ukrainians and Russians

Languages: Ukrainian, Russian

Currency: Ruble

Major Religion: Eastern Orthodox

Orphans Admitted into United States
Fiscal year 1996: 1
Fiscal year 1995: 4

Adoption Information: On January 28, 1996, the Rada (Ukrainian parliament) amended the Family and Marriage Code of Ukraine, thereby lifting the moratorium on adoption of Ukrainian children (orphaned or abandoned) by foreign nationals, effective April 1, 1996. The amended law places new burdens on prospective adopting families and bars the use of third-party adoption facilitators.

Citizens of foreign countries may adopt Ukrainian children after those children have been registered with the Adoption Center for one year and if within this year no Ukrainian family expresses a desire to adopt them or become their guardians. If citizens of the foreign countries are relatives of the child, the one-year requirement may be waived. If the child is suffering from a disease (the Ministry of Health protection has a list of those diseases), the one-year requirement may also be waived. Citizens of foreign countries may adopt Ukrainian children only if they have permission from the Adoption Center. Citizens of countries which have signed bilateral agreements on adoption have priority.

Under the new law, a hospital, orphanage, or any other place which keeps, or has information about the orphan or abandoned child, must notify the local guardianship board about this within one week. Orphans or abandoned children, who may be adopted, as well as citizens of Ukraine willing to adopt, should be registered with local guardianship boards and the Adoption Center (a new structure with the Ministry of Education of Ukraine). Citizens of foreign countries willing to adopt Ukrainian children should also register with the adoption center.

Citizens of foreign countries interested in adopting a child residing in Ukraine should submit their request to the Adoption Center of the Ministry of Education of Ukraine. International adoptions must by law be open adoptions.

Adoption Authority	*U.S. Embassy/Visa Issuing Post*
Adoption Center	U.S. Embassy, Consular Section
Ministry of Education	10 Yuria Kotsubynskoho
Ukraine	254053 Kiev 53
	Ukraine
	Tel: [380] (44) 244-7345
	Fax: [380] (44) 244-7350

*Visas are issued by the U.S. Embassy in Warsaw, Poland.

*UZBEKISTAN (CIS)

Geography: A republic of 447,400 square kilometers bordered by Kazakhstan, Turkmenistan, Tajikistan, Kyrgyzstan, and Afghanistan

Capital: Tashkent

Demography: Population of 19,906,000 Uzbekis and Russians

Languages: Uzbeki and Russian

Currency: Ruble

Major Religion: Islam

Orphans Admitted into the United States
Fiscal year 1996: 14
Fiscal year 1995: 47

Adoption Information: The government office responsible for adoptions in Uzbekistan is the Ministry of Education. Parent-initiated and agency-initiated adoptions are permitted.

The following steps outline the Uzbeki adoption process:

An agent or the prospective parents select a child from an orphanage; They present the child's documents to the adoption inspector of the regional Department of Education (Rayonniy Otdel Narodnovo Obrazovaniya, or RAY-ONO) for review; The inspector passes the documents to the city's mayor's office (Hokimiate) for approval;

The city Hokimiate sends approval to a local district (Hokimiate), which grants final authority for the adoption; The local ZAGS (registration office of civil acts) issues a certificate of adoption based on the local Hokimiate's decision (Note: the certificate can also legalize a name change based on the adopting parents' wishes.); UVVG (the Administration for Exit, Entry, and Citizenship, formerly known as OVIR) issues a passport to the child based on the local Hokimiate's permission, the ZAGS certificate, and a notarized invitation for permanent residence abroad.

Adopted orphans retain their Uzbekistan citizenship until they reach the majority age of sixteen. In order to monitor the rights of its citizens adopted overseas, in 1992 the Cabinet of Ministers officially delegated this responsibility to the Red Crescent Society (an Islamic version of the Red Cross). The Red Crescent Society, in turn, delegated this reponsibility to a sub-organization called Tayanach.

Tayanach, a not-for-profit organization, has become an active participant in the process of foreign adoptions. Although it has no official authority to do so, this organization has been accepting the documents and bona fides of various adoption agencies and granting them permission to operate in Uzbekistan. Since it works to ensure that children adopted from Uzbekistan have good living conditions and receive necessary medical treatment once overseas, it also requests regular reports about the children's life and health abroad during the first five years after adoption.

Adoption Authority	***U.S. Embassy/Visa Issuing Post***
Ministry of Education	U.S. Embassy, Consular Section
Tashkent, Uzbekistan	82 Chilanzanrskaya
	Tashkent
	Uzbekistan
	Tel: [7] (3712) 77-1407
	Fax: [7] (3712) 89-13-35

*Visas are issued by the U.S. Embassy in Moscow, Russia.

YUGOSLAVIA

Former republic which now includes Serbia-Montenegro, Croatia, Slovenia, Macedonia, and Bosnia-Herzegovina

* BOSNIA-HERZEGOVINA

Geography: A newly formed republic whose borders were still in dispute in early 1997
Capital: Sarajevo

Demography: Population of approximately 3, 594,000

Languages: Serbian and Croatian

Currency: BH Dinar

Major Religions: Islam, Roman Catholic, and Eastern Orthodox

Orphans Admitted into the United States
Fiscal year 1996: 0
Fiscal year 1995: 0

Adoption Information: In June of 1996, the U.S. Embassy noted that all adoptions of Bosnian children by foreign citizens have been suspended until further notice.
Excerpts from a U.S. Consulate report follow:
Para4: Regarding children orphaned by the war, according to the international conventions for protection of children, decisions regarding permanent protection of the child, such as adoption, may not be made until a lasting peace has been effected. A possibility exists that the child has a living parent or a close relative (brother, sister, uncle, aunt, grandparent) who will take over the care of the child, which would be the most favorable means of providing protection for the child.
Para5: Children from Bosnia-Herzegovina are given shelter in the Republic of Serbia and are accorded complete protection in the way of housing, providing for, education, in institutions for social protection. Decisions regarding the permanent form of protection may be brought only by the Social Security Office (SSO) having jurisdiction over the child's place of permanent residence. This means that if the child is, for example, from Sarajevo, Bosnia-Herzegovina, such a decision may be made by SSO in Sarajevo, not an SSO in the Republic of Serbia.

U.S. Embassy/Visa Issuing Post
U.S. Embassy, Consular Section
43 Ul. Dure Dakovica
Sarajevo, Bosnia-Herzegovina
Tel: [387] (71) 445-700
Fax: [387] (71) 659-722

CROATIA

Geography: Large republic split off from former Yugoslavia bordered by Slovenia, Hungary, Romania, Bosnia-Herzegovina, and Serbia
Capital: Zagreb

Demography: Approximately 1,700,000 Croatians and Serbs

Languages: Croatian, Serbian, Slovenian

Currency: Kuna

Major Religions: Eastern Orthodox and Roman Catholic

Orphans Admitted into the United States
Fiscal year 1996: 2
Fiscal year 1995: 0

Adoption Information: Under normal circumstances, only Croatian citizens may adopt children from Croatia. In some "extraordinary circumstances" persons of Croatian ethnic origins who have lived in Croatia for some time or persons willing to adopt children with special needs were allowed to adopt.

Adoption Authority
Minisarstvo Radai Socijalne
Skrbi Hrvatske
(Croatian Ministry of
Labor and Social Service)
10000 Zagreb
Prisculje 14 Zagreb
Attn. Ms. Helena Ujevic

U.S. Embassy/Visa Issuing Post
U.S. Embassy, Consular Section
Andrije Hebranga 2, Unit 1345
Zagreb, Croatia
Tel: [385] (1) 455-5500

Mailing Address:
APO, AE 09213-1345

MACEDONIA

Geography: A former republic of Yugoslavia bordering Albania, Greece, Bulgaria, and Kosova

Capital: Skoplje

Demography: Approximately 1,500,000 Macedonians of Serbian, Greek, and other minorities

Languages: Serbian, Greek, Albanian

Currency: Macedonian Dinar

Major Religions: Greek Orthodox, Roman Catholic, and Muslim

Orphans Admitted into the United States
Fiscal year 1996: 3
Fiscal year 1995: 0

Adoption Information: The waiting list of qualified Macedonian traditional couples seeking to adopt Macedonian children far exceeds the availability. In fact,
in recent times, the only foreign couples who successfully adopted locally have
been persons holding dual nationality (Macedonian and another) and who have
long-standing family and ethnic ties to Macedonia. Nonetheless, responsible
officials are not totally closed to the possibility of adoption by foreigners, but are
considering future procedures and revision to law in order to ensure the best
interests of those few children who may become available for adoption. Among
options presently under consideration by the Ministry of Labor and Social Affairs
is the designation of a sole U.S. agency for U.S. adoptions.

Adoption Authority	**U.S. Embassy/Visa Issuing Post**
Mr. Ilija Rajcinovski	U.S. Embassy, Consular Section
Ministry of Labor and Social Affairs	Bul Llinden BB
91000 Skoplje	9100 Skoplje
F.Y.R.O. Macedonia	Macedonia
	Tel: [389](91) 116-180
	Fax: (389] (91) 117-103

*SERBIA-MONTENEGRO

Geography: The largest of the former Yugoslavia republics, Serbia also still
controls Kosova, Montenegro, and Vojvodina.

Capital: Belgrade

Demography: Approximately 10,800,000 Serbs, Kosovans, Montenegrins,
Vojvodinans

Languages: Serbian, Croatian, Slovenian, and other languages and dialects of
former Yugoslavia

Currency: Dinar

Major Religions: Eastern Orthodox and Roman Catholic

Orphans Admitted into the United States
Fiscal year 1996: 6
Fiscal year 1995: 47

Adoption Information: An excerpt from a U.S. Consulate report states that according to the Law of Marriage and Marital Affairs, adoption of orphans by foreign citizens is only allowed under unusual circumstances. For example, a few exceptions may be made for diplomats and foreign citizens of Yugoslav origin or dual nationals when an adoptive parent is not found within national boundaries.

U.S. Embassy/Visa Issuing Post

U.S. Embassy, Consular Section
Kneza Milosa 50
11000 Belgrade, Serbia
Tel: [381] (11) 645-655
Fax: [381] (11) 645-332

Mailing Address:
APO AE 09213-1310

*SLOVENIA

Geography: Formerly a part of Yugoslavia, this republic became independent and, for the most part, escaped the civil war that followed the break-up. Slovenia shares a border with Italy, Austria, Croatia, and Hungary.

Capital: Ljubljana

Demography: 1,625,000 people of Slovenian, Italian, and Croatian ethnicity

Languages: Slovenian, Serbian, Croatian

Currency: Slovenian Dinar

Major Religion: Roman Catholic

Orphans Admitted into the United States

Fiscal year 1996: 0
Fiscal year 1995: 5

Adoption Information: Usually only Slovenians can adopt children who have been relinquished to a "competent body." There are no central institutions for adoption, rather 52 centers of social work carry out social services. Approximately 200 Slovenian couples are waiting to adopt-a high number for a relatively small population.

U.S. Embassy/Visa Issuing Post

U.S. Embassy, Consular Section
P.O. Box 254
Prazakova 4
61000 Ljubljana,
Slovenia
Tel: [386] (61) 301-427/472/485   Fax: [386] (61) 301-401/472/485

SLOVAK REPUBLIC

Geography: Separated from the former Czechoslovakia, the Slovak Republic shares borders with the new Czech Republic, Austria, Poland, Hungary, and the Ukraine.

Capital: Bratislava

Demography: Approximately 5,000,000 Slovaks and Czechs

Languages: Slovak, Czechoslavak

Currency: Koruna

Major Religions: Roman Catholic, Protestant

Orphans Admitted into the United States
Fiscal year 1996: 0
Fiscal year 1995: 0

Adoption Information: The authority in charge of the legal regulations for adoptions and child-placing matters in Slovakia is the Ministry of Social Affairs, Labor, and Family. A written request must be presented to the appropriate guardian authority, usually the Department of Youth at the local Town Hall.

Slovak orphanages house about 2,500 children aged 3-18 in 56 orphanages in Slovakia. About 10 percent of these children are in the process of being adopted; 40 percent have different guardians from their parents, and the remaining 40 percent were placed in orphanages for legal institutional care. Due to the small number of children who are "legally free for adoption" combined with defective Slovak legislation, there were no Slovak children adopted by foreigners until recently.

Slovak parliament has passed a new law on adoptions No. 48-1996 Coll. This law is an amendment to the currently valid law 97-1963 about the international private and process law and which at the same time changes legal conditions for international adoptions of children who are citizens of the Slovak Republic. This new law may make future international adoptions more common.

Contact the U.S. Consulate for the names of lawyers who can assist with adoptions.

U.S. Embassy/Visa Issuing Post
U.S. Embassy, Consular Section
Hviezdoslavovo Namestie 4
81102 Bratislava
Telephone: [42] (7) 533-0861
Fax: [42] (7) 533-5439

SPAIN

Geography: A large country of 504,745 square kilometers in western Europe bordering France and Portugal

Capital: Madrid

Demography: 39,187,000 of Spanish, Basque, Catalan, and Galician descent

Language: Spanish

Currency: Peseta

Major Religion: Roman Catholic

Orphans Admitted into the United States
Fiscal year 1996: 0
Fiscal year 1995: 0

Adoption Information: Spanish law provides for the adoption of Spanish children by foreigners when all requirements and qualifications are met. The different Autonomous Communities (equivalent to State Government) in Spain are responsible for adoptions in their regions. Available children are turned over to the Autonomous Communities for adoption. These institutions in turn send the children to foster parents who after a period of time (usually nine months to a year), can become the adopting parents. It is mandatory that the institution in charge of adoptions in the area makes a statement supporting the adoption by the applicants. Applicants must be prepared to remain in Spain for the entire procedure.

Applicants must personally contact the Autonomous Community office in Madrid at the address listed below. This institution selects families for the children they have available. The selection is made by the institution's social worker and a psychologist who try to find the most suitable home for the child. There is an estimated waiting period of nine months from the time an application is accepted by the Community until a child is turned over to the requesting family for custody. After the child is placed, the institution maintains contact to assure the adjustment of the foster parents and the child. The Autonomous Community attorney takes charge of all legal processing for the adoption.

Adoption Authority
Servicio Regional de
  Beinestar Social
Unidad de Acogimiento
  Familiar y Adopciones
c/o O'Donnell , 52
28009 Madrid
Tel: [34] (1) 574-3875
and 573-3829

U.S. Embassy/Visa Issuing Post
U.S. Embassy, Consular Section
Serrano 75
28006 Madrid
Tel: [34] (1) 587-2200
Fax: [34] (1) 587-2303

Mailing address:
APO AE 09642

TURKEY

Geography: A nation located between southwestern Europe and the Middle East Peninsula

Capital: Ankara

Demography: 55,900,000 persons of Mediterranean, Caucasian, and Mongolian heritage

Language: Turkish

Currency: Turkish Lira

Major Religion: Islam

Orphans Admitted into the United States
Fiscal year 1996: 1
Fiscal year 1995: 9

Adoption Information: Adoptions are governed by the Turkish Civil Code, which requires the adopting parents to be at least 40 years of age, at least 18 years older than the child to be adopted, and have no biological children. The final adoption decree is issued in court.

Government Authority in Charge of Adoptions
General Directorate of Social Services
and Child Protection Agency
Anafartalar Caddes i, No. 70
Ankara, Turkey

U.S. Embassy/Visa Issuing Post
American Embassy, Consular Section
110 Ataturk Blvd.
Ankara, Turkey
Tel: [90] (312) 468-6110
Fax: [90] (312) 467-0019

Mailing Address:
PSC 93
Box 5000
APO AE 09823

Latin America

The geographic designation of Latin America includes Mexico, the countries of Central and South America, and the Caribbean Islands.

ARGENTINA

Geography: Argentina, the eighth largest country in the world, forms the southeastern part of South America.

Capital: Buenos Aires

Demography: Argentina's population of 32,300,000 is made up mainly of people of European descent, including Spanish, Italian, German, French, and other nationalities. In the northern parts of the country about two percent of the people are mestizos; a few Amerindians remain in southern Patagonia, the Chaco, and the northwestern highlands.

Language: Spanish; little English is spoken

Currency: Peso

Major Religion: Roman Catholic

Adoption Information: Individuals over 35 years old who have been married for at least five years, and who do not have children, may adopt in Argentina. Medical evidence of sterility must be presented. Persons over 35 who are widowed, divorced, or single may also adopt. It is extremely difficult for nonresidents to adopt in Argentina.

Another approach to adoption in Argentina is through judges who are willing to arrange guardianships for foreign adopters. The final adoption can then be granted abroad. The law states (Chapter V, Article 32): "The rights and duties of the adopter(s) and the adopted will be ruled by the law of the address of the adopted at the time of the adoption, when granted abroad."

Adoption Authority

Dirección de la Minoridad General
Humberto 1762, Cuarto piso, 1103 Capital Federal
Buenos Aires, Argentina
Tel: [54] (1) 27-9707

Private Adoption Agency

Director por el Equipo de Adopción
Movimiento Familiar Cristiano
Concepción Arenal 3540, 1427 Capital Federal
Buenos Aires, Argentina

U.S. Embassy/Visa Issuing Post

U.S. Embassy   *Mailing Address:*
4300 Colombia   APO AA 34034 Unit 4334
1425 Buenos Aires, Argentina
Tel: [54] (1) 777-4533
Fax: [54] (1) 777-0197

BAHAMAS

Geography: The Bahamas are made up of about 3,000 coral islands and reefs extending from the Straits of Florida to the northeastern tip of Cuba.

Capital: Nassau

Demography: About 80 percent of the population of 250,000 are descendants of slaves who were brought to the islands by the British loyalists after the Revolutionary War; the rest of the people are whites and mulattoes (persons of mixed Caucasian and Negro ancestry).

Language: English

Currency: Bahamian Dollar

Major Religions: Protestant, Anglican

Adoption Information: Bahamian law allows adoption by any person with legal status in the Bahamas, including tourists. The entire adoption procedure requires a minimum of three months, with the Department of Social Services acting as the representative of the child's interests. A lawyer must guide the process through the supreme court. Children are required to be adopted in the

Bahamas, unless the guardian grants permission for a guardianship. While there are no court fees, the lawyers charge a fee for their services (between $400 to $1,000).

Personal contact between adopters and adoption sources is preferable. Private adoptions are arranged by local attorneys, and prospective adopters should contact an attorney recommended by the U.S. Embassy or another reputable person.

Adoption Authority
Department of Social Services

U.S. Embassy/Visa Issuing Post
U.S. Embassy
Mosmar Building, Queen Street
Nassau, Bahamas
Tel: (809) 322-1181/328-2206
Fax: (809) 328-7838

Mailing Address:
P.O. Box N-8197
Nassau, Bahamas

BARBADOS

Geography: The U.S. Consular district of Barbados also includes Anguilla, Antigua, the British Virgin Islands, Dominica, Grenada, Saint Kitts-Nevis, Saint Lucia, and Saint Vincent. The islands of Barbados, Dominica, Grenada, Saint Lucia, and Saint Vincent are independent nations in the West Indies; the islands of Anguilla, Antigua, and Saint Kitts-Nevis are states in association with Great Britain; the British Virgin Islands is a British possession.

Capital: Bridgetown

Demography: Although the 255,000 people of these islands represent many different races and nationalities, most are Blacks whose ancestors were brought to the West Indies as slaves. Other groups include people of Chinese, Danish, Dutch, East Indian, English, French, Portuguese, Spanish, and Carib-Indian heritage.

Languages: English, Spanish, French, and Creole (an English/African patois)

Currency: Barbados Dollar

Major Religion: Anglican, African religions, Roman Catholic

Orphans Admitted into the United States
Fiscal year 1996: 1
Fiscal year 1995: 0

Adoption Information: Citizens of countries with which Barbados has diplomatic or consular relations may adopt Barbadian children. This includes U.S. citizens. Adoptive parents who are non-nationals may obtain a final decree if they are domiciled and residing in Barbados. If they live abroad, they must obtain authorization for guardianship with the intent of adopting abroad. The judge must be satisfied that the minor will be lawfully admitted to the adoptive parent's country. Normally it takes non-nationals between six months and a year to adopt a child in Barbados.

In St. Vincent, the Child Care Board makes arrangements for adoptions and carries out investigations. The Adoption Board is chaired by the Senior Magistrate in St. Vincent. The application to the court in St. Vincent for an adoption order shall not be made by the adopter until the expiration of a period of six months from the date the child was delivered into the care and possession of the adopter pursuant to the arrangements made by the Adoption Board.

Any married couple domiciled and resident in St. Vincent and at least 25 years of age may adopt as may any relative of the child at least 21 years old or the mother or father of the child. A married person adopting a child must have the consent of his/her spouse and the parent of the child. All adoptions must take place in St. Vincent. British subjects may obtain a license permitting adoption outside of St. Vincent.

Adoption Authority

Barbados Child Care Board
Cotton Park Complex, Waldron St.
Bridgetown, Barbados, West Indies
General Office: [246] 426-2577
Director's Tel: [246] 429-3691

U.S. Embassy/Visa Issuing Post

U.S. Embassy
Canadian Imperial Bank of
  Commerce Building
Broad Street
Bridgetown, Barbados, West Indies
Tel: [246] 436-4950
Fax: [246] 429-5246

Mailing Address:
P.O. Box 302
Bridgetown, Barbados, W.I.

or FPO AA 34055

BELIZE

Geography: Located on the east coast of Central America, Belize is about the size of Massachusetts and is bordered by Mexico and Guatemala. A former British colony, Belize gained its independence in 1981.

Capital: In 1975 the capital was moved from Belize City, which is on the coast, inland to Belmopan, which offers more protection from hurricanes. The U.S. Consulate is still located in Belize City (40,000).

Demography: Creole (African/English), Mestizo, Maya, and Carib-Indian groups, as well as East Indian, African, Asian, and Caucasian minorities make up the population of about 187,000.

Languages: English, Spanish, and Mayan

Currency: Belizean dollar

Major Religion: Anglican

Orphans Admitted into the United States
Fiscal year 1996: 7
Fiscal year 1995: 1

Adoption Information: Belizean adoption law is not fully delineated and is in the process of revision. While U.S. citizens may adopt in Belize, Belizean adoption law requires that both the adoptive parents and the child reside in Belize. However, Belizean law does not specify residence requirements, which have often been liberally interpreted to mean being physically present long enough to accomplish the adoption. Adoptive parents must be at least 25 years of age and 21 years older than the child. The process of adoption in Belize can take as long as two years. Cases are processed by the Belize Supreme Court and do not require the services of a private attorney.

U.S. Embassy/Visa Issuing Post
U.S. Embassy
Gabourel Lane and Hutson Street
Belize City, Belize, Central America
Tel: [501] (2) 77161
Fax: [501] (2) 30802

Mailing Address:
P.O. Box 286
Belize City, Belize
Central America

or APO AA 34025

BERMUDA

Geography: Britain's oldest self-governing colony, Bermuda is comprised of a group of about 365 islands, of which 16 are inhabited.

Capital: Hamilton

Demography: 58,000, the majority of whom are either of African descent or biracial. There is a minority of Anglo-Saxons.

Language: English

Currency: Bermuda Dollar

Major Religion: Anglican

Orphans Admitted into the United States
Fiscal year 1996: 0
Fiscal year 1995: 0

Adoption Information: Private adoptions in Bermuda are handled through lawyers.

Adoption Authority
Ministry of Health,
  Social Services, and Housing
Old Hospital Building
7 Point Finger Road
Paget DV 04,
P.O. Box HM 380
Hamilton HM BX, Bermuda

U.S. Embassy/Visa Issuing Post
U.S. Consular General
Crown Hill, 16 Middle Road,
Devonshire
P.O. Box HM325
Hamilton HMBX, Bermuda
Tel: (441) 295-1342
Fax: (441) 295-1592

Mailing Address:
PSC 1002
FPO AE 09727-1002

BOLIVIA

Geography: Bolivia is the fifth largest country in South America. It is bordered by Brazil on the north and east; Paraguay on the southeast; Argentina on the south; and Chile and Peru on the west.

Demography: More than half of Bolivia's 7,300,000 people are Amerindians; the rest are mestizos and Europeans.

Capital: La Paz

Languages: Although Spanish is the official language, Aymará and Quechuan are more widely used. Little English is spoken.

Currency: Bolivian Peso

Major Religion: Roman Catholic

Orphans Admitted into the United States
Fiscal year 1996: 33
Fiscal year 1995: 21

Adoption Information: A new adoption law exists in Bolivia, which now legalizes foreign adoption. Adopters must be at least 30 years old and unable to have biological children. They must prove their inability to have children by presenting a medical certificate. At least one of the adopters usually stays in Bolivia for two to three weeks. Adoptions are under the jurisdiction of the Court of Family and the National Department of Social Services (NDSS). The National Organization of Minors, Women, and Family is in charge of orphanages.

Adoption Authority

Secretaría Nacional de Servicios Sociales, NDSS
(National Department of Social Services)
La Paz, Bolivia

and

Organismo Nacional de Memores, mujer y familia (ONAMFA)
(National Organization of Minors, Women, and Family)
Casillas 5960
Edificio Lotería Nacional
La Paz, Bolivia
Tel: [591] (2) 376862
Fax: [591] (11) 366763

U.S. Embassy/Visa Issuing Post

U.S. Embassy
Consular Section
Arce No. 2780
La Paz, Bolivia
Tel: [591] (2) 430251
Fax: [591] (2) 433900

Mailing Address:
APO AA 34032

BRAZIL

Geography: Colossal Brazil is the largest country in Latin America and the fifth largest country in the world. Its 21 states, four territories, and federal district are slightly larger than the 48 continental United States.

Capital: Brasília

Demography: 150,400,000. About 60 percent of the Brazilian people have European ancestry (Italian, Portuguese, Spanish, and German); more than 25 percent are of mixed ancestry (European, African, and Indian). About 10 percent of the people are Black, and one percent are Amerindian. Most of the people who live in northern, northwestern, and central Brazil are Indians; those in the northeastern coastal area are of African ancestry; those in the southeastern area are of European ancestry; and those within the triangle formed by Brasília, Sao Paulo, and Rio de Janeiro are mixed. Brazil's estimated population of 150 million is about half of the entire population of Latin America. One-half of all Brazilians are less than 25 years of age.

Languages: Portuguese; some English is spoken in major cities.

Currency: Cruzeiro

Major Religion: Roman Catholic

Orphans Admitted into the United States
Fiscal year 1996: 103
Fiscal year 1995: 146

Adoption Information: Singles and couples over 21 may adopt. They must be at least 16 years older than the orphan. Only approved adoption agencies are allowed to act on behalf of the adopting parents.

In accordance with the new law, priority in adoptions is given to Brazilian citizens. Brazilians most often prefer to adopt healthy white infants. Judges do not like to split up sibling groups. As a result, foreigners willing to adopt more than one child, an older or non-white child, or one with medical problems or deformities have the greatest chance of adopting in Brazil.

In the case of adoption by a foreigner resident or domiciled outside of Brazil, there is a probationary period of joint residence which must be completed within Brazilian territory before a final decree of adoption will be granted. The period of joint residence is at least 15 days for children less than two years of age and at least 30 days for children more than two.

Approximately two million abandoned children live in the streets of Brazil's cities; many of them struggle for survival in Rio de Janeiro, Recife, and Belém.

Adoption Authority
Brazilian states have a Febem (Department of Social Service). The address for Brasília is:

Febem
Fundacao do Servico
Social do Distrito Federal
E. IRB -11 Andai
Sector Bancário - SBS
CEP 70.00 - Brasília-DF

U.S. Embassy/Visa Issuing Post
U.S. Consul General
Avenida das Nacoes, Lote 3
Rio de Janeiro Unit 3501
Tel: [55] (61) 321-7272
Fax: [55] (61) 225-9136

Mailing Address:
APO AA 34030

CHILE

Geography: Chile is the southernmost country of Latin America. It occupies a long, narrow ribbon of land between the Pacific Ocean and the Andes Mountains.

Capital: Santiago

Demography: About one-third of Chile's 13.2 million people are mestizos, two percent are Araucanian Indians, and most of the rest are descended from Spanish or other European settlers.

Languages: Spanish; some English is spoken in the cities

Currency: Peso

Major Religion: Roman Catholic

Orphans Admitted into the United States
Fiscal year 1996: 63
Fiscal year 1995: 90

Adoption Information: Couples must be 20 years older than the child to be adopted and married for at least three years. Singles are seldom accepted, even for older children. To be adopted, a child with a living parent must be declared abandoned by a family court with jurisdiction over the child's place of residence. Such a declaration is based on the mother's irrevocable and final release of the child to the court or to the prospective adoptive parents.

Because non-resident foreigners may not adopt, they are given guardianship and authority to take the child out of Chile. This authority is transmitted through a court order. A huge disparity in fees is the result of a system dominated entirely by private attorneys. SENAME, the Chilean Child Welfare Service, has been appointed to handle all applications before presentation in court.

The Chilean Consul with jurisdiction over your state must issue a certificate that all state and U.S. preadoption requirements have been met, before a dossier is accepted by SENAME. The adopting parents must appear personally before a judge in Chile. Married couples may request the judge to require the presence of only one spouse. The adoptive parent usually stays in Chile about two weeks in order to obtain the guardianship and emigrate the child. A new law is under discussion to change from guardianships to final decrees.

Adoption Authority
SENAME
Avenida Pedro de Valdivia #40-70
Santiago, Chile

U.S. Embassy/Visa Issuing Post
U.S. Embassy
Ave. Andres Bello 2800
Santiago, Chile
South America
Tel: [56] (2) 232-2600
Fax: [56] (2) 330-3710

Mailing Address:
APO AA 34030

COLOMBIA

Geography: Colombia is the fourth largest country in South America, with coastlines on both the Atlantic and Pacific oceans. Columbia shares a border with Panama.

Capital: Bogotá

Demography: Of Colombia's 33,000,000 population, about 40 percent are mestizos; 30 percent whites, mostly of Spanish descent; 15 percent mulattoes; seven percent Amerindians (Colombia has 398 distinct tribes); and five percent Blacks. Bogotá has a high percentage of mestizos, while Medellín has a high percentage of people with European ancestry, and Cali has a tri-ethnic mixture of mestizos, Blacks, and people of European descent.

Languages: Spanish; English is spoken widely in major cities.

Currency: Peso

Major Religion: Roman Catholic

Orphans Admitted into the United States
Fiscal year 1996: 255
Fiscal year 1995: 350

Adoption Information: Singles are accepted, although couples are preferred. For married couples, at least one of the adopting parents must be over 25 years of age and be physically, emotionally, and economically capable of supporting a child. In practice, newborns are assigned to younger couples, and older children are assigned to older couples. The child to be adopted must not be over 16 years of age.

The law establishes that only sources licensed by the ICBF (Instituto Colombiano de Bienestar Familiar or Colombian Family Welfare Institute) and licensed Colombian adoption agencies can offer children for adoption. A short waiting period for orphaned, abandoned, and relinquished children takes place while relatives are sought. If none appear, a certificate of abandonment is issued by the court. Then when the child is placed, a final adoption decree is soon issued, which negates the possibility of the birth parents or adoptive parents overturning the adoption.

Private adoption agencies shelter abandoned children and some wards of the ICBF. Wards of the family welfare institute are usually housed in government orphanages. Since government orphanages usually provide minimal care, adopters may find it possible and desirable to arrange foster care for a child who has been assigned to them.

The ICBF, as well as most of the private agencies, works with adoption agencies rather than individuals. The exception is Casa de la Madre y el Niño, which will only place children directly with couples.

Adoption Authority
Dr. Mariá Jesus Dussan L.
Jefa de la Division de Adopciones
ICBF
Ave. 68 Calle 64
Santa Fe de Bogotá
Apartado Aéreo 18116
Colombia, South America
Tel: [57] (1) 231-4558

Licensed Adoption Agencies
Ayudame
Calle 128 No. 8-53
Apartado Aéreo #53761
Bogotá, Colombia
Tel: [57] (1) 213-5923

Fundacón Los Pisingos
Avenida 7a. No. 157-91
Bogotá, Colombia
Tel: [57] (1) 671-8591

Casa de la Madre y el Niño
Calle 48 #28-30
Apartado Aéreo 28263
Bogotá, Colombia
Tel: [57] (1) 244-2510

Centro de Adopción Chiquitines
Avenida Aguacatal No. 15-325
Juanambú
Apartado Aéreo 034516
Cali, Colombia
Tel: [57] (1) 880-1040

CRAN
Transversal 66 No. 164-90, Suba
Bogotá, Colombia
Tel: [57] (1) 681-4940

Casita de Nicolas
Carrera 50 No. #65-23
Apartado Aéreo 3800
Medellín, Colombia
Tel: [57] (4) 263-8086

FANA
Calle 155 No. 93-04
Bogotá, Colombia
Tel: [57] (1) 681-5037

U.S. Embassy/Visa Issuing Post
U.S. Embassy
Consular Section
Calle 22D-BIS
Bogotá, Colombia
Tel: [57] (1) 315-0811
Fax: [57] (1) 315-2197

Mailing Address:
APO AA 34038

COSTA RICA

Geography: Costa Rica is a small, mountainous country in Central America, which has coastlines on both the Atlantic and Pacific oceans.

Capital: San José

Demography: More than 97 percent of Costa Rica's population of 3,015,000 are either mestizos or whites of unmixed European ancestry. Amerindians and blacks make up two small minority groups.

Languages: Spanish; some English is spoken in the larger cities.

Currency: Colón

Major Religion: Roman Catholic

Orphans Admitted into the United States
Fiscal year 1996: 20
Fiscal year 1995: 11

Adoption Information: Patronanto Nacional de la Infancia (PANI) requires that adoptive couples must be between 25 and 60 years of age and at least 15 years older than the adopted child. Children four years old or more may be adopted. They may be younger than four if they are part of a sibling group adopted together. Both spouses must travel to Costa Rica. Adoptions are processed through PANI.

Once a child is assigned, the couple must stay in Costa Rica for two weeks to initiate the adoption. Then, the child can be placed in foster care and both spouses can return home, or one can stay and care for the child. One spouse must return in 45 to 60 days for the final adoption decree and to obtain the child's U.S. visa before immigrating the child.

The Patronato does not charge a fee for child care or legal work. Excellent medical and psychological evaluations on each child are provided at the time of assignment. Adoptions through private attorneys or agencies must be authorized by the Patronato.

Adoption Authority
Patronato Nacional
    de la Infancia (PANI)
Apartado 5000
San José, Costa Rica

U.S. Embassy/Visa Issuing Post
U.S. Embassy
Consular Section
Pavas
San José, Costa Rica
Tel: [506] 220-3939
Fax: [506] 220-2305

Mailing Address:
APO AA 34020

CUBA

Geography: An island in the Caribbean of 114,524 square kilometers

Capital: Havana

Demography: The population is 10,600,000.

Language: Spanish

Currency: Cuban Peso

Major Religions: Roman Catholic, Voodoo

Orphans Admitted into the United States
Fiscal year 1996: 0
Fiscal year 1995: 0

Adoption Information: The United States does not have diplomatic relations with Cuba, and U.S. citizens generally are not allowed to travel to Cuba. The Swiss Embassy, U.S. Interest Section provided this information.

Foreigners are permitted to adopt in Cuba, but not surprisingly the standards they must adhere to are different from those that apply to Cuban nationals. Orphanages are run by local social workers under the direction of the Ministry of Education. For Cubans, legal adoptions are under the administration of the Ministry of Justice. For foreigners, however, legal jurisdiction for adoption matters start with the quasi-governmental institution known as the "Consultoria Juridica Internacional," located at 16th Street between 3rd and 5th Streets. Foreigners are required to contact a lawyer at the Consultoria to begin the adoption procedures.

Adoption Authority
Consultoría Juridíca Internacional
16th Street, between 3rd and 5th Streets
Mirimar, Havana
Tel: 33-24-37

or 33-26-97
33-28-61
33-29-90

Swiss Embassy/U.S. Interest Section
(USINT) Calzada between
L&M Street
Vedardo
Havana, Cuba
Tel: 33-3551/9
Fax: 33-3700

DOMINICAN REPUBLIC

Geography: The Dominican Republic makes up the eastern two-thirds of the island of Hispaniola in the Caribbean Sea; Haiti occupies the western third of the island.

Capital: Santo Domingo

Demography: About 65 percent of the 7,170,000 population are biracial, 20 percent are Blacks, and 15 percent are whites of European ancestry.

Language: Spanish

Currency: Peso

Major Religion: Roman Catholic

Orphans Admitted into the United States
Fiscal year 1996: 13
Fiscal year 1995: 15

Adoption Information: Preadoptive parents must be 40 years of age; however, if they are childless and have been married 20 years, only one spouse need be over 35 years. Adopters may already have adopted children, but they are not eligible to adopt if they have biological children. Although adopters must be 15 years older than the child they are adopting, this age difference may be reduced or waived by a judge in the Dominican Republic.

Only one spouse is required to travel to the Dominican Republic; the absent spouse signs a power of attorney form that authorizes the other spouse to act on his or her behalf. The government adoption department does not charge a fee for adoption services. Private attorneys also arrange adoptions. A final adoption decree is issued.

Adoption Authority
Doctora Martha Brown
Secretaría de Estado de Salud Pública y Asistencia Social
Avenida San Cristobal
Santo Domingo, Dominican Republic
Tel: [809] 565-3218

U.S. Embassy/Visa Issuing Post
U.S. Embassy
Consular Section
Corner of Calle Cesar Nicolas
Penson & Calle Leopoldo Navarro
Santo Domingo, Dominican Republic
Tel: [809] 541-2171
Fax: [809] 686-7437

Mailing Address:
APO AA 34041

ECUADOR

Geography: Ecuador is a small, mountainous country in South America that lies on the west coast of the continent between Colombia to the north and Peru to the south.

Capital: Quito. The largest city is Guayaquil, where the U.S. Consulate is located.

Demography: The population of 10,600,000 consists of about 40 percent mestizos, about 40 percent Amerindians, and about 10 percent whites of European ancestry.
Languages: Spanish; some English is spoken in the cities.

Currency: Sucre

Major Religion: Roman Catholic

Orphans Admitted into the United States
Fiscal year 1996: 51
Fiscal year 1995: 67

Adoption Information: Husbands must be between 30 and 50 years of age, and wives must be between 25 and 40. No prior divorce is permitted, and the couple must be married at least five years. Childless couples are given preference. If the couple has a biological child, they must present a statement of infertility in order to adopt a child of the opposite sex to the one they already have. If they have an adopted child, they may adopt a child of either sex. Some exceptions may be made for couples wishing to adopt a special needs child.

The wait between the assignment of the child and the adoption trip is about one week. Both spouses travel to Ecuador for a stay of about two weeks in Guayaquil. They receive custody during their stay. The final decree is issued five to six weeks later. Children can only be placed in Ecuador through licensed Ecuadorian agencies or the Ministerio de Bienestar Social who, in turn, license U.S. adoption agencies to place children.

Adoption Authority
Dirección Nacional de Protección de Menores
Departamento Técnico de Adopciones
Ministerio de Bienestar Social
Lizardo Garcia y Andes Xaura 123
Quito, Ecuador
Tel: [593] (2) 541-871

U.S. Embassy/Visa Issuing Post
Although the U.S. Embassy is in Quito, immigrant visas are processed at the U.S. Consulate General in Guayaquil.

U.S. Consulate General
Ave. 12 de Octubre y Av. Patria
Guayaquil, Ecuador
Tel: [593] (2) 562-890
Fax: [593] (2) 502-052

Mailing Address:
APO AA 34039

EL SALVADOR

Geography: Located on the Pacific coast between Guatemala and Honduras, El Salvador is the smallest and most densely populated country in Central America.

Capital: San Salvador

Demography: About 92 percent of El Salvador's 5,300,000 people are mestizos; nearly five percent are whites of unmixed ancestry, and three percent are U.S. citizens.

Language: Spanish; some English is spoken in the major cities.

Currency: Colón

Major Religion: Roman Catholic

Orphans Admitted into the United States
Fiscal year 1996: 17
Fiscal year 1995: 30

Adoption Information: Adopters must be more than 25 years old, and couples must be married at least two years. Generally, an orphan's birth documents are sent to preadoptive parents shortly after the child is assigned to them. Only one spouse is required to travel to El Salvador to obtain custody of the child; adopters stay in the country about one week. Proxy adoptions are permitted, as is the escorting of children. Juvenile court judges permit orphans to leave El Salvador provided that the adoptive parents agree to notify the court when the child is readopted in the United States. Guardianships, as well as final decrees, are granted. All adoption dossiers must be reviewed and the decrees granted by the government welfare department in San Salvador (The Procaclaria). Most orphans available for adoption are in government institutions which provide minimal care. Foster care may be arranged.

Adoption Authority
Jefe de Sección de Adopciónes
Procuradoría
General de la República
13 a Calle Poniente
Centro de Gobierno
San Salvador
Tel: (503) 22-444 or (503) 22-4133

also

Instituto Salvadoreño de Protección Menor
Ave. Irazu
Final Calle Santa Marta, Colonia, Costa Rica #2
San Salvador
Tel: (503) 270-4142

U.S. Embassy/Visa Issuing Post

U.S. Embassy   *Mailing Address:*
Consular Section   APO AA 34023
Final Blvd. Santa Elena
Antigua Cuscatlan
San Salvador, El Salvador
Central America
Tel: (503) 26-7100
Fax: (503) 26-5839

GRENADA

Geography: Small island off the coast of Venezuela, consisting of 344 square kilometers

Capital: St. George's

Demography: Population of 85,000, mostly of African and mixed heritage

Languages: English, French patois

Currency: East Caribbean Dollar

Major Religions: Christian, Protestant

Adoption Information: Although limited detailed information is available, international adoption is allowed in Grenada.

Adoption Authority

Adoptions are usually
    handled by this law firm:
Renwick & Payne
Church Street
St. George's, Grenada
Tel: (809) 440-2479

U.S. Embassy/Visa Issuing Post

U.S. Embassy
P.O. Box 54
St. George's,
Grenada, West Indies
Tel: (809) 444-1173
Fax: (809) 444-4820

Orphanage

The Queen Elizabeth Home for Children
Tempe Street
St. George's, Grenada
Tel: (809) 440-2327

GUATEMALA

Geography: With 108,888 square kilometers, Guatemala is the third largest of the Central American countries. Guatemala shares a long border with Mexico and has coastlines on both the Atlantic and Pacific oceans.

Capital: Guatemala City

Demography: About 55 percent of Guatemala's 9,200,000 people are mestizos; most of the remaining 45 percent are Amerindians. The infant mortality rate is 95 per 1,000 births; 82 percent of urban children and 95 percent of rural children suffer from chronic malnutrition.

Languages: Spanish and Mayan; some English is spoken in the larger cities.

Currency: Quetzal

Major Religion: Roman Catholic

Orphans Admitted into the United States
Fiscal year 1996: 427
Fiscal year 1995: 449

Adoption Information: Couples between 25 and 50, married at least one year, as well as single women over 25, may adopt. Adoptable children must be orphans or, if there is a living parent, must be unconditionally released for adoption through a declaration to a private attorney. Private and church-run agencies may have additional requirements.

Adoptions in Guatemala follow either the public (judicial) or the private (extrajudicial) route, depending on the status of the child to be adopted. Public adoptions, which require a court decree declaring that the child has been abandoned, are only processed when the biological parents are known to have died or deserted the child. This process grants considerable discretion to the judge and normally takes about a year to complete. Public adoptions are under the jurisdiction of the Dirección de Bienestar Infantil y Familiar (see address below).

Under the private adoption procedure, the natural parent makes a declaration of release of the child to an attorney who represents both the natural and the adoptive parents. Guatemalan adoption law requires a document review by the Attorney General's office and a social worker's report on the natural and adoptive parents. The private adoption process usually takes about six months to complete. All Guatemalan children must be adopted there; however, adopters are not required to remain in Guatemala during the entire adoption process.

In private adoptions, the private adoption agencies of Guatemala place children through a child-placing contract with several U.S. adoption agencies and help arrange final adoptions or guardianships. Some provide an escort service for orphans from newborn to grade school age.

Adoption Authority

Hogar Elisa Martinez
Director of Adoption Program
Secretaria de Bienestar Infantil y Familar
4a Avenida 15-64, Zona 1
Guatemala City, Guatemala
Tel: [502] (2) 22-67-47

(for abandoned children)

Private Guatemalan Adoption Agencies

Alycon Ruth Fleck
Hogar Campestre Adventista "Los Pinos"
(Seventh Day Adventist couples)
15 Avenida 19-62, Zona 13
Guatemala City, Guatemala
Apartado 35-C,
Tel: [502] (2) 31-00-56

Joyce Heinlein
Agua Viva (located at Km.
18, Carretera Roosevelt)
Apartado 10
Guatemala City, Guatemala
Tel: [502] (2) 92-12-07

Roberto Wer
Asociación Amigos
 de Todos Los Niños
19 Calle 12-57, Zona 11
Guatemala City, Guatemala
Tel: [502] (2) 48-14-23

Sor Josephina Fumagalli
Mater Orphanorum
Km. 14 and 1/2 Carretera
 San Juan
Sacatepequez
Guatemala City, Guatemala
Tel: [502] (2) 91-00-87

Luz del Carmen
 Morales Catalán de Paredes
Patronato Contra la Mendicidad
5a Avenida 4-26, Zona 1
Guatemala City, Guatemala
Tel: [502] (2) 58-86-96

AGAND
15 Calle 5-20
Zona 11
Guatemala City, Guatemala
Tel: [502] (2) 73-18-00

U.S. Embassy/Visa Issuing Post

U.S. Embassy
Consular Section
7-01 Avenida de la Reforma, Zone 10
Guatemala City, Guatemala
Central America
Tel: [502] (2) 31-15-41
Fax: [502] (2) 31-88-85

Mailing Address:
APO AA 34024

HAITI

Geography: Haiti occupies the western third of the Caribbean island of Hispaniola, which lies between Cuba and Puerto Rico.

Capital: Port-au-Prince

Demography: Most of Haiti's 6,513,000 people are descendants of Africans who were brought to Haiti as slaves; about five percent are biracial.

Languages: French and Creole (a French/African patois).

Currency: Gourde

Major Religions: Roman Catholic, Voodoo

Orphans Admitted into the United States
Fiscal year 1996: 68
Fiscal year 1995: 49

Adoption Information: As of February 1991, Haitian law requires that a completed final adoption decree must be issued in Haiti before a child can leave the country. The adoption process normally takes from two to six months, but can stretch to longer than a year. The host government is involved in two distinct stages. The court issues adoption decrees, and· The Ministry of Social Affairs provides adoption authorizations. While it is possible to complete the adoption process without the use of a local attorney, the U.S. Embassy will refer you to competent Haitian counsel.

Adoption Authority	**U.S. Embassy/Visa Issuing Post**
Ministry of Social Affairs	U.S. Embassy
	Harry Truman Boulevard
	P.O. Box 1761
	Port-au-Prince, Haiti
	Tel: (509) 22-0354, 22-0368
	Fax: (509) 23-1614

HONDURAS

Geography: Second largest of the Central American countries, Honduras is bordered by Guatemala and Nicaragua. Honduras has a long coastline on the Caribbean Sea and a small strip of coastline on the Pacific Ocean.

Capital: Tegucigalpa

Demography: With 5,138,000 people, about 95 percent are mestizos; the rest are small minorities of Amerindians and Blacks.

Languages: Spanish; some English is spoken in the larger cities.

Currency: Lempira

Major Religion: Roman Catholic

Orphans Admitted into the United States
Fiscal year 1996: 28
Fiscal year 1995: 28

Adoption Information: At least one member of the adoptive couple must be 25 years of age. Both prospective parents must be of good conduct and reputation and have the means to feed, educate, and care for the child. A single person may adopt if she or he is at least 25 years old. The above provisions are strictly enforced by the Junta Nacional de Bienestar Social (JNBS), the Honduran government agency that oversees the adoption process. The Junta will only work with agencies accredited by them.

Children eligible for adoption must be at least 15 years younger than the youngest adopting parent. The child must be either abandoned or relinquished. Honduran law defines a child as abandoned if its parents are unknown, cannot be found, or have refused to care for the child. A relinquished child is one whose parent(s) voluntarily release the child for adoption. The parent(s) must appear before a court to renounce all parental rights before the child can be adopted.

Honduran adoption takes about eight to ten months. All children must be assigned by the Junta. U.S. citizens wishing to adopt in Honduras must plan to be there for about two weeks for the initial assessment sessions. In the case of a couple, both adoptive parents must be present. After these sessions, the prospective parents may leave the country and allow their attorney to handle the rest of the proceedings. Honduran law requires that a final adoption decree be issued in Honduras before a child leaves the country.

Adoption Authority
Junta Nacional de Bienestar Social (JNBS)
J.R. Molina, #518
Tegucigalpa, D.C., Honduras
Tel: (504) 22-1030 or (504) 22-3735

U.S. Embassy/Visa Issuing Post
U.S. Embassy
Consular Section
Avenida La Paz
Tegucigalpa, Honduras
Tel: (504) 36-9320
Fax: (504) 36-9037

Mailing Address:
APO AA 34022

JAMAICA

Geography: Jamaica is a Caribbean island that lies 480 miles south of Florida.

Capital: Kingston

Demography: About 90 percent of Jamaica's population of 2,500,000 are descendants of Africans who were brought to Jamaica as slaves.

Languages: English and Creole (an English/African patois)

Currency: Jamaican Dollar

Major Religions: Protestant, Roman Catholic

Orphans Admitted into the United States
Fiscal year 1996: 34
Fiscal year 1995: 45

Adoption Information: Only Jamaicans who have become naturalized U.S. citizens can obtain a final adoption decree. All others must obtain a guardianship and adopt the child in their home country.

Adoptions are completed in Jamaica in three to six months. The adoption board oversees a home study and other preadoption requirements, then issues a license to adopt. Next, a court hearing is scheduled and at least one of the adopting parents must appear. Since the Adoption Board prepares all of the necessary documents, private attorneys are not necessary. At present, there are no official fees for a Jamaican adoption; however, the U.S. Embassy in Kingston expects this policy to change in the future. The only costs borne by prospective parents are payments toward foster care during the processing period.

Adoption Authority
The Adoption Board Children's Services
10 Chelsea Ave.
Kingston 10, Jamaica
West Indies

U.S. Embassy/Visa Issuing Post
U.S. Embassy
Consular Section
Jamaica Mutual Life Center
2 Oxford Road, 3rd Floor
Kingston, Jamaica
Tel: (809) 929-4850
Fax: (809) 926-6743

MEXICO

Geography: Mexico is the northernmost country of Latin America. High mountains and rolling plateaus cover more than two-thirds of the country. Mexico also has tropical forests, barren deserts, and fertile valleys.

Capital: Mexico City

Demography: More than 70 percent of Mexico's 88.6 million people are mestizos; about 20 percent are Amerindians, and less than 10 percent are whites of European ancestry. Maya Indians live mainly in the Mexican states of Campeche, Quintana Roo, and Yucatán.

Languages: Although Spanish is the official language, more than ninety Amerindian languages are still in use. About one million Indians speak only their native language.

Currency: Peso

Major Religion: Roman Catholic

Orphans Admitted into the United States
Fiscal year 1996: 76
Fiscal year 1995: 83

Adoption Information: The adopting parents may be married or single, and male or female. All adopters must be at least 25 years of age and at least 17 years older than the child. In the case of a married couple, only one of the adoptive parents must meet the 17-year seniority requirement. If the child is over 14 years old, he or she must agree to the adoption.

The Mexican government welfare department, Sistema Nacional Para el Desarrollo Integral de la Famila (DIF), in each state is assigned responsibility for determining a child's eligibility for adoption. A child is considered legally abandoned six months after a determination by the public ministry of the municipality in which the child lives.

Mexico ratified the Hague Convention and prefers to work with other countries that also ratified.

Approximately 700,000 abandoned children live on the streets of the cities in Mexico's 31 states and the federal district of Mexico City.

Adoption Authority
Sistema Nacional Para el
  Desarrollo Integral de la Famila (DIF)
Prolongación Xochialco 960
Colonia Santa Cruz Atoyae
Cóctigo Postal 03300
Mexico, DF
Tel: [52] (5) 601-2222 ext. 6031

U.S. Embassy/Visa Issuing Posts
U.S. Consulate-General
Paseo de la Reforma 305
Mexico DF
Tel: [52] (5) 211-0042
Fax: [52] (5) 208-3373

Mailing Address:
P.O. Box 10545
El Paso, Texas 79995-0545

NICARAGUA

Geography: Nicaragua, the largest of the Central American countries, is bordered by Honduras to the north and Costa Rica to the south.

Capital: Managua (400,000)

Demography: Mestizos make up about 75 percent of the population of 3,871,000; Black and Amerindian minorities live in the coastal areas near the Caribbean Sea.

Languages: Spanish; some English is spoken in the larger cities.

Currency: Córdoba

Major Religion: Roman Catholic

Orphans Admitted into the United States
Fiscal year 1996: 14
Fiscal year 1995: 10

Adoption Information: The adoptive parents must work directly with the FONIF (see address below) until the final stage of the adoption. Once the FONIF authorizes the adoption, the adopting parents may hire a lawyer to complete the adoption procedures. Adoptions arranged by foreigners directly with the birth parents or private orphanages whether personally or through the offices of an attorney or adoption agency are almost universally disapproved by FONIF. Though in some cases local attorneys have managed to obtain court decrees for such arrangements, these adoptions are not valid under Nicaraguan law without FONIF approval. Lists of attorneys are available from the American Embassy or the Department of State Office of American Citizens Services.

Adoption Authority
FONIF (Fondo Nicaraguense Para la Niñez la Familia
Managua, Nicaragua

U.S. Embassy/Visa Issuing Post
U.S. Embassy
Km. 4-1/2 Carretera Sur.
Managua, Nicaragua
Tel: [505] (2) 666010, 666013, 666015 through 18
Fax: [505] (2) 666074

Mailing Address:
APO AA 34021

PANAMA

Geography: Panama is the southernmost country in Central America; it is divided by the Panama Canal, which runs through the Canal Zone between the Atlantic and Pacific oceans.

Capital: Panama City

Demography: Most of Panama's 2,418,000 people are of mixed white, Indian, and African ancestry; 14 percent are Black, nine percent are whites of European ancestry, and seven percent are Amerindians.

Languages: Spanish; English is widely understood.

Currency: Balboa (which is really the U.S. dollar)

Major Religion: Roman Catholic

Orphans Admitted into the United States
Fiscal year 1996: 10
Fiscal year 1995: 24

Adoption Information: The Tribunal Tutelar de Menores (Minors' Court) has jurisdiction over the adoption case if the child is an orphan, legally abandoned, or declared a ward of the court. The Juzagados de Circuito (Circuit Courts) have jurisdiction when the child has been voluntarily surrendered by the biological parent(s) to the adopting parent(s). Persons interested in adopting through a circuit court should contact the American Embassy to determine if the child meets the definition of orphan, or if the child must reside for at least two years with the adoptive parents in Panama before becoming eligible for an immigrant visa.

If adopting through the Minor's Court, a judge will appoint the prospective adoptive parents as the child's legal guardians for a trial period. At the end of the trial period-which is usually six months or less-the judge will determine if the child's adjustment has been successful. If so, the adoption is finalized. If the judge is concerned about the child's welfare, he or she may extend the trial period, or cancel the adoption process altogether. Cancellation is extremely rare. If adopting through a circuit court, no trial period is required.

Adoption Authority
Tribunal Tutelar de Menores
Avenida de los Poetas
Chorillo, Panama

U.S. Embassy/Visa Issuing Post
U.S. Embassy
Apartado 6959,
Panama City, 5 Panama
Tel: (507) 227-1777
Fax: (507) 227-1964

Mailing Address:
APO AA 34002

PARAGUAY

Geography: Paraguay is a landlocked country in the heart of South America, bordered by Brazil, Argentina, and Bolivia.

Capital: Asuncion

Demography: Most of the population of 2,804,000 are mestizos; the rest are Guarani Indians.

Languages: Although Spanish is the official language, Guarani, the language of the Guarani Indians, is spoken almost as widely as Spanish.

Currency: Guaraní

Major Religion: Roman Catholic

Orphans Admitted into the United States
Fiscal year 1996: 258 (old cases, finally completed)
Fiscal year 1995: 351

Adoption Information: Paraguay suspended new international adoption cases effective September 18, 1995, pending the promulgation of new family law codes. No new cases are currently being accepted by the courts. Cases that are already in the courts have been subject to lengthy delays, and have received considerable negative media attention. The prospect for resumption of international adoptions in Paraguay is uncertain, but it is doubtful that you can expect to look to Paraguay as a source for international adoptions in the near future.

U.S. Embassy/Visa Issuing Post
U.S. Embassy
1776 Mariscal Lopez Ave.
Asunción, Paraguay
Telephone: [595] (21) 213-715
Fax: [595] (21) 213-728

Mailing Address:
APO AA 34036-0001

PERU

Geography: Located on the northern half of South America's west coast, Peru has three main land regions: the arid coastal area, the highland of the Andes Mountains, and the thick rainforests and jungles to the east of the Andes.

Capital: Lima

Demography: About 46 percent of Peru's 21.5 million people are Amerindians; about 43 percent are mestizos, and about 10 percent are whites of unmixed European ancestry.

Languages: Spanish and Quechua, the language of the Incas, are the official languages; some highland Indians speak Aymara.

Currency: Nuevo Sol

Major Religion: Roman Catholic

Orphans Admitted into the United States
Fiscal year 1996: 17
Fiscal year 1995: 15

Adoption Information: All adoptions are handled through agencies approved by the central authority in Lima.

Adoption Authority
> Secretariá Técnica de Adopciónes
> Av. Pablo Cazziguiry No. 415-Córpac
> San Isidro, Lima 27 Peru
> Tel: [51] (12) 224-2918

U.S. Embassy/Visa Issuing Post
U.S. Embassy
Av. Encalada, Cuadra 17, Monterrico
Lima 1, Peru
Tel: [51] (12) 21-1202
Fax: [51] (12) 21-3543

Mailing Address:
P.O. Box 1995
Lima, Peru

or: APO AA 34031

PUERTO RICO (U.S. POSSESSION)

Geography: Puerto Rico is a fertile, mountainous island in the West Indies about 1,000 miles southeast of Florida. It is a self-governing commonwealth associated with the United States.

Capital: San Juan

Demography: Most of Puerto Rico's three million people are mixed race, Spanish, Indian, Black, with minorities of mestizo, and whites of Spanish descent.

Languages: English and Spanish

Currency: U.S. Dollar

Major Religions: Roman Catholic, Protestant

Adoption Information: Because Puerto Rico is a United States Commonwealth, it does not have entry requirements for adoptive parents from the United States, and no immigration visas are necessary for orphans adopted by U.S. citizens. Private, independent adoptions are arranged by third parties such as relatives of the adopted child. Puerto Rico does not have child welfare services at this time.

Adoption Authority
Program Director of Services to Family and Children
Miramar Naval Base
P.O. Box 11398, Fernandez Juncof Station
Santurce, Puerto Rico 00910

SURINAME

Geography: Suriname is a small country on the northern coast of South America, which is covered mostly by mountainous rainforests.

Capital: Paramaribo (150,000)

Demography: More than one-third of the population of 481,000 are Hindustanis whose ancestors came from India; another third of the people are Creoles who have mixed African and European ancestry.

Languages: Dutch is the official language; English is widely spoken. The lingua franca is Sranang Tongo, also called taki-taki.

Currency: Guilder

Major Religions: Christian, Hindu, Islam

Adoption Information: Although Surinamese nationals are given priority in adopting, U.S. citizens may adopt in Suriname. Most Surinamese children in adoptive placements are from unmarried mothers. Almost ninety percent come from ethnically East Indian mothers.

The adoption process in Suriname begins when a mother declares in writing that she wishes to place her child in adoption. The Suriname government strongly encourages all arrangements be conducted by them. U.S. citizens not resident in Suriname must allow for a six- to eight-week stay in Suriname in order to adopt a Surinamese child. The authorities will release the child into the custody of the new family only after they can demonstrate that the child has permission to travel and to reside in the country of destination. There is no charge for adoption in Suriname.

Adoption Authority
Bureau voor Familie
  rechttelijke Zaken
Minstry of Justice and Police
De Voodijraad
Grote Combeweg P.O. Box 67
Paramaribo, Suriname,
  South America
Tel: (597) 475-763

U.S. Embassy/Visa Issuing Post
U.S. Embassy
Dr. Sophie Redmondstraat 129
P.O. Box 1821
Paramaribo, Suriname
Tel: (597) 472900
Fax: (597) 410972

TRINIDAD AND TOBAGO

Geography: Trinidad and Tobago are two islands in the West Indies, located 10 miles from the coast of Venezuela.

Capital: Port-of-Spain (250,000)

Demography: More than one-third of the population of 1,281,000 are Blacks of African ancestry; about a third are descendants of people from India. Other groups are Creoles, whites of unmixed European ancestry, and people of Chinese heritage.

Languages: English; French, Spanish, and Hindi are also spoken.

Currency: West Indian Dollar

Major Religions: Roman Catholic, Protestant

Orphans Admitted into the United States
Fiscal year 1996: 4
Fiscal year 1995: 9

Adoption Information: According to the Adoption of Children Ordinance, residents of several years and citizens of Trinidad and Tobago may apply for an adoption. Information concerning adoption and residency requirements is available from the Adoption Board at the address below.

Adoption Authority
Ministry of Social Development & Family Services
c/o Mrs. Hyacinth Whiteman, Secretary
Adoption Board, Fourth Floor
Salvation Building, Frederick Street
Port-of-Spain, Trinidad
Tel: (809) 625-1926

U.S. Embassy/Visa Issuing Post

U.S. Embassy
Consular Section
15 Queen's Park West
Port-of-Spain, Trinidad
Tel: (809) 622-6372 or 622-6376, 6176
Fax: (809) 628-5462

Mailing Address:
P.O. Box 752
Port-of-Spain, Trinidad

VIRGIN ISLANDS OF THE UNITED STATES (U.S. POSSESSION)

Geography: Located a short distance east of Puerto Rico, this U.S. territory is made up of three main islands: Saint Croix, Saint John, and Saint Thomas, together with many nearby islets.

Capital: Charlotte Amalie

Demography: About 70 percent of the population of 104,000 are Blacks of African descent, and about 18 percent are whites of European ancestry.

Languages: English; Spanish and Creole are also spoken.

Currency: U.S. Dollar

Major Religions: Various American religious denominations

Adoption Information: The Virgin Islands of the United States are under the jurisdiction of the U.S. Department of Interior. The adoption law states that only residents may adopt. To obtain the residency requirements and specific adoption information, write to the address below.

Adoption Authority

Governor of The Virgin Islands
P.O. Box 599
Charlotte Amalie
St. Thomas, Virgin Islands 00801

URUGUAY

Geography: Uruguay is the smallest republic in South America. It lies between Brazil and Argentina on the southeast coast of the continent.

Capital: Montevideo

Demography: Most of Uruguay's three million people are whites of Spanish or Italian ancestry. About 10 percent are mestizos, and about eight percent are Charrua Indians.

Language: Spanish

Currency: Peso

Major Religion: Roman Catholic

Orphans Admitted into the United States
Fiscal year 1996: 0
Fiscal year 1995: 0

Adoption Information: U.S. citizens are eligible to adopt in Uruguay, but there are different parental and adoptive child requirements for the two types of adoption, *adopción* and *legitimación adoptiva*. A child adopted through the *adopción* method is not irrevocably relinquished by birth relatives and therefore does not meet INS criteria.

Under *legitimación adoptiva* adoptive parents must be married for at least five years, be over the age of 30, be more than 15 years older than the child, be morally fit and financially able, and have had the child under their guardianship or custody for at least one year. To be eligible for *legitimación adoptiva*, a child must be abandoned, an orphan, a ward of the state, or the child of unknown parents.

A child adopted through *legitimación adoptiva* is irrevocably registered as the legitimate child of the adopting parents with the same rights and duties as a natural child. An adoption is approved by the judge after the child has been in the guardianship of the adoptive parents for at least a year and when the judge believes the adoption to be in the child's best interest.

Adoption Authority
Instituto Nacional del Menor (National Institute for Minors)
Instituto de Adopción
Rio Branco 1394
Montevideo, Uruguay

U.S. Embassy/Visa Issuing Post
U.S. Embassy
Consular Section
Calle Lauro Muller 1776
Montevideo, Uruguay
Tel: [598] (2) 23-60-61
Fax: [598] (2) 48-86-11

Mailing Address:
APO AA 34035

VENEZUELA

Geography: Located on the north coast of South America, Venezuela is bordered by Colombia, Brazil, and Guyana.

Capital: Caracas

Demography: About two-thirds of Venezuela's 19,700,000 people are of mixed Spanish, African, and Indian ancestry; the rest of the people are whites, Blacks, and Amerindians of unmixed ancestry.

Languages: Spanish; English is spoken in the major cities.

Currency: Bolívar

Major Religion: Roman Catholic

Orphans Admitted into the United States
Fiscal year 1996: 14
Fiscal year 1995: 6

Adoption Information: There are basically two ways to adopt a child in Venezuela—through the Instituto Nacional de Menores (INAM), or through an "entrega directa." INAM is the Venezuelan child protection service. They deal with adoptions of children over the age of two who have been abandoned by their parents. "Entrega directa" is an adoption in which the mother gives up her child, through the court, directly to the prospective parents.

Venezuelan law does not specifically address completion of an adoption outside of Venezuela but it can be done. Parents may be granted provisional custody of a child by a Venezuelan judge and permission to take the child out of Venezuela. Parents should be sure that the court has made it clear, in writing, that the child may travel to the United States for the purpose of emigration. Once the embassy concludes its investigation and determines that the orphan criteria have been met and that all other legal requirements such as the medical exam and home study are in order, an immigrant visa may be issued.

Venezuelan law mandates a three-month probationary period after custody has been granted. During this time, a home study may be conducted by a social worker in Venezuela. However, home studies which have been completed in the United States, and approved by an international service agency, may be acceptable to the court. In such cases, the three-month waiting period may take place outside.

Adoption Authority

Instituto Nacional del Menor (INAM)
Servicio de Colocaciónes Familiares y Adopciónes
Avda. San Martin
Edif. Jta. Beneficencia Pub.
San Martin, Caracas 1020
Venezuela
Tel: 461-7866

U.S. Embassy/Visa Issuing Post

U.S. Embassy
Calle F con Calle Suapure
Colinas de Valle Arriba
Caracas 1060-A, Venezuela
Tel: [58] (2) 977-2011
Fax: [58] (2) 977-3253

Mailing Address:
P.O. Box 62291
Caracas 1060-A, Venezuela

or   APO AA 34037

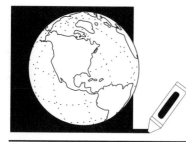

Resources and Contacts

NATIONAL ADOPTIVE PARENT SUPPORT GROUPS

Organizations exist throughout the United States. Those listed support foreign as well as domestic adoptions. They also provide information and literature on adoption-related issues.

Adoptive Families of America
Chapters organized throughout the United States for adoptive families.
>3333 Highway 100
>North Minneapolis, MN 55422
>Telephone: (612) 535-4829

Joint Council for International Children's Services
Organization of licensed, child-placing agencies.
>Holt International Children's Services
>P.O. Box 2880
>Eugene, OR 97402-9970
>Telephone: (541) 687-2202

National Council for Adoption
Organization for individuals as well as licensed nonprofit agencies.
>1930 17th St. N.W.
>Washington, D.C. 20009-6207
>Telephone: (202) 328-1200

IMMIGRATION & NATURALIZATION SERVICE (INS) OFFICES

INS Regional Offices in the United States
INS has four regional offices.

Eastern Region
Regional Commissioner
U.S. Immigration & Naturalization Service
Burlington, VT 95401
Telephone: (802) 951-6201

Northern Region
Regional Commissioner
U.S. Immigration & Naturalization Service
Federal Bldg., Fort Snelling
St. Paul, MN 55111
Telephone: (612) 854-7754

Southern Region
Regional Commissioner
U.S. Immigration & Naturalization Service
P.O. Box 152122, Dept. A
Irving, TX 75015-2122
Telephone: (214) 767-7769 thru 7773

Western Region
Regional Commissioner
U.S. Immigration & Naturalization Service
400 Oceangate
Long Beach, CA 90802
Telephone: (213) 514-6512

INS District Offices in the United States

These offices process the I-600A (Application for Advance Processing), I-600 (Petition to Classify an Orphan as an Immediate Relative), and the FD-258 (Fingerprint Chart).

Anchorage, AK 99513
New Federal Bldg.
701 C St., Room D-229

Atlanta, GA 30303
Richard B. Russell
Federal Annex Bldg.
77 Forsyth St. SW
Room G-85

Baltimore, MD 21201
E.A. Garmatz Federal Bldg.
101 West Lombard St.

Boston, MA 02203
John Fitzgerald Kennedy
Federal Bldg.
Government Center

Buffalo, NY 14202
68 Court St.

Chicago, IL 60604
Dirsken Federal Office Bldg.
219 S. Dearborn St.

Cleveland, OH 44199
Anthony J. Celebreeze
Federal Office Bldg., Room 1917
1240 E. 9th St.

Dallas, TX 75247
8101 N. Stemmons Freeway

Dallas, TX 75242
Fm. 6A21, Federal Bldg.
1100 Commerce St.

Denver, CO 80294-1799
1787 Federal Bldg.
1961 Stout St.

Detroit, MI 48207
Federal Bldg
333 Mt. Elliott St.

El Paso, TX 79925
1545 Hawkins

Houston, TX 77060
509 N. Sam Houston Parkway

Hartford, CT 06103-3060
Ribicoff Federal Bldg.
450 Main St.

Helena, MT 59626
Federal Bldg., Room 512
310 South Park
Drawer 10036

Honolulu, HI 96809
P.O. Box 461
595 Ala Moana Blvd.

Houston, TX 77060
509 N. Belt

Kansas City, MO 64153
9747 N. Conant Ave.

Los Angeles, CA 90012
300 N. Los Angeles St.

Miami, FL 33138
7880 Biscayne Blvd.

Newark, NJ 07102
Federal Bldg.
970 Broad St.

New Orleans, LA 70113
Postal Service Bldg.
Room T-8005
701 Loyola Avenue

New York, NY 10278
26 Federal Plaza

Omaha, NE 68102
Federal Office Bldg.
Room 1008
106 S. 15th St.

Philadelphia, PA 19103
1600 Callowhill St.

Phoenix, AZ 85025
Federal Bldg.
230 N. 1st Ave.

Portland, ME 04103
739 Warren Ave.

Portland, OR 92709
Federal Office Bldg.
511 N.W. Broadway

St. Paul, MN 55101
923 Main Post Office Bldg.
180 E. Kellogg Blvd.

San Antonio, TX 78239
8940 Four Winds.

San Diego, CA 92188
880 Front St.

San Francisco, CA 94111
Appraisers Bldg.
630 Sansome St.

San Juan, PR 00936
GPO Box 5068

Seattle, WA 98134
815 Airport Way South

Washington, D.C. 22203
4420 N. Fairfax Dr.
Arlington, VA

INS Service Offices in Foreign Countries

Athens, Greece
U.S. Immigration and
    Naturalization Service
c/o American Embassy
APO 09253
Telephone: [30] (1) 721-2951
    or 721-8401

Bangkok, Thailand
U.S. Immigration and
    Naturalization Service
c/o American Embassy, Box 12
APO 96546, San Francisco, CA
96346-0001
Telephone: [66] (2) 252-5040

Cuidad Juarez
U.S. Immigration and
    Naturalization Service
c/o American Consulate General
P.O. Box 10545
El Paso, TX 79995-0545
Telephone [52] (16) 11300

Frankfurt, Germany
U.S. Immigration and
    Naturalization Service
c/o American Consulate General
Box 12, APO NY 09213
Telephone: [49] (69) 7535-0

Hong Kong, British Crown Colony
U.S. Immigration and
    Naturalization Service
c/o American Consulate General
Box 30,
FPO San Francisco, CA 96659-
0002
Telephone: [65] 338-0251

Manila, Philippines
U.S. Immigration and
    Naturalization Service
c/o American Embassy
APO San Francisco, CA 96528
Telephone: [63] (2) 521-7116

Mexico City, Mexico
U.S. Immigration and
    Naturalization Service
P.O. Box 3087, Rm. 118
Laredo, TX 78044
Telephone: [52] (5) 211-0042

Monterrey, N.L., Mexico
U.S. Immigration and
    Naturalization Service
c/o American Consulate General
P.O. Box 3098
Laredo, TX 78041
Telephone: [52] (83) 45-2120

Rome, Italy
U.S. Immigration and
    Naturalization Service
c/o American Embassy
APO NY 09794-0007
Telephone: [82] (2) 732-2601

Seoul, Korea
U.S. Immigration and
    Naturalization Service
c/o American Embassy
APO San Francisco, CA 96301
Telephone: [49] (69) 7535-0

Singapore, Republic of
U.S. Immigration and
    Naturalization Service
c/o American Embassy
FPO San Francisco, CA 96699-001
Telephone: [65] 338-0251

1010 Vienna, Austria
U.S. Immigration and
    Naturalization Service
c/o American Embassy
APO AE 09108-0001
Telephone: [43] (1) 31-55-11

State Departments of Public Welfare or Social Services

ALABAMA
Alabama Department
    of Human Resources
Gordon Person Bldg., Box 30400
50 N. Ripley St.
Montgomery, AL 36130-1801
Telephone: (334) 242-1160

ALASKA
Alaska Department of Health
    and Social Services
Pouch H-05
Juneau, AK 99811
Telephone: (907) 465-3023

ARIZONA
Adoption Coordinator
Arizona Dept. of Economic Security
1789 W. Jefferson (Zip code: 85007)
P.O. Box 6123
Phoenix, AZ 85005
Telephone: (602) 542-2415

ARKANSAS
Permanency Planning Unit Manager
Arkansas Department
    of Human Services
Division of Children & Family Services
626 Donaghey Bldg., Room 1038
P.O. Box 1437, Slot 808
Little Rock, AR 72203

CALIFORNIA
James W. Brown
Chief, Adoptions Branch
California Department
    of Social Services
744 P St., M/S 19-69
Sacramento, CA 95814
Telephone: (916) 445-3146

COLORADO
Colorado Department
    of Social Services
1575 Sherman St., 2nd Floor
Denver, CO 80203
Telephone: (303) 866-3209

CONNECTICUT
Adoptions Services Coordinator
Connecticut Department
    of Children & Youth Services
White Hall, Bldg. 2, 3rd Floor
Undercliff Road
Meriden, CT 06450
Telephone: (203) 238-6640

DELAWARE
Delaware Department
    of Social Services
1st State Executive Plaza
630 East 30th Street, 3rd Floor
Wilmington, DE 19802
Telephone: (302) 633-2676

DISTRICT OF COLUMBIA
District of Columbia Department
    of Human Services
500 1st Street, N.W., Room 8040
Washington, DC 20001
Telephone: (202) 724-2093

FLORIDA
Florida Department of Health
    & Rehabilitation Services
Children, Youth & Family Services
1317 Winewood Boulevard
Tallahassee, FL 32399-0700
Telephone: (904) 488-8000

GEORGIA
Georgia Department
    of Human Resources
State Adoption Unit
878 Peachtree Street, N.E., Room 501
Atlanta, GA 30309-3917
Telephone: (404) 894-3376

HAWAII
Beatrice Yuh
Hawaii Department
    of Human Services
Family and Children's Services
810 Richards Street, 4th Floor
P.O. Box 339
Honolulu, HI 96809-0339
Telephone: (808) 548-6407

IDAHO
State Adoptions Coordinator
Idaho Department of Human Services
Division of Family
   and Children's Services
450 West State Street, 3rd Floor
Boise, ID 83720
Telephone: (208) 334-5700
   or 334-5697

ILLINOIS
Illinois Department of Children
   and Family Services
406 East Monroe, Station 55
Springhill, IL 62706-1498
Telephone: (817) 785-8080

INDIANA
Indiana Department of Public Welfare
Family Protection
402 W. Washington St., Room 364
Indianapolis, IN 46204
Telephone: (317) 232-4427

IOWA
Iowa Department of Human Services
Hoover State Office Building, 5th Floor
Des Moines, IA 50319
Telephone: (515) 281-5358

KENTUCKY
Kansas Department of Social
   & Rehabilitative Services
300 S.W. Oakley St.
Topeka, KS 66606
Telephone: (502) 564-2136

LOUISIANA
Adoption Program Manager
Louisiana Department of Health
   & Social Services
Division of Children, Youth
   & Family Services
Office of Community Services
P.O. Box 3318
Baton Rouge, LA 70821
Telephone: (504) 342-9925

MAINE
Maine Department of Human Services
State House, Station 11
221 State St.
Augusta, ME 04333
Telephone: (207)289-3271

MASSACHUSETTS
Massachusetts Department
   of Social Services
150 Causeway St.
Boston, MA 04333

MICHGAN
Michigan Department
   of Social Services
Child Care Resources Division
235 S. Grand Ave., 5th Floor
Zip code: 48933
   or P.O. Box 30037
Lansing, MI 48909
Telephone: (517) 373-3513

MINNESOTA
Minnesota Department
   of Human Services
444 Lafayette Road
St. Paul, MN 55155-3831
Telephone: (612) 296-5288

MISSISSIPPI
Mississippi Department
   of Human Services
Division of Family
   and Children's Services
939 North President Street, 2nd Floor,
   Suite 201
Zip Code: 39202
Telephone: (601) 354-0341

MISSOURI
Missouri Division of Family Services
Broadway State Office Bldg.
615 Howerton, Zip code 65109
   or P.O. Box 88
Jefferson City, MO 65103-0088

MONTANA
Montana Department
   of Family Services
P.O. Box 8005
Helena, MT 59604
Telephone: (406) 444-5900

NEBRASKA
Nebraska Department
   of Social Services
301 Centennial Mall, South, 5th Floor
P.O. Box 95026
Lincoln, NE 68509
Telephone: (402) 471-3121

NEVADA
Social Services
Nevada Hampshire Division
    for Children & Youth Services
Adoption Unit
711 East 5th St., Capitol Complex
Carson City, NV 89710
Telephone: (702) 687-4979

NEW HAMPSHIRE
New Hampshire Division
    for Children & Youth Services
Adoption Unit
6 Hazen Drive
Concord, NH 03301-6522
Telephone: (603) 271-4707

NEW JERSEY
New Jersey Division of Youth
    & Family Services
50 E. State St., C.N. 717
Trenton, NJ 08625-0717
Telephone: (609) 633-3991

NEW MEXICO
Adoption Unit
New Mexico Human Services Dept.
PERA Bldg., Room 515
(2009 S. Pancheo, zip code 87505)
P.O. Box 2348
Santa Fe, NM 87504-2348
Telephone: (505) 827-4109

NEW YORK
New York State Department
    of Social Services
40 N. Pearl St., Mezzanine
Albany, NY 12243
Telephone: (518) 473-0855

NORTH CAROLINA
North Carolina Division
    of Social Services
325 N. Salisbury St.
Raleigh, NC 27611
Telephone: (919) 733-3801

OHIO
Ohio Department
    of Human Services
Bureau of Children's Services
65 East State St., 5th Floor
Columbus, OH 43215
Telephone: (614) 466-8520

OKLAHOMA
Oklahoma Department
    of Human Services
Sequoia Bldg., Room 308
2300 N. Lincoln Boulevard
P.O. Box 25352
Oklahoma City, OK 73125
Telephone: (405) 521-2475

OREGON
Oregon Department
    of Human Services
Children's Services Division
198 Commercial St., S.E.
Salem, OR 97310
Telephone: (503) 581-6198

PENNSYLVANIA
Pennsylvania Department
    of Public Welfare
Office of Children, Youth, & Families
Health & Welfare Bldg. Annex
    (Harrisburg State Hospital, Lanco
    Ladge 2nd Floor, zip code 17103)
P.O. Box 2675
Harrisburg, PA 17105
Telephone: (717) 787-7015

RHODE ISLAND
Rhode Island Department for
    Children, youth & Families
610 Mt. Pleasant Avenue, Bldg. 3
Providence, RI 02908
Telephone: (401) 457-5389

SOUTH CAROLINA
Deputy for Adoption
Office of Children, Family
    & Adult Services
South Carolina Department
    of Social Services
1535 Confederate Ave., #421
P.O. Box 1520
Columbia, SC 29202

SOUTH DAKOTA
South Dakota Department
    of Social Services
Children, Youth & Family Services
Richard F. Kneip Bldg.
700 Governor's Drive
Pierre, SD 57501-2291
Telephone: (605) 773-3227

TENNESSEE
Tennessee Department
   of Human Services
Social Services Division
Citizens Plaza
400 Deaderick St., 14th Floor
Nashville, TN 37219
Telephone: (615) 741-5935

TEXAS
Texas Department
   of Human Services
701 West 51st St., 4th Floor West
Austin, TX 78751
Telephone: (512) 450-3302

UTAH
Utah Department of Social Services
   Division of Family Services
120 N. 200 West, 4th Floor
Salt Lake City, UT 84102

VERMONT
Vermont Department of Social
   & Rehabilitative Services
103 S. Main St.
Waterbury, VT 05676
Telephone: (802) 241-2131

WASHINGTON
Washington Department
   of Social & Health Services
Division of Children
   & Family Services
14th & Jefferson, OB-41-C
P.O. Box 45711
Olympia, WA 98504-5711
Telephone: (206) 586-2612

WEST VIRGINIA
West Virginia Department
   of Health & Human Services
Office of Social Services
Capitol Complex, Bldg. 6, Room B-850
Charleston, WV 25305
Telephone: (304) 348-7980

WISONSIN
Wisconsin Department of Health
   & Human Services
Division of Community Services
(1 West Wilson Street, zip code 53702)
P.O. Box 7851
Madison, WI 53707
Telephone: (608) 266-0700

WYOMING
Division of Public Assistance
   & Social Services
Wyoming Department
   of Social Services
Hathaway Bldg., Room 319
Cheyenne, WY 82002-0710
Telephone: (307) 777-6789

PUERTO RICO
Puerto Rico Department
   of Social Services
San Juan, Puerto Rico
Telephone: (809) 724-8135
   or 722-7400

VIRGIN ISLANDS
Virgin Islands Department
   of Human Services
Management Review
3011 Golden Rock
Christiansted, Virgin Islands
00820-4355

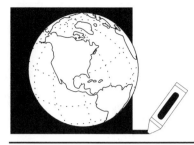

Bibliography

Adoption Resources

Agency Adoption

Alexander- Roberts, Colleen. "Adoption Agencies: How They Work."
    AdoptNet 4, no.4 (July/August 1992): 32-33, 47.
Burgess, Linda C. *The Art of Adoption*. Rev. ed. New York: W.W.
    Norton and Company, 1981.

Adoption Agency Listings

International Concerns Committee for Children (I.C.C.C). *Report on Foreign
    Adoption*. Boulder, CO: ICCC, 1993.
National Adoption Information Clearinghouse. Rev. ed. *National Adoption
    Directory*. Rockville, MD: NAIC, 1992.
Paul, Ellen. *The Adoption Resource Guide*. Washington, D.C.: Child Welfare
    League of America, Inc., 1990.
Drake, Sylvia, *Directory for Adoptive Parents Over 40*. Walters Communications.
    Place orders through Box 509, Welcome, NC 27374, 910-731-3348.
Posner, Julia L. *Adoptive Agency Directory*. Washington, D.C.: CWLA.

Adoption- General Information

Adamec, Christine and William Pierce. *The Encyclopedia of Adoption*,
    New York: Facts on File, 1991.
"As Adoptions Get More Difficult." *U.S. News and World Report*,
    June 25, 1984, 32.
Bartholet, Elizabeth. *Family Bonds*: *Adoption and the Politics of Parenting*.
    Houghton Mifflin, 1994.
Child Welfare League of America. *National Adoption Task Force:
    A CWLA Report*. Washington, D.C.: CWLA, 1987.
Gilman, Lois, *The Adoption Resource Book*. New York:
    Harper & Row, 1987.
Lindsay, Jeanne and Catherine Monserrat. *Adoption Awareness: A Guide for
    Teachers, Counselors, Nurses, and Caring Others*. Buena Park,
    California: Morning Glory Press, 1989.

National Committee for Adoption. *Adoption Factbook: United States Data, Issues, Regulations and Resources.* Washington, D.C.: National Committee for Adoption, 1989.

Pierce, William. "Taking Adoption Seriously." *Society*, July/August 1990, 23-24.

Plumer, Jacqueline. "Families: The Adoption Option." *Working Woman*, May 1983, 148+

Quindlen, Anna. "Baby Craving." *Life*, June 1987, 23-24.

Riben, Marsha. *The Dark Side of Adoption.* Detriot: Harlo Press, 1988.

Schooler, Jayne. *The Whole Life Adoption Book.* Pinon Press, 1993.

Adoption of Older Children and Children with Special Needs

Brockhaus, J. and R. Brockhaus. "Adopting and Older Child: The Emotional Process." *American Journal of Nursing* 82 (1982): 288-294.

Cox, Caroline, ed. *Trajectories of Despair: Misdiagnosis and Maltreatment of Soviet Orphans.* Available as a photocopy. Send $10.00 to Parent Network for the Post-institutionalized Child, Box 613, Meadow Lands, PA 15247.

Dunn, Linda, ed. *Adopting Children with Special Needs: A Sequel.* Washington, D.C.: North American Council on Adoptable Children, 1983.

Jarratt, Claudia Jewett. *Helping Children Cope With Separation and Loss.* Boston: Harvard Common Press, 1982.

Jewett, Claudia L. *Adopting the Older Child.* Boston: Harvard Common Press, 1978.

Kravi, Patricia, ed. *Adopting Children with Special Needs.* Riverside, Cailifornia: North American Council on Adoptable Children, 1976.

Leof, Joan. "Adopting Children with Developmental Disabilities." Rockville, Maryland: National Adoption Information Clearinghouse.

Marks, Jane. "We Have A Problem." *Parents*, October 1987, 62-68.

Welch, Martha. *Holding Time.* Order through Heartland Catalog, P.O. Box 1974, La Porte, TX 77572-1974.

Adoption Support and Awareness (for Family and Friends)

Bloom S. *A Family for Jaime, An Adoption Story.* New York: Potter, 1991.

Bothun, Linda. *When Friends Ask About Adoption: A Question & Answer Guide for Non-Adoptive Parents & Other Caring Adults.* Chevy Chase, Maryland: Swan Publications, 1987.

Holmes, Pat. *Supporting an Adoption.* Wayne, Pennsylvania: Our Child Press, 1982.

Children's Books

Brodzinsky, Anne. *The Mulberry Bird: Story of an Adoption.* Ft. Wayne, Indiana: Perspectives Press, 1986.

Bunin, Sherry and Catherine Bunin. *Is that Your Sister? A True Story of Adoption.* Wayne, PA: Our Child Press, 1992.

Freudber, J. and T. Geiss. *Susan and Gordon Adopt a Baby.* New York: Random House, 1989.

Girard, Linda. *Adoption Is for Always.* Niles, Illinois: Albert Whitman and Co., 1986.

Kindersley, Barnabas and Anabel, *Children Just Like Me*, UNICEF, DK Publishing, Inc.

Koch, Janet. *Our Baby: A Birth and Adoption Story.* Ft. Wayne, Indiana: Perspectives Press, 1986.

Koehler, P. (1990). *The Day We Met You.* New York: Bradbury Press. Book about adoption for pre-schoolers.

Krementz, Jill. *How It Feels to Be Adopted.* New York: Knopf, 1988.

Livingston, Carole. *Why Was I Adopted?* Secaucus, New Jersey: Lyle Stuart, 1986.

Lowe, Darla. *Story of Adoption: Why Do I Look Different?* Minneapolis, Minnesota: East West Press, 1987.

Rosenberg, Maxine B. *Being Adopted.* New York: Lathrop, Lee, Shepard Books, 1984.

Schwartz, Perry *Carolyn's Story.* Lerner Publications, 1996.

Schnitter, Jane T. *William Is My Brother.* Indianapolis, Indiana: Perspectives Press, 1991.

Stein, Stephanie. *Lucy's Feet.* Indianapolis, Indiana: Perspectives Press, 1992.

Tax, Meredith. *Families.* Boston: Little, Brown and Co., 1981.

Wasson, Valentina. *The Chosen Baby.* Philadelphia: J.B. Lippincott, 1977.

Welch, Sheila Kelly. *Don't Call Me Marda.* Wayne, Pennsylvania: Our Child Press, 1990.

Wickstrom, Lois. *Oliver: A Story about Adoption.* Wayne, Pennsylvania: Our Child Press, 1991.

Walvoord-Girard, Linda. *We Adopted You, Benjamin Koo.* Morton Grove, Illinois: Albert Whiteman and Company, 1992.

Waybill, Majorie Ann. *Chinese Eyes.* Scottdale, Pennsylvania: Herald Press, 1974.

Cultural Enrichment

Against All Odds Productions/Melcher Media. *Passage to Vietnam.* Publishers Group West, 1994.

D'Aluisio, Faith. *Women in the Material World.* Sierra Book Club, 1996. Menzel, Peter. *Material World.* Sierra Book Club, 1994.

How To Adopt Resources

Adamec, Christine A. T*here are Babies to Adopt: A Resource Guide for Prospective Parents.* New York: Pinnacle, 1991.

Adopt a Boy. *OURS,* 21, no. 4 (July/August 1988): 30-31.

Alexander-Roberts, Colleen. *The Essential Adoption Handbook.* Dallas, Texas: Taylor Publishing, 1993.

Gilman, Lois. *The Adoption Resource Book.* Borgo Press, 1991.

Plumez, Jacqueline Horner. *Successful Adoption.* New York: Crown Publishers, 1982.

Walker, Elaine. *Loving Journeys Guide to Adoption.* Available from Loving Journeys, PO Box 755, Peterborough, NH 03458.

Home Studies

O'Rourke, Lisa and Ruth Hubbell. "*Adopting a Foreign Child through an Agency.*" Rockville, Maryland: National Adoption Information Clearinghouse.

Setterberg, Fred, T*he Triumphs of Foreign Adoption.* For back issues call 800/822-2822.

Smith, Debra. *The Adoption Home Study Process.* Rockville, Maryland: National Adoption Information Clearinghouse.

The World and I, March 1993, A Chronicle of Our Changing Era, A Publication of The Washington Times Corporation.

Infertility and Adoption

Johnston, Patricia Irwin. *An Adopter's Advocate.* Indianapolis: Perspectives Press, 1984.

Johnston, Patricia Irwin. *Adopting After Infertility.* Indianapolis: Perspectives Press, 1992.

Johnston, Patricia Irwin. *Taking Charge of Infertility.* Indianapolis: Perspectives Press, 1994.

Melina, Lois. "Pros, Cons of Adopting During Infertility Treatment." *Adopted Child* (newsletter), June 1986.

Menning, Barbara Eck. *Infertility: A Guide for the Infertile Couple.* Englewood, New Jersey: Resolve, 1977.

International Adoption

Dey, Carol and LeAnn Theiman. *This Must Be My Brother.* Victor Brooks, 1995.

F.A.C.E. *F.A.C.E. Resource Manual.* Provides a listing of regional and extraregional programs in the regional and international fields of adoption. Order from Families Adopting Children Everywhere, Inc., PO Box 28058, Northwood Station, Baltimore, Maryland 21239.

International Concerns Committee for Children (I.C.C.C.). *Report on Foreign Adoption.* Boulder, Colorado: ICCC, 1997.

Koh, Frances. *Oriental Children in American Homes.* Minneapolis, Minnesota: East-West Press, 1988.

Redlich, Susan. "Baby of Mine." *First,* July 8, 1991.

Register, Cheri. *Are Those Kids Yours?* American Families with Children Adopted from Other Countries. New York: The Free Press, 1991.

Van Loon, J.H.A. *Report on Intercountry Adoption.* Social and legal history of international adoption leading toward a convention on international cooperation for the protection of children in connection with intercountry adoption. Order from: Permanent Bureau of the Conference, Scheveingseweg 6, The Hague, Netherlands.

Interracial Adoption

Alstein, Howard and Rita Simon. *Intercountry Adoption.* Praeger Publishers, 1991.

Aldridge, Jane (ed.) and Ivor Gabor. *In the Best Interests of the Child: Culture, Identity and Transracial Adoption.* Free Association Books, 1995.

Simon, Rita J. *Adoption, Race, and Identity: From Infancy Through Adolescence.* Praeger Publishers, 1992.

Simon, Rita J., Howard Alstein and Marygold S. Melli. T*he Case for Transracial Adoption.* American University Press, 1993.

Learning Disabilities, ADHD, and Adopted Children

Alexander-Roberts, Colleen. *The ADHD Parenting Handbook.* Dallas, Texas: Taylor Publishing, 1994.

Bordwell, Martha, Ph.D. "The Link Between Adoption and Learning Disabilities." *OURS,* September/October, 1992, 22-25.

Parenting Adopted Children

Boyd, Brian. *When You Were Born In Korea: A Memory Book for Children Adopted from Korea.* Available from Adoptive Families Bookstore, 800/372-3300.

Brazelton, M.D. T. Barry. *Touchpoints: Your Child's Emotional and Behavioral Development.* Addison-Wesley Publishing Company, 1992.

Clark, Jean Illsley and Connie Dawson. *Growing Up Again: Parenting Ourselves, Parenting Our Children.* Hazetzen Publishing, 1989.

Dorow, Sara. *When You Were Born In China.* Available from Adoptive Families Bookstore, 800/372-3300.

Greenspan, MD, Stanley. *First Feeling: Milestones of the Emotional Development of Your Baby and Child.* Penguin Books, 1985.

Hallenbeck, Carol. *Our Child: Preparation for Parenting in Adoption.* Wayne, Pennsylvania: Our Child Press, 1988.

Hormann, Elizabeth. *After the Adoption.* New Jersey: Revell Company, 1987.

Jarratt, Claudia Jewett. *Helping Children Cope with Separation and Loss.* Harvard Common Press, revised 1994.

Katz, Lilian G. "Adopted Children." *Parents*, January 1987, 116.

Karen, Robert. *Becoming Attached: Unfolding the Mystery of the Infant Mother Bond and Its Impact on Later Life.* New York: Time-Warner Co, 1994.

Komar, Marian. *Communicating with the Adopted Child.* New York: Walker and Company, 1991.

Leach, Penelope. *Your Baby and Child from Birth to Age Five.* New York: Alfred A. Knopf. 1981.

Melina, Lois R. *Making Sense of Adoption: A Parent's Guide.* New York: Harper and Row, 1989.

Melina, Lois R. *Raising Adopted Children: A Manual for Adoptive Parents.* New York: Harper and Row, 1986.

Miller, Margi and Nancy Ward. *With Eyes Wide Open: A Workbook for Parents Adopting International Children Over Age One.* Available from Children's Home Society of Minnesota, 2230 Como Ave, St. Paul, MN 55108.

Sachs, Andrea. "When the Lullaby Ends." *Time*, June 4, 1990, 82.

Schaffer, Judith and Christina Lindstrom. *How to Raise an Adopted Child.* New York: Crown, 1989.

Silber, Kathleen and Speedlin, Phylis. *Dear Birthmother: Thank You For Our Baby.* Using actual correspondence between birth parents and adoptive parents, this book proves that most birth parents care a lot about their children and think about them later. It also helps adoptive parents and adopted persons understand birth parents. Order from: Corona Publishers, 1037 South Alamo, San Antonio, Texas 78210.

Van Gulden, Holly and Lisa Bartles-Rabb, *Real Parents, Real Children: Parenting the Adopted Child.* New York: Crossroad Press, 1993.

Watkins, Mary and Susan Fisher. *Talking with Young Children About Adoption.* Yale University Press, 1995.

Personal Adoption Experiences (Adoptive Parents)

Ciccarelli, Dave. *Steppe Children: Gifts from Mother Russia.* FACE FACTS, July/Aug, 1996.

Erichsen, Jean and Heino. *Butterflies in the Wind: Spanish/ Indian Children with White Parents.* Available from Los Ninos International, 281/363-2892.

Pohl, Constance. *Transracial Adoption: Children and Parents Speak.* Franklin Watts, 1992.

Sheehy, Gail. *Spirit of Survival.* New York: William Morrow, 1986.

Viguers, Susan T. *With Child: One Couple's Journey to Their Adopted Children.* San Diego: Harcourt Brace Jovanovich, 1986.

Post Adoption Support

Macaskill, C. "Postadoption Support: Is It Essential?" *Adoption and Fostering* (1985): 45-49.

Psychological Issues

Brodzinsky, David and Marshall Schechter, eds. T*he Psychology of Adoption.* New York: Oxford University Press, 1990.

Brodzinsky, David M., Ph.D., Marshall D. Schecter, M.D., and Robin Marantz Henig. *Being Adopted: The Lifelong Search for Self.* New York: Doubleday, 1992.

Benson, Dr. Peter and Dr. Anu Sharma, L.P. and Eugene C. Roehlkepartain. *Growing Up Adopted.*

Da, Dr. Frank, et al. "Infants and Young Children in Orphanages: One View from Pediatrics and Child Psychiatry." *Pediatrics,* Vol 97 no.4, pp.569-578, 1996.

Fahlberg, M.D., Vera. *A Child's Journey Through Placement.* Indiana: Perspectives Press, 1995.

Single Adoptive Parents

Doughtery, Sharon Ann. "Single Adoptive Mothers and Their Children." (*The Philadelphia Inquirer*). June 13, 1990.

Groze, Victor K. and James A. Rosenthal. "Single Parents and Their Adopted Children: A Psychosocial Analysis." *Families in Society* 72, no. 2 (February 1991): 67-77.

Marindian, Hope. *The Handbook for Single Parents.* Chevy Chase, Maryland: Committee for Single Adoptive Parents, 1992.

Mattes, C.S.W., Jane. *Single Mothers by Choice: A Guidebook for Single Women Who are Considering or Have Chosen Motherhood.* New York: Times Books, 1994.

Oliver, Stephanie Stokes. "Single Adoptive Fathers." *Essence* 12 (1988) 114-116, 146.

Prowler, Mady. "Single Parent Adoption: What You Need To Know." Rockville, Maryland: National Adoption Information Clearinghouse.

Sullivan, Marylou. "Perceptions of Single Adoptive Parents: How We View Ourselves, How Others View Us." *OURS* 22, no.6 (November/December 1989): 34-35.

State Laws

National Adoption Information Clearinghouse. "Adoption Laws: Answers to the Most Asked Questions." Rockville, Maryland: NAIC.

Other Resources

Films

Erichsen, Jean. *How to Adopt Internationally.* Distributed by Los Ninos International.

Melina, L.R. (1990) *While You Wait to Adopt.*

Goodwins. *Visible Differences.* North Bay Adoption, 9068 Brooks Road South, Windsor, CA 95492.

Tai Kai Productions. *Tai Li Comes Homes.* 1340 W. Irving Park, #348, Chicago, IL 60613-1901.

Rashad, Phyllis. *Baby Alive.* Action Films & Video LTD. Yao, Dr. Esther. *Interactive Parenting.* To order call 888/Baby-Play.

Magazines and Newsletters of Adoptive Parents' Groups

Adopted Child. Published monthly. U.S. subscriptions $22.00 for 1 year, $38.00 for 2; foreign subscribers add $10.00 per year. Order from Lois R. Medina, PO Box 9362, Moscow, ID 83843.

Adoption Today. Published quarterly. $15.00 annually. 32 pages; information on all aspects of adoption. Order from WACAP, PO Box 88948, Seattle, WA 98138.

Buenas Noticias. Order from Latin American Parents Association (LAPA), PO Box 4403, Silver Springs, MD 20914-4403.

Connections. For families with children from India and Indian Subcontinent. $14.00 annually for 4 issues. Order from Address: 1417 E. Miner, Arlington Heights, IL 60004.

F.A.C.E. F.A.C.T.S. Published bi-monthly. Newsletter and membership, $20.00 annually. Order from Families Adopting Children Everywhere. PO Box 28058, Northwood Station, Baltimore, MD 21239.

FAIR Newsletter. Published 6 times a year; membership and newsletter, $20.00 annually. Address: PO Box 51436, Palo Alto, CA 94303.

Families with Children from China. 255 W. 90th St., Apt. 11C, New York, NY 10024. Similar groups exist in nearly every major city.

Families for Russian and Ukranian Adoption. Box 2944, Merrifield, VA 22116-2944. Telephone: (202) 429-3385.

Romanian Children's Connection. 5180 Huntcliff Trail. Winston-Salem, NC 27104.

The Adoption Advocate. Published three times a year. $10.00/year. Order from Adoptive Advocates International. 136 Old Black Diamond Road, Port Angeles, WA 98362.

The African Connection. $20.00/yr. Focuses on Africa. Order from Americans for African Adoptions, Inc., 8910 Timberwood Dr., Indianapolis, IN 46234.

The Children's Voice. Family/individual = $10.00 yearly. Organizations = $25.00 yearly. Order from National Coalition to End Racism (in America's Child Care System), 22075 Koths, Taylor, MI 48180.

The Communique. For interracial marriages and interracial families. Order form Interracial Family Alliance, PO Box 16248, Houston, TX 77222.

Resources for Travelers

English Magazines and Newspapers

Africa News: Box 3851, Burham, NC 27702. Twice monthly digest of African affairs, news, and culture.

Asia: P.O. Box 1308-A Fort Lee, NJ 07024. Magazine published every other month on Asian affairs, news, and cultures.

Europe: 2100 M. Street, N.W., Washington, DC 20037. $6.00 per year. Magazine published every other month on European affairs, news, and culture.

UNICEF: A beautiful catalog which reports on the needs of children in developing countries and offers an outstanding array of international cards, books, games, stationary as well as a growth chart. Order from: UNICEF, United Nations Children's Fund, 475 Oberlin Ave. South, CN 2110, Lakewood, NJ 08701.

Health Care for Travelers

A Foreign Language Guide to Health Care. A free guide which explains how to say phrases like "It hurts here" in four languages, including Spanish, Order from: Communication Department, Blue Cross and Blue Shield of Greater New York, 3 Park Ave., 27th Floor, New York, NY 10016.

International Association of Medical Assistance to Travelers. A free directory (donations appreciated) of English-speaking doctors abroad who charge set fees. Order from: International Association of Medical Assistance to Travelers, 735 Center St., Lewiston, NY 14092. Telephone: (716) 754-4883.

Other publications:

Notes: A unique series of short, authoritative pamphlets on every country of the world. Concise information on culture, climate, clothing, health precautions, transportation, visa requirements, tourist attractions, etc. $16.00 per year. Order from: Superintendent of Documents, Government Printing Office, Washington, DC 20402.

"A Guide to Visas, Passports, and Consular Services." Washington, D.C., Department of State, bureau of Consular Affairs. 1978.

"Consumer's Guide to Travel Information." Washington, DC: Travel Service, Department of Commerce, 1978. A kit of nine brochures which explain how to obtain the best travel prices, how to obtain information for travelers with special needs, and if necessary, where to complain.

U.S. Government Printing Office. "Area Handbooks." Washington, D.C., Government Printing Office. A highly regarded U.S. Army series from: Public Documents Distribution Center, Department 20, Pueblo, CO 81009.

World Travel Directory. Vol.8. New York, Ziff-Davis. Published annually. A library reference book which is a source of addresses to write to for free information provided by the U.S.-based tourist information services.

Languages

Language Guides. Originally issued to armed services personnel, these U.S. government guides emphasize speaking rather writing skills. Order from Superintendent of Documents, Washington, DC 20402. Spanish #37N9. Portuguese #35N9.

Local Ethnic Organizations:

Consult the History Department of the public library in large cities. Their "Club File" holds cards for local ethnic group organizations. Names of the organizations as well as current presidents are listed.

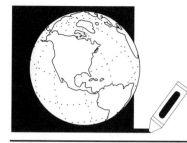

Glossary

abandonment	Term used to define a child as an orphan by his or her government's setting a specific time limit, such as three months, in which a relative may reclaim the child. If not, a decree of abandonment is issued.
adoptee	Person who is adopted.
adopter	Adult who adopts a child.
adoption	Consummation, or finalization of a child's placement with a couple or single in the child's native country or in the new country of residence.
adoption agency, U.S.	Performs social work and home study as required by state licensing standards.
agency-initiated adoption	A placement and/or adoption facilitated or processed by an agency.
ambassador	The highest ranking representative appointed by one country or government to represent it in another.
Americans	All the citizens of the Americas. Latin Americans consider themselves Americans, as do Canadians.
apgar score	Health check of a newborn at birth and five minutes later for the quality of the heartbeat, respiratory effort, muscle tone, and reflex action. A perfect score is 10, which is rare. An eight or nine is considered excellent. A low Apgar score is usually found in infants with complicated pregnancies or deliveries.
apostille	A form from the state verifying a notary's date of commission.
authentication	There are two types of authentication. The consul of the country from which you wish to adopt attests to the authenticity of your certificate and original documents by his or her seal or signature. The U.S Department of state attests to the authenticity of your documents with red seals and ribbons.
biological parent	Birth mother and birth father.
bonding	The loving, caring, emotional attachment for a successful parent-child relationship.
certification	Issued by the department of vital statistics in the country where the birth, marriage, divorce or death took place.
closed adoption	No exchange of information is agreed upon by both parties.
consulate	Office or residence of a consul.
consul	Citizen appointed by his or her government to live in a certain city in a foreign country to look after his country's citizens and business interests there.
cooperative adoption	Information is exchanged between birth parents and adoptive parents. Usually, pictures and letters are sent once a month until adoption, then once a year on the child's birthday.

consummation	An adoption decree, issued after the documents have been reviewed by a judge.
custody transfer	When an orphan is escorted from one state or country to another for the purpose of adoption, the government of the agency in authority formally transfers custody of the child to the adoption agency or DPW at the child's destination.
DHS or DPW	Department of Human Services or Department of Public Welfare, or similarly named agencies in each U.S. state where adoption of out-of-state and foreign-born children are approved. DPW studies and records the orphan's documents before the INS gives approval.
disruption	Adoptive placement is interrupted prior to consummation. (Nationally, this accounts for ten to fifteen percent of placements.)
dossier	Envelope containing the application, pictures, legalized documents, and so forth, required by a foreign adoption source.
embassy	Official office or residence of an ambassador in a foreign country; foreign embassies are in Washington, D.C., and U.S. Embassies are usually located in the capital cities of foreign countries with which we have diplomatic relations.
emigration	The act of leaving a country legally.
escort	A child already adopted or to be adopted is brought to the United States by an authorized adult.
ethnicity	A minority within an existing racial group.
finalization	Adoption is complete and the adoption decree is issued.
guardianship	A formal paper is issued by the judge in court which grants legal guardianship of a child to a prospective adoptive couple with the understanding (in foreign countries) that they will adopt the child under the laws of the country in which the child will reside.
hard-to-place children	Children over five, large sibling groups, older sibling groups, babies or children with a correctable or noncorrectable handicap.
home study	An evaluation by a social worker with at least a bachelor's degree in social science.
I-600	Orphan visa petition form.
immigration	The act of entering a country legally.
INS	Immigration and Naturalization Services, a federal agency in each state and in Washington, D.C.
invitation	A letter from the ministry of a foreign country granting permission to obtain a visa.
locating fee	Fee from an unlicensed U.S. individual for finding a foreign orphan for an adopter. Unnecessary and, in some states, illegal.
managing conservator	The legal guardian of the child.
nationality	Nation or colony in which a person is born. (Nationality and race are not the same thing, although this mistake is often made.)
natural child	English expression for a child of birth-parents, wed or unwed.
natural parents	English expression for birth parents.
networking	Formal or informal agreements between adoption agencies and U.S.-based international agencies to cooperate with home studies for international placements.
notarization	A notary public verifies that the signatures on your original documents are valid.
open adoption	Personal visits between birth parents and child continue after placement with the adoptive parents. This is impractical in foreign adoptions.

original document	Documents generated on your behalf, such as letters of reference.
orphan	Child released for adoption by an immediate relative, or abandoned for a legally prescribed time.
passport	A document required by most countries for entry.
parent-initiated adoption	Direct or independent adoption of a foreign child without the use of a U.S. based international adoption agency.
permission to leave	A form required for orphans in some countries which must be signed by a child-placing authority.
placement	Physical placing of orphan with adoptive parent(s).
postplacement study	A report of a supervisory study in an adoptive home.
power of attorney	A form signed by adopters for use by foreign attorney to initiate the adoption before the adopter arrives, or to arrange an adoption by proxy of a child to be escorted to the United States.
pro se adoption	Adoption without a lawyer.
proxy adoption	Child adopted through power of attorney and escorted to the United States; an arrangement usually made by agencies or liaisons.
readoption	A second adoption in the United States, under the laws of the child's new county of residence.
referral	Assignment of a child to an adopter, either by phone call or letter, and followed up with medical and social reports and photos.
release/relinquishment	A release form signed by the orphan's mother or orphanage, and necessary, along with a birth certificate, or the orphan's visa petition and visa issuance.
replacement	Child relinquished by adoptive parents and placed again in a new home.
semi-open adoption	Adoptive and birth parents meet at the child's placement or in court, then proceed as in cooperative adoption.
siblings	Brothers and/or sisters.
social worker	An individual with a bachelor of science, or master of science from an accredited college of social work. Most social workers obtain certification form the state board.
street child	Two types: 1. Child who lives in the street who does not have a caretaker or a home. 2. Child who lives mainly in the streets, but who does have a caretaker of sorts.
Third World	Developing countries, as opposed to First World, (the U.S.A. and other industrially developed nations).
U.S.-based international agency	Hold legal contracts with foreign adoption sources to make child placements.
verification	A form from the state verifying the notary's commission.
visa	For adults, an endorsement granting entry into a particular country for a specified length of stay. Adopted orphans are an exception.
waiting children	Children over five, large sibling groups, older sibling groups, babies or children with a correctable or noncorrectable handicap.
waiting pool	A group of prospective adoptive parents who have completed their preadoption requirements for the foreign court and have INS clearance.

Index